GOD CALLS US

DAUGHTERS
EXTRAVAGANTLY LOVED

GOD CALLS US

DAUGHTERS
EXTRAVAGANTLY LOVED

BY

KIMBERLY GIBSON JOHNSON

God Calls Us: *Daughters Extravagantly Loved*

© 2019 Kimberly Gibson Johnson

Published by

Gibson, Johnson & Company, Inc.

P.O. Box 250646

Atlanta, GA 30325

kimberlygibsonjohnson.org

Cover Design: Megan Fechter, Painted Parcels, www.paintedparcels.com

Editorial assistance: Leonard G. Goss, GoodEditors.com, www.goodeditors.com

ISBN: 9781733871808 (sc)
ISBN: 9781733871815 (e)

Library of Congress Control Number: 2019903335

Unless otherwise noted, all Scripture references are from the New International Version edition, published by Zondervan Publishing House. Copyright © 1973, 1978, 1984, 2011

Printed in the United State of America.

Gibson, Johnson & Company, Inc., July 15, 2019

To the One and Only
Father God in Jesus Christ,
who loves us extravagantly
and calls us his own

CONTENTS

ACKNOWLEDGEMENTS

To my fellow sojourners, family members, and friends who have gone before, walked along beside, and stand with me as I write and share God's story in my life. I am grateful for who you are to me and all those around you. You have profoundly affected the lives of so many, and God's heart for his daughters and sons shines brightly through you and your stories. Your lives are full of the love and grace of our Savior, and they speak of him in remarkable ways, like caring for others, serving those in need, and honoring him as you share your lives.

To my daughter, Julie, I am eternally grateful for God's great gift of you as my daughter. Although this book is not specifically about you, it is about us as the Father's daughters for such a time as this. Thank you for encouraging me to write and share God's story. And thank you for your understanding and kindness; you bless me and so many others by your kind and generous heart and spirit. I want to be more like you.

To my husband, Gray, who inspires me to live with courage and joy. You speak encouragement and love in greater measure and in more ways than you know. Thank you for your grace, which you give freely and generously.

To my son, Alan, whose heart, courage, and words of wisdom give me great joy. I am so privileged and honored to be your mother. Thank you for being a steadfast supporter.

And to Ben, my son-in-law. Your encouragement to share my passion means more than you know. Thank you.

To Megan Fechter, of Painted Parcels. Your enthusiasm for this book cover design is truly matched by your creativity. The heart of joy in your art is contagious. I am so honored and thrilled that you would work with me on this book cover to invite readers to know God and the love he has for his children. Thank you for the privilege of getting to know you.

I also want to thank my editor, Len Goss, of GoodEditors.com. I am grateful for your editorial and theological expertise and for the privilege of working with you again. You made me think a second book was possible. Your work as a theologian and your faithfulness to God's Word give me great assurance that through this book I can share the deep heartfelt love of our Father God with all his sons and daughters.

For each of you I am eternally grateful for your lives and stories of the hope of Jesus Christ. This has given me immeasurably more than I could ask or imagine!

Now let me address my readers: I write to each of you, God's children—those who already know the Father, but also those who have not responded to his pursuing love. I write to you, daughter or son, already in the church or in Christian ministry, yet who yearns for more. Your heart asks, "Is this all there is?" I also write to God's children who feel there is no way that God loves you. You feel separated from him because you are struggling and in pain, or perhaps because you have rejected him. You ask, "Does God really love me?" Or, "How is it that God shows his love?" Or even, "How could God allow such horrible things in my life?" In reality, we all ask these questions or others like them at different points in our lives. The answer from our Father God and our Savior Jesus Christ is always, "You are extravagantly loved." When we look for God, we know he is the one who loves us extravagantly and calls us his own.

PREFACE

DAUGHTERS OF THE KING

Through the Lens of the Inheritance of God

What is the lens by which we view life, the one for which we have been created and chosen for such a time as this? Is it through past shame and disappointment, or fear of either in the present or future? Or is it through the lens of the inheritance of a child of God, an heir and co-heir with Jesus Christ? The Lord gives us a new view, one of hope and victory, for now and eternity. Isaiah 61:7 assures us that "Instead of your shame you will receive a double portion, and instead of disgrace you will rejoice in your inheritance. And so you will inherit a double portion in your land, and everlasting joy will be yours." This is a beautiful illustration of the Messiah and our inheritance as children of God.

The apostle Paul also describes the beauty of the hope poured into our hearts as receivers of God's love when we follow him while also enduring trials as Jesus did:

> Therefore, since we have been justified through faith, we have peace with God through our Lord Jesus Christ, through whom we have gained access by faith into this grace in which we now stand. And we boast in the hope of the glory of God. Not only so, but we also glory in our sufferings, because we know that suffering produces perseverance; perseverance, character; and character, hope. And hope does not put us to shame, because God's love has been poured out into our hearts through the Holy Spirit, who has been given to us. (Rom. 5:1-5)

Scripture says we will not be disappointed in hope; it is not deceiving, nor will it fail. We believe by the power of the Holy Spirit in us as his children.

When we fear shame or disappointment, we have either placed our hope in something other than Jesus Christ, or we believe a lie that there is something to fear in the form of shame or disappointment. Most often, our hope in things turning out as we expected becomes a lens by which we view life and God's blessings. Our God is so much bigger than our hopes and dreams; he will not fail, and he always loves us and never leaves us. The lie the world would have us believe is that things turning out as we think they should is the good life; however, the prophet Isaiah said, "For my thoughts are not your thoughts, neither are your ways my ways," declares the Lord. "As the heavens are higher than the earth, so are my ways higher than your ways and my thoughts than your thoughts" (Isa. 55:8-9). The truth is that God is sovereign, and he works out his purposes for his glory and our good so that the entire world will know him. He created us, knows us, and has a plan uniquely for us for such a time as this.

Fearing shame is another lie. We fail, but God does not. He offers us a clean slate through the death and resurrection of his Only Son, Jesus—our shame for his righteousness. Jesus washed away our sins, past, present, and future. We are in right relationship with God. To fear our sin is to be enslaved to it still. God has given us freedom to be tightly tethered to him instead.

Trusting the Lord in the midst of our disappointments and shame is the way for God's children. When we trust him, hope becomes the lens through which we see all of life, including shame, disappointment, suffering, and trials. As sons and daughters of God, may we choose to view our days in his presence as the inheritance he has given, so much more than we hope, dream, or imagine.

Crossing Over to the Life He has Imagined for Us

As I listen to God's instruction for the new day, I hear, "Come. Wait. Watch." I know he has actively pursued me to listen, so I hear him, or notice small things that are of him, or remember things and people who have spoken truth and love into my life. It is in the waiting that he prepares me for what is next without my knowing what or who or when. But when it does come, I know God watched over me in the process and during the hard waiting. The preparation is not for naught when I see the very wonder of the divine watchful eye and loving hand.

It is in this relationship with the Almighty, the Creator, and the Savior that we find the very thing for which we seek—hope, beauty, love, treasure, dreams, and truth. When we listen, we know that for this new day, we continue to seek:

Cause me to come.

Show me the wonder of your great love.

Because … it is true of him. It is the essence of him. It is everything. I must come and be filled with God's wonder.

The Next …

When we have come and waited and watched for him in our midst, we are attuned to his presence where he is where we are. It is in the present that we know he is. God comes in the present and reminds us of who he is. When he fills us with his wonder, we remember what he has done, and we know that wherever we are, we can rely on him. We can trust him with whatever is next.

The wonder …

It is through the wonder of his great love that we know who God is, and it is in knowing him that we receive the life he has imagined for us.

And oh, what a life he has imagined for us. Come, Wait, Watch. He has great wonder to show us. Jesus has come already. He is waiting for us. His watchful eye and loving heart and hand extend for us. Come. Receive the wonder of his great love.

Five Questions (for which the Creator and Savior Requires a Response)

Our almighty and merciful Creator and Savior, our heavenly Father God, loves us and pursues us as we live on planet Earth, so beautiful and full of his creation, including us. As the Lord mightily displays his majestic and complex intricate natural forms, he also knows us intimately and shows us his love. What is our response to the one who creates and sustains all, loves and pursues us, and knows us and our innermost desires and dreams, as well as our flaws and dark places?

When we acknowledge him as our Savior, he gives us all of himself in Jesus Christ. It is in the receiving of all he offers that we know him, believe him, and become the persons we were created to be for his glory and our good. The journey only begins with salvation, the beginning of "life to the full." There is so much more from him who promised life to the full if we are willing to participate in his great calling on our lives. Will we respond with a *yes* to all of him, our Creator and Savior God?

What or whom are we going to seek as we live out our days here? Will it be to fulfill a dream or passion, satisfy a desire, perform good deeds, continue a generation, or lead an enterprise? Our almighty and sovereign Creator made us with a desire to create and to be filled. He requires a response from us.

If we acknowledge our Creator and Sovereign God, will we confess our rebellion and sin and our need for salvation? Our affirmative answer to this question gives us life in him for eternity. Yet, there are several questions for us if we are to receive the fullness of which Jesus spoke and the promises of God for those he saves.

Will we receive all of God — his unfailing love, his mercy, his presence, his rescue, and his promises? All he offers us?

Will we allow him to teach us from his Word by making our minds and hearts available? Will we get to know Him—who he is and what he has done for us?

As we receive him, will we make our hearts available to him and continue to make our hearts available as we walk with him?

If we receive what God has given through Jesus, we will have life to the full. During our days on this earth, he has given us the power of Jesus flowing through us, the love of the Savior in us, and the Truth written on our hearts. Are we going to live out his truth and grace in our lives? Will we truly believe and receive what he has given us in Jesus? Will we accept life as he imagined for us, life to the full?

INTRODUCTION

GOD CALLS US

DAUGHTERS EXTRAVAGANTLY LOVED

God's Call on Our Lives Requires a Response

Not only does God call us his children, he also calls us by name to his anointing and plan for our lives as his own. His pursuing love is given freely to all he creates and he invites each one of us to his grace and truth. But his invitation requires a response. In failing to respond to the Creator of the universe and Savior of our souls, we have rejected his invitation. In his will to give us free will of our own, God does not coerce or force us, but he does not want even one to miss out on his grace and truth.

God fully loves his sons and daughters, and he promises never to leave us or forsake us. He does not change, and he always keeps his promises. When we receive his grace and truth as followers of Jesus, we become the Father's sons and daughters. As we follow him with our lives, he provides his all, and our days and lives become a response to his unfailing love and truth.

God first loved us. His call on our lives requires that we make a decision, namely that we respond to his love. As we live our lives as God's children, we not only know him, but he gives us a desire to please him, and to honor him with our lives.

Receiving as a Response

It has taken me quite a few years to learn some things about the nature of being a child of God. If you were to say that I am a slow learner, you would be right. When God calls us to become his children, he wants to be in relationship with us. By virtue of our being in relationship with the Almighty God of the universe, there are things one must know on face value. First of all, there is nothing that we can give our great God. He has it all. Also, there is nothing he does not know about us. He is all knowing. And then, there is nothing he would withhold from us as his children. God is faithful and true, loving and compassionate, and slow to get angry with us. Whether we choose to believe it or not, he enjoys us. After all, he created us to be in relationship with him, and his great joy is in loving us. *Thus, in relationship with God, we must receive what he has to offer. It is all about receiving his truth and grace.*

In order to live as followers of our Father and Savior God, we must receive the offer of his Son and thereafter receive his lead in our lives. With each decision we encounter, or fork in the road we take thereafter, we must receive divine direction, forgiveness, comfort, strength, healing, or victory. It is in our believing who he says he is and what he says he will do that we come to know him. He will give us the faith to believe as we step first into his grace and truth and then with each step to receive what he has to offer us. *As we take each step, the effort we make must be in our trusting that He is all we need for life and walking this journey of faith with Him.*

Living a Life of Praise is also a Response to His Great Love and Call

As daughters of the King who trust in the One True God, we must respond by offering ourselves to him. This active response of the heart motivated to love and share what we have been given is offering back what has been given to us. The walk of faith and our response to his truth and grace has momentum because it is collaboration with our God, the author of all. We want to please God by responding to his great love. We do this by living a life of praise; pleasing God is the means by which he continues to give us lives fully loved.

The book you now hold in your hands, *Daughters Extravagantly Loved*, is an account of God's pursuing love and the unfolding journey when one receives it. Like no other, our Father God gives full and abounding life to his children. As sons and daughters, we must respond to God's offer. It is in the receiving of all that God has to offer that a daughter of the King comes to know she is fully loved by our Savior, Father, and King of kings.

Daughters Fully Loved and the Lives to which God Calls Them—Lives to the Full

God created us to be in a relationship with him for his direction and objectives. When we say we have been created for God's glory, this is what we mean. God is God, and there is no other; thus, we are made for *his* glory. An inherent part of being God's children, God's own people, is that through us he makes himself known to the world. This is an enormous privilege and honor, and it is also an exciting and fulfilling purpose.

Through the Bible, which has rightly been called God's love letter to humankind, we learn of the journey God had in the past with the creation he called his own, including their trials, triumphs, wanderings, and wayward ways. We learn from Scripture about the fallen world and fallen relationships of our ancestors. We live in the same world. Still, God loves us unfailingly and pursues us with his grace and truth. God is still the God of the universe who has called each one of us to be His own for such a time as this.

Not only is God revealed through Jesus Christ to his people— unfaithful, doubting, and sinful as we are—he also meets us in our brokenness. *It is in our broken places that God continues to show us the wonders of his love.* He comes to show us our sin and then to give us his mercy in Jesus Christ, through whom we have salvation. And when we determine to accept heaven's offer of truth and grace, the Sovereign God comes to dwell within us to continue pouring out his love on us. God's heart is bigger than we can dream, and his plans for us are wilder than our imagination can summon. Such is the way the heavenly hound pursues us.

God offers his unfailing love, to which he requires a response. *It is in responding "yes" to him that his children receive what God gives*—transformation into the persons they are created to be, with the desire to live out the plans he intended for his purposes and his glory.

God's heart keeps on giving to his children. Extravagantly loved by our Father God, we have his word on it, and his Holy Spirit to guide us in it:

- God's love letter, the Bible, is our guide for living in a fallen world with fallen relationships

- God shows us his heart by meeting us in the broken places of our lives

- God gives us more faith as we respond by faith

- God works in us from the inside out when we receive his offer of love and truth (private transformation to public proclamation)

- Our lives become fulfilled as we acknowledge and live out who God is and whose we are (living to please and praise him)

Story of the Red Dress

Do you have a red dress story? After you read mine, please consider that you have a story to tell, one that has given you insight into your own life. We are not to hide our stories. And our stories are not for our own limelight, but for the reader or listener to know who God is and what he has done for us. Perhaps our stories will draw others to the truth they have not known, or to a deeper meaning they can apply to their lives.

My story is about a daughter who is hopeless and heartsick. She is riddled by shame and unrest because of the dysfunction in her family system, mostly as a result of a mother who needs to be the most beautiful and talented person in the room, and who is untiring in her resolve to be the center of attention. Not only does she possess the requisite beauty and talent, she is also driven to attain it by whatever means the moment presents, even at the insult or injury to her children. My story is not different from so many in that God uses the broken places in our lives to bring us to him, to know him, to know his truth, and for him to bring healing to our hopeless and heartsick souls. The story of the red dress is my awakening to certain themes in my life and how God uses them for his glory and our good.

The red dress became a symbol in my life for all the ways things were out of whack. Yet God used the theme for his purposes in ways I could not see until he showed them to me.

The gown my mother wore as mother of the bride on my wedding day was red and flowing and perfectly magnificent. I believe it had not consciously occurred to her that she was upstaging the bride (me). When I called this to her attention, she would not choose another dress to wear. Consequently, my mother became the most visible member in the wedding procession and the celebration thereafter.

The rejection of another, particularly your own mother, is difficult to say the least. The red dress incident was not the first time something like this occurred. But it became a revelation of something I did not want to face. I enjoyed my wedding day despite the glaring reminder of our human flaws.

Memory has a way of giving us fodder for unforgiveness, shame, and unbelief. But God has another plan for us if we will allow him to reveal it. In my case, it took many years of stuffing the memories back and searching for ways to make myself lovable, lovely, and significant in my own eyes. And, of course, these often-tried ways were not going to fill the hole in my heart where rejection and hopelessness thrived. In addition to the paradox of wanting to be significant and yet not wanting the spotlight on me (because I had seen what it brought out in my mother), I thought the problem was center stage and visible in a red dress. This was not true.

Shortly after we were married, my mother-in-law gave me a red dress for Christmas. It was beautiful, and she had chosen it for me. As a daughter-in-law in a new family, it was particularly meaningful. I felt chosen, loved, and lovely. God was at work even when I could not recognize him.

The red dress Mary gave me was also elegant, flowing, and beautiful. But I did not particularly feel beautiful in it. It was not the dress itself but what was going on inside of me. This is what happens when we are not ready to receive a gift. Receiving is not something many are comfortable with. Yet, this is the great grace God has in mind for us. We have to reach for the very thing that is being given and allow ourselves to receive it. In receiving God's precious gift of a Savior, we become the very persons God had in mind in creating us. Wearing the red dress and having fully received it would have given me the very thing for which I was seeking, which was love and loveliness. God was there in Mary's gift at Christmas.

I have had a few red dresses over the years, and it has taken time for the significance of the symbol to become apparent to me. The light God gives us in our stories is for the recognition not only of who we are, but also for who he is, what he has given us, and who he has created us to be. When God gives us a gift and we receive his gift, we are to wear it. It is in the wearing, the receiving of him, that we become who he has set us apart to be and also part of his greater story. We are not to believe the lie that we must remain hidden. Rather, we come to know the truth that we become visible for God's story to be known. He does not have to give us a part in his great story, but he does. We need to receive the true gift and let it be as he has said: "I am the Lord, and there is no other; apart from me there is no God" (Isa. 45:5).

The red dress is a symbol to me of how God uses hard things and brokenness to bring his redemption to his children. The lie that the Evil One wanted me to believe so that I would remain hopeless and heartsick became the groundwork, the broken place, that God used for his purposes in my life and for others who hear the story of his pursuing love and plan for all of his creation.

I ask you as daughters of Jesus Christ, our King of all kings, to recall your story of God. Receive his story and wear Jesus for the entire world to see. That is how our lives can become lives to the full, lives for which we were created as he planned for his purposes.

CHAPTER ONE

GOD CALLS US
TO MORE OF HIMSELF

Since ancient times no one has heard,

no ear has perceived,

no eye has seen any God besides you,

who acts on behalf of those who wait for him.

(Isa. 64:4)

Whoever has will be given more, and they will have an abundance.
Whoever does not have, even what they have
will be taken from them.

(Matt. 13:12)

God Calls Us to More

Viewing our journey of faith like a walk along the road, we take God's hand wherever he leads. We live with him along the way as he teaches and we listen. It is beautiful and wonderful if we go with him in this way, but we rarely do. He knows all this, and still he loves us.

We are puny and unreliable on this journey of faith. We want our way and not God's way. We believe, but only by struggling, that God can take us where we want to go. We know he is God and there is no other. Yet we have trouble allowing him to be our Father God and living in relationship with him as his children. The Father demonstrated his love for us and his desire to be in relationship with us through the ultimate sacrifice of his only Son, Jesus. In this, he made it possible for the creation to be in right standing with the Creator.

Are we still trying to be right with God? We want to get things right while we walk our own path and feel we have done something for God. God, however, requires only that we walk and live with him as our Father on the journey. When I use the word *walk*, I mean an active participation in a relationship with God the Father. For many of us, *walking* is still something we do to earn or achieve a relationship with heaven. But that is not what the journey is about at all.

I am a walker, and I love moving about in God's creation. For me, this is a special time with God when I can breathe in and enjoy his handiwork in nature. Often, he demonstrates his love and teaches me. It is a wonder that we have the privilege to visit with nature's Creator in this way.

Recently, God reminded me that I am his daughter. There is no earning or achieving this status. There is no manner of walking that makes me more or less his daughter. I am simply God's daughter and I have inherited the status to walk with him. For all Christians, he is our Father, and we are his heirs.

As God continues teaching me about being his daughter, he has given me many things to ponder of late. Some seem to be questions, and some are reminders of who he is and what he has promised. As he writes his truth on my heart, he also peels away layer upon layer of what is not the inheritance of a daughter. He takes away the parts of me that keep me from him, whether it is self-protection, or my desire to be comfortable, or my need to be in control of my life. In peeling these things away, he has something good in mind: his best for us. Could it be we are not receptive to God's best because we feel we are not worthy? And of course, we feel that way because in fact we are not worthy. Only God has made us worthy through the sacrifice of God the Son.

Some of our questions suggest we doubt God's plan for us as his children:

o Who am I to be taught by him?

o Who am I to receive a word from God?

o Why would the Father reveal himself to me?

o Why would the Son rescue me?

o Why would Jesus die so I could be made right with God?

o Why would the Lord give me a clean slate over and over again?

The question God poses for us as his children is, "If you really knew how much I loved you, would you live differently?" Do we really know how much the Almighty loves us? And if so, what difference is that making in our lives? Knowing he loves us as he does is a quest that has turned into an incredible lesson on being God's daughter. His Word shows us how to know him as our Father and what he intends for us, his children—including joy, laughter, and dancing—merely because he delights in us. He wants us to receive heaven's riches, the riches of daughter of the King, God himself.

God calls us to more. He awakens us to more, to know him more and to know what it is to be his daughter. He wants us to cross the threshold instead of wandering alone on our journey. He wants us to receive fully what is on offer: life to the full. Will we cross over to experience what he has in mind, what love he has in his heart for us? Or will we stay back and keep our distance from the fullness so readably available in Christ Jesus?

It is overwhelming at times to glimpse the love of God. As God reminds us that we are his daughters and sons and that his love is real and abundant and not dependent on what we did or did not do, we perhaps understandably begin finding ways we are not worthy. At least that is what I do at times. Neither my head nor my heart was definitely ready for the wonderful plan God had for me. When we are not ready to receive the gift he has for us (in my case, the lesson of being his daughter), God knows and loves and waits for us. He hides us for a time, as he hid me, so he could pour out his love and assurance and allow time for rest and growth. He did not abandon his plan because I doubted him or had little faith. Perhaps I was not ready to see what he had to offer, or maybe I needed a respite. Maybe he was preparing the road.

Sometimes God allows us to glimpse in hindsight who he is and what he has done for us. During these times we see he has not abandoned us to our own pitiful devices. Just as God told Moses he could not see him and live, God hid Moses in the cleft of the rock and allowed the prophet to see his back and know that God was with him. As I look back, I see God showed me himself as I wrestled with him and with his plan for rest and stillness. He had hidden me in the cleft of the rock for a season to show me how he cares for me and wants me to receive all he has to offer, including his provision for rest and restoration. Truly my great Father God took me away from earning and achieving my "walk" to resting and being restored to his path. When I glimpsed my God in hindsight, I said, "It has been you, Great God!" That is the way of our God for his children: he poses the questions, allows our sight, and then he poises us for listening to him.

God wants us to receive. We will only be filled when we receive what he offers. As I saw a glimpse of his hand, he also opened my heart for what was next—the invitation to come and rest as his daughter. This is a difficult task, because we believe we need to work at being his children. But it is in trusting him that we come to know him and who he says he is. Placing our trust in God brings rest.

No matter what stage we are in our Christian walk, there is so much more to know about our God. There is no better way to know him than to come into his presence and rest. He shares many things with his children who want to know him more, including what the heart of a Father is like, how his healing is accomplished, and what he does in his harvest. He delights also in assuring us that he is our advocate, our true defense, and that our loving and just Father is also the sovereign God of the universe.

If we remain with our Advocate on the road to knowing him better and to crossing the threshold to more of God in our lives, we will have "life to the full." As we are assured in the gospel of John, "The thief comes only to steal and kill and destroy; I have come that they may have life, and have it to the full" (10:10). While God softens our hearts and offers his bounty, he shares with us that the quest is for more of him. No matter what spiritual stage we are in, we will never get to the end of God. If we surrender, and get to the end of ourselves, we will be closer to the Source of all, for he is the counterpart to our every need, physical, emotional, and spiritual. He is the best counselor, comforter, and teacher. He offers his riches to us in relationships, forgiveness, love, grace, delight and pleasure, peace, and joy.

We suffer when we refuse divine bounty. When we supply our own, which leads to emptiness, or when we pursue other good things, which also leads to emptiness, we miss out on God's rich supply. Often, we do not receive his bounty because it seems "too good to be true." But it is good, and it is true. Humbling ourselves as children to the almighty and compassionate God, we surrender and trust him to reveal knowledge of himself, the one, true God. When he draws us near, we must call upon him; it is then he shows us the table of his grace.

We can only join God at the table of grace due to the capacity we have in the Holy Spirit. God knows our every need, and he offers his table to fit our good. As we humble ourselves and lean in to partake of the Father himself, we become the thriving children of God planned before the creation of the world. He has bounty in store, and he draws us closer to discover "life to the full."

To share his grace and bounty, God waits with his loving hand upon us to offer the best he has—his Son Jesus—so we can be his own, too.

"Loving Father God"

God goes before
And awakens me to more
God closes in behind
Shows me His hand kind

Guides He does, draws us to His side
With His word He teaches and confides
His sons and daughters in Him they abide
As they come, His rest He provides

When they know Him as their Father
He shares His heart, healing, and harvest
Then He opens their minds, heart, eyes, and ears
To know assuredly His advocacy and not to fear

Knowing and believing He takes us deep
We children approach Him at His table a heap
Full of good food, plentiful and right
To us for our souls and bodies alike

To partake of His bounty true
Our hearts bow before Him and bodies lean too
His rightness received; we are alive
Life is full; in Him we abide

He fills us to become more of Him alike
So that when we see Him, we will know aright
Thriving children of our loving Father
Truly as He desires and delights

"He Loves You So"

Each layer of pretense or armor
He requires us to shed
To know His honor, His cover
Come to Him and rest your head

He comes from on high
For Him to us is not too low
Because He dearly loves us so
He makes the journey with us to go

Your weary head and heart stone cold
Not too difficult for Him to take hold
He invites poor souls to come to His table
Full of bounty and rest — and He makes us able

To come, to know, to trust Him above
Only because He is full of love
His plan you see was to give His all
So that you and I would know Him above all

Yearning

What do you yearn for? My own answer to that question is
that I yearn for purpose, calling, right relationships, home,
community, intimacy, hopes and dreams, and rest, peace, and joy.
These are not uniquely my yearnings, but I believe they are
common to all. God wired us this way to desire the things that
ultimately lead to him. This past year I came to a place where I
yearned for something I could not describe.

God invited me to be still, to allow my head to rest and my
heart to know more of him. There is always more of God to know,
so I am not referring to head knowledge. What I mean by getting to
know the Father is understanding his love for us. God wanted me
to trust his love. I was just to come and sit with him—and let him
do the rest. And I do mean "rest." What the Lord began teaching
me as he drew me closer was that he is enough. In fact, he is more
than enough, and he wanted me to know this in my heart. I do not

have to know anything else, and I do not have to do anything else. Resting in God's love is difficult for us because somehow resting does not seem enough. We want to do something to earn our rest beside God. But we can never earn his love; it is his gift to us.

If we really knew God's heart for his sons and daughters, we would expect our yearnings to take us to him, just as he planned. It is only required that we go to him with them. God wants to lavish his love upon us; he is extravagant in this life-affirming way.

Other Yearnings

I do yearn for right relationships, especially with my family of origin, and particularly with my mother. Instead of completely trusting God, and I do believe I have trusted him with this in large ways, I am still searching inside of myself for ways to make it work. God has healed me in so many ways beyond my comprehension, yet with right relationships I am still struggling to make things "right" myself. I hold to the fact that I may not have done everything I could to make the situation right. This has turned out to be another form of working for God's approval instead of resting in his righteousness. He has other plans, but as of yet I do not know what they are. Instead of making family relationships fall in line so the hole in my heart will be filled up, God has called me to be his daughter and a member of his family—the perfect way for all of heaven's children to be complete and whole. I must not search for ways to do the filling itself but seek him who completes us in extraordinary ways.

Yearning in Psalm 84

The psalmist describes it best in Psalm 84—"yearning" as his heart and body cry out to the living One, to be in his dwelling, close to God. Our inner beings desire a place near and with God. We gather strength in his presence especially if we are in desperate and barren times. God looks on us, his children, with favor and honor and he withholds nothing good from us while shielding us from harm.

Psalm 84

How lovely is your dwelling place,
O Lord Almighty!
My soul yearns, even faints,
for the courts of the Lord;
my heart and my flesh cry out
for the living God.
Even the sparrow has found a home,
and the swallow a nest for herself,
where she may have her young—
a place near your altar,
O Lord Almighty, my King and my God.
Blessed are those who dwell in your house;
they are ever praising you. "Selah"
Blessed are those whose strength is in you,
who have set their hearts on pilgrimage.
As they pass through the Valley of Baca,
they make it a place of springs;
the autumn rains also cover it with pools.
They go from strength to strength,
till each appears before God in Zion.
Hear my prayer, O Lord God Almighty;
listen to me, O God of Jacob. "Selah"
Look upon our shield, O God;
look with favor on your anointed one.
Better is one day in your courts
than a thousand elsewhere;
I would rather be a doorkeeper in the house of my God
than dwell in the tents of the wicked.
For the Lord God is a sun and shield;
The Lord bestows favor and honor;
no good thing does he withhold
from those whose walk is blameless.
O Lord Almighty, blessed is the man who trusts in you.

The Heart Set on a Pilgrimage—The Walk of Faith in Psalm 84

Who is this living God who cares for even the sparrow and the swallow? God sets our hearts on this walk of faith, this yearning for him. The psalmist knows he needs the One who withholds no good thing, the One whose home and dwelling beckons him, the One and Only who is worthy of praise. He says "Blessed are those whose strength is in you, who have set their hearts on pilgrimage." Here it is again, the pilgrimage, the walk of faith which is the provision God has made for those whose hearts know the need for a Savior who is Jesus Christ. When the heart knows and believes that Jesus is Lord, it is grace indeed that opens it up and grace abounding that pours more as the heart yearns.

The first four verses of Psalm 84 demonstrate the findings of a child of God whose rest is in God and who wants to remain with him. "Blessed are those who dwell in your house; they are ever praising you." As he recalls God's small creatures, also provided for by the Almighty, his claim is clear: he resolves and cries out for more of God in his life. In the next verses of the psalm, five through eight, the revelations of the truth of God in the Psalmist's life become more apparent. When we experience God, we want more of him, just as the psalmist proclaims. As God pours himself into us, we know him more, and even our trials become places of God's blessing if we turn to him.

The pilgrimage in this psalm is expressed in an anthem of the joy of God's presence. We hear him beckoning through our deepest yearnings. When we come to him, we find in him that for which we yearn—God Himself. The heart on a pilgrimage knows that God is near, and the psalmist demonstrates that God provides for him, protects him, and wants good things for him. God's presence provides the journey and the One for whom we are seeking. The King of Glory provides his children with the walk of faith, a trek for our hearts to know God's heart.

The Greatest Journey is with Your Father

The greatest journey of life is one where our deepest desires are met and our wildest dreams are possible. The One who takes us, holds us, guides us, and makes it possible has our very best interests at heart. He will not lead us to a place he is not. Nor will he ever leave us. He is the Father we have yearned for our whole life, the One who knows our deepest desires and wildest imaginations. He will not fail or disappoint.

We had no choice in who our physical parents were, and neither did we have a voice in who became our family. However, we do have a decision to make on whether we will allow God to be our Father. He created us, knew us, and loved us before the creation of the world. He loves us and fathers us even without our knowing or reciprocating his love, and he gives us free will to decide whether to allow him to become active in our lives. He loves us so and pursues us to be his sons and daughters. If we girls choose, it is a daring adventure of ultimate grace—the highest, total empowering relationship with our creator God and eternal Father. Being a daughter to our Great God is a

Daring

Adventure

Ultimate

Grace

Highest

Total

Empowering

Relationship

Our eternal Savior and Father God protects and provides for us. He loves and shows affection, teaches and leads, and disciplines and corrects us. His gifts are always his best for our good, and as he fathers us, he pours himself into us. And through the saving grace of his Son, our sins are atoned for and forgiven.

Through God's gifts we have a meaningful relationship with him for eternity.

If we allow God to come into our lives and enjoy him as a Father, he will give us rest, joy, peace, hope, and the capacity to trust him and persevere through whatever life on earth throws us. Not only will we know him, we will be changed into the daughters he designed us to be. Our Father God is the perfect guide who provides perfect love.

As the Father's beloved daughters, we can take the greatest journey ever.

"Closer to God"

Closer to God, I want to be
For Him to be all I see
Thank you, Jesus, for eyes to behold
Your mercy, love, and compassion instead of me

Loving eyes upon me
Instruction and guidance You give
You will not leave or forsake me
Help me to trust You more

How many ways of rescue
Of providing Your hand to me
Outstretched arms You extend
'Til I am safely home in Your fold

I cannot outrun You
Or live outside Your love
You've saved me now and forever
Blessed with assurance, grow me closer to You.

From Anxious Child in the Cluttered Closet to God's Daughter at the Bountiful Table

From hiding in the cluttered closet to sitting at the Lord's Table, I have arrived. God knocked on the door and asked permission to enter my tiny space. I peeked around and reluctantly answered. I feared he already knew I was hopeless and despairing, and that it was not what he had in mind for me. I knew the great God of the universe, but I could not reconcile the pain I felt from living. God does not want us merely to live; he wants us to live as his sons and daughters, as recipients of divine grace and bounty.

As the Lord gave me courage to come out of the closet and remain in his presence, I entered his table of plenty. He does not have requirements for this—if he did, no one could meet them. But because he has already settled the account between himself and humankind, we can sit with him at his table.

I write as one child to another. We must become small in order to gain the awesome privilege of knowing the grandeur of our Great and Holy God who came down to us, brought us up to him, and loves us without fail. When we open the door of our hearts to him, then our adventure begins.

Living as God's Daughter in the House of God

Even in the tiny cluttered closet, I knew I was a child of God. I think one of the hardest things about that time period was that I couldn't reconcile being God's child living in darkness and defeat. As I came to know the God of all hope and the truth in his Word, as described in my earlier book, *Real Struggles, Real Hope: A Journey to Truth, Trust, and Freedom*, I left the tiny cluttered space and the life of defeat to graduate to more spacious accommodations and victory in him.

As he clothed me in his rich mercy and kindness, and took away my shame, God encouraged me to enter into his presence at the table he set for us as his children. He wants us to fully experience his bounty, not shy away from it because we feel we are not deserving. As God opened my heart, eyes, and mind to the fullness of life he promised, I awakened from what seemed like a deep sleep.

While wrestling with God over resting in him, I knew he wanted me to know him better. After all, he is a loving, kind, and generous God. Why was I wrestling with him? I must receive what he has to offer. I needed to wait to take the step of faith in believing he was working on my behalf. He had the table set, but I was not ready to receive. He wanted me to be ready to receive.

Perhaps I was awakening from the deep sleep that had been shrouding my eyes. Still groggy, I am awaking to God's great love and mercy. And better yet, he is awakening in me the woman who knows the Author of Abundant Life itself.

"Revelation"

To know the truth in front of me
My view is often narrow, too small you see
Less than your Truth, certainly not free
Transform my heart to trust you, not me

Through a window that frames the view
I come to know only what's within it too
Beyond the eyes, to know your heart
You, great God, your love impart

Your presence lights the room
Without the beams from the windows bloom
Like the view where I cannot see
You make my heart know only Thee

Where am I going, what step do I take
To go the distance with you to make
It's only from head to heart you see
A small leap I trust Thee to keep

Open my heart, my ears, my eyes
To know, to hear, to see Thee on high
I cannot do this journey on my own
For you come with me, I'm not alone

As you love and hold and go ahead of me
To prepare the way, to set our hearts free
Eyes fixed on your truth, your beauty unfolds
I'm transformed by the sight of you to behold

God Awakens Us to More

God has certainly given me more than I ever dreamed. And yet, he has shown me how to seek him out on what it means to have life and have it to the full. God will show me a way not to stand at the threshold with him but to step out and cross over the chasm keeping me from living the abundant life. This he will do for anyone.

God offers us more and pursues us with more of himself. If I am at the crossroads of living life to the full, what then is keeping me from stepping over? What are the hindrances in my life? Have I kept my eyes on Jesus, the pioneer and perfecter of faith (Heb. 12:2)? God is faithful. He will also help us to choose him and keep our eyes on him for the journey.

Perhaps you have crossed the river like me in a huge step of faith, but there is something still holding you back. There will always be obstacles on the journey, but God promises that if we follow him, we will have life to the full. The evil one has come to steal, kill, and destroy, but he came to give abundant life (John 10:10). In the midst of the obstacles and roads not taken on life's journey, we may have "life to the full" as God has promised.

With God's intentional and extravagant gift, he guides us on the journey to know him better. Leaning into him, he creates us as new women, daughters for such at time as this. I do not want to miss him. He is faithful, and he will do it—he will show himself to me and to us. The heavenly plan has always been and still is to show how much God loves and pursues us.

Our God is an Awesome God

- God chooses to call us his children, not because of anything we have done but because of who he is

- God upholds us as we walk by faith

- God gives us hope, expectancy, and joy

- God causes us to notice and remember

God is our help and our strength for walking by faith. In fact, we must take his hand in order for him to uphold us along the journey. The Father's righteousness has rescued us from deserved wrath, aid he provided in his Son Jesus. He continues showing us his kindness and mercy as we travel with him on the walk of faith.

The one thing we must do to complete the journey with God is consciously to choose to follow him. When one is safely on board with Christ and his offer of salvation, the way to live the new life that the Father has given in the Son becomes possible. This is the walk of faith. With each step of the walk of faith, the Lord gives us more of himself. He changes us by faith, and he gives us hope, expectancy, and joy. He causes us to notice the things of God surrounding us, and to remember what he has done for us in the past and in the present—and what he has promised us for the future.

We have the capacity to walk by faith only through the Holy Spirit, who dwells within us after we choose to follow Jesus. The step-by-step process is God's provision to know Jesus and draw closer and closer to him. As we depend on him, he increases the measure of his fullness in our lives. As we walk by faith, by searching for the ultimate and living in the journey, we are offered the spiritual abundance he provided for us to live life to the full.

Searching for the Ultimate and Living in the Journey—Walking by Faith

Does time get by you as you live out the day meeting its demands and doing what needs to be done to keep your head above water for the hour? It seems we yearn for something more, and yet we live our days just getting by. What does this say about our hopes and dreams for today and the future?

I believe God created in us a need to dream, hope, and yearn for something better. We have free will to choose our dreams and how we go about obtaining them. But at our human core is a void only God can fill. Our dreams and hopes are a means by which God pursues us to meet him. He holds all we imagine and envision, yet he sets us all on a journey for such a time as this. The Father's children live in search of him. He has numbered our days to find him and all he has set apart for us—a life lived in him full of God's love and truth: the abundant life. While we live in the journey we search for the ultimate, just as our Creator and Savior fulfills in us the abundant life when we choose to follow him.

The journey God gives us is full of hope and promise, but it is not something everyone receives automatically. We have to choose it. If we do, we will have the ultimate ride. If we do not, we will attempt to fill our lives with all kinds of things, none of which satisfies the yearning we have deep inside. When God meets our deepest needs, we are complete. The journey and the search are one; our dependence on him yields a life of purpose and pleasure, trial and joy, and hope and peace.

When the Israelites entered the Promised Land, they had to believe it was theirs by virtue of the fact that God promised it to them. Their belief in God determined their destiny; God made a covenant with their forefathers, a covenant that determined the trajectory of their lives. In their faith, they seized the Promised Land. The God of Abraham, Isaac, and Jacob made the covenant and promised the land to them; their walking by faith in him made it possible for them to enter and receive the gift he promised.

When we walk by faith, when we know who and what our ultimate is, and when we believe that God is who he says he is, the same holds true. It determines our journey as well as how we receive the gifts already given us. Just as our forefathers in the faith did, we must walk in faith to receive them. As they searched for the ultimate, they believed he had gone before them and was with them, and they lived their journeys by walking by faith. As they stood at the border to the Promised Land, they knew they were receiving the very thing for which they were headed—a land full of promise and lives full of hope. They knew it because they depended on the One who gave it. As we live in hope of the ultimate, our One and Only, we find the journey filled with the dreams he has for us and the full life he planned for each of his children.

What They Received as They Believed—Some Biblical Heroes of the Faith

Each of the following biblical characters lived their lives by faith in Israel's God. They knew the Great God of the universe, sought him for direction, and worshipped him as a practice of their faith. And as they believed, they received what he had promised—for some, it was hope for better lives to be found in the presence of God in heaven; for others, it was the hope of the generations, the long awaited Messiah. Each received the God of Abraham, Isaac, and Jacob as they walked in faith through their lives. They knew whom they served. Some received positions, and others received their heart's desires; all were given more as a result of their faith. All were flawed and yet transformed by the power of God in their lives. Each one had a unique story to be told. In fact, their stories are a huge part of what God gave them as they walked by faith.

What does God want us to have that he has already given? What is our story and how are we receiving all God wants to give us?

Abraham

Abraham left his homeland because God told him to do so, and he did not know where he was going. Yet he became the father of the faith, the father of the generations of people who were chosen by God.

Moses

Moses also did as God told him when he was instructed to go to Pharaoh to demand the release of the Hebrew people from slavery. He knew he was not welcomed by the Egyptians any longer, but he was welcomed by God who met with Moses. Moses became the leader of the Israelites.

Joshua

With great courage and resolve Joshua entered the Promised Land with the Israelites as God directed. He knew God would defeat their enemies, though there were many in the land.

Deborah

Deborah was the prophetess and judge who settled disputes and went into battle with the Lord as her guide. She would not allow credit to go to her protégé, who needed her with him to fight. Deborah sought victory and justice in the land and for the people she led for God.

Rahab

The Hebrew people needed Rahab to hide them and not tell of their whereabouts. Rahab was a prostitute who risked her own life and her family's lives for the sake of the Hebrews. God showed great mercy and grace for her and her family when all the others were killed. Rahab is in the lineage of Jesus.

David

David waited to be king for fifteen years. He ran from Saul, who wanted to kill him, and he failed at marriage and fidelity. But David loved God and enjoyed worshipping and serving him. Of David, God said he had a heart after God's own heart. David is in the lineage of Jesus.

Elizabeth

Though Elizabeth waited to be a mother for many years, she knew God heard her pleas. She was the mother of John the Baptist, who heralded the way of Jesus Christ. She was pregnant with John at the same time Mary was pregnant with the long awaited Messiah.

Anna

Anna was widowed for most of her life while she fasted and prayed for the long awaited Messiah. She knew when Mary and Joseph brought Jesus to the temple that he was the One.

Peter

Peter was a fisherman who followed Jesus. He became a fisher of men, then one who denied Christ, and then he became the rock upon which Jesus built his church.

Mary Magdalene

Mary Magdalene saw Jesus as the resurrected One after his crucifixion. He had healed her of demons, and she was his ardent follower. After Mary saw the resurrected Lord, she was the messenger who announced his resurrection to the disciples.

Paul

Paul was a well-educated Jew who persecuted Christians. He became a convert to Christ on the Damascus Road and ministered the gospel of Jesus Christ by preaching about the boundless riches of Christ. He was a dramatically transformed zealot and persecutor who displayed great joy in serving the One who gave him life.

Lydia

Lydia was a purple cloth merchant who answered the voice of God when Paul spoke and used her home as a meeting place for the Jews who were also converts under Paul. Lydia was the first convert in Philippi.

Questions for Followers of Jesus

1. If we really believed what God has given us in full, would we live differently? What is "life to the full"?

2. What is your passion?

3. Who is your fellowship?

4. What are your obstacles in walking by faith?

5. What have you received as a byproduct of your beliefs?

6. What has your walking by faith shown you about God and his character?

7. What has your walking by faith shown you about yourself?

God's Vast Love

God's unfailing love far surpasses all things, even our imaginations. We cannot get to the end of it. This does not mean evil does not exist, nor does it mean bad things do not happen. There is hurt, disappointment, and even death in our lives. However, we can count on God's love; he is with us always and will not leave us, even when darkness seems to prevail.

When hurt and rejection occur, God's vast love is with us. He will come in to the hurt place if we let him in. If we hold on to the hurt, we are not allowing ourselves to receive his profoundly healing and transforming love, love to which there is no equal. Yet, if we tether ourselves to God, he will cover us, hold us, and teach us how to withstand the sorrows of this world. We get to know him better while setting our eyes on him and relying on his power and love. He is enough: God's love through Jesus Christ counters all injustice. Jesus conquered death and sin and resides within every person who believes in him. He reaches out to the broken, the imprisoned, and the ones in darkness, and he says there is hope. His love reaches down and lifts us up; we cannot find him without his pursuing us. The good news is that the Lord loves us intentionally. His hand extends to all, and his heart is big enough for all creation.

God appears to us in a whisper, in a prayer, through a friend, through his Word, in his and in many other ways. Let us say *yes* to him through our listening, our attention, and our devotion to the One who loved us first.

What is God's Invitation?

In God's invitation we are given an opportunity in the moment. There are patterns in the way God works in our lives—not like a rulebook to follow, or a prescription, or a predictable circumstance. God works much more wonderfully and greater than anything we could dream. His work in our lives is like a mysterious opening where I know God is teaching me something and I want to learn from it what he has for me.

Something new is appearing; the Holy Spirit awakens us to the Lord's presence and work. The veils over our hearts are taken away; we do not fear or deny the grace and truth he has already given and we have yet to receive. May his truth and grace sustain us through this opportunity in the moment to know him better.

In the spiritual realm (and actually all of life is spiritual), God in Jesus Christ has given each of his children a God-sized life. We may individually and collectively know his huge love and mercy; he has already given us "life to the full." As we turn to him and trust, we may receive more of what he has already graciously given through Jesus Christ and the Holy Spirit, who now lives within us as we have come to faith in Christ.

Is the question perhaps not what is going on but who is working? And is it not the actual work itself to be realized but the result in us that is the point? And even more, for whose glory is the result? Only God can produce it. The One and Only returns the harvest. We must wait, fix our eyes on him, and lean totally on him during the season. So the invitation is to draw close, to remain in Christ, and to know him better. When the harvest comes, all will be revealed.

God will clothe us in something new, which will reveal more about him than about us. We will be changed with the invitation received and the opportunity seized, and even more significantly, God will be more present to us while his name will establish itself in world renown.

What is the opportunity in life at the moment that feels like an interruption, or one that makes us fear the future, or one that seems like a wrecking ball in the present? If we lean on the Father, we may find him. He has more for us than we ever dreamed. Is this God's invitation to "life to the full?"

God's Pursuit of Us with the Abundant Life

Everything starts with God. He describes the abundant life he desires for us, and then he pursues us to receive and embrace it. Out of God's great love for us, he pursues us with a loving-kindness that cannot be measured or even comprehended. Only he can meet the void in us he created. We cannot approach him unless prompted, yet we must "Seek the Lord while he may be found" (Isa. 55:6). He loves us and pursues us and knows our hearts for him. We may think that we can put him off forever, but we cannot.

God desires that we all have abundant life, and he allows all kinds of "field trips" to get our attention and transform us into the people he created us to be. But the Creator will not coerce us into choosing him or the life he desires for us.

God is faithful, generous, and he keeps his Word. He pursues us with the abundant life; his intention is for us to know him better and grow more mature in him. Without the working of the Holy Spirit, we cannot even conceive of the greatness of God. Nor can we praise, worship, or serve the Father without the capacity of God the Holy Spirit. In the final analysis, asking God questions about the abounding life he means for us to have would be impossible without the Holy Spirit.

Do I Believe in Abundance?

Jesus came to give us life in the fullest sense—an abundant life. He sacrificed his own life so we might gain eternity and live with him forever. He said, "The thief comes only to steal and kill and destroy; I have come that they may have life, and have it to the full" (John 10:10). The Enemy will fight to take this life away, but Jesus has won the battle for all eternity. Abundance is in the transformative work of the Holy Spirit; it is not only in the transformation of the character of a person, but also in the person's perspective on life and its purpose. Without the work of the Holy Spirit in us, there would be no abundant life, nor would there be capacity to believe in Jesus Christ. There is no beginning or end to God; his riches, love, and power are incomparable. Through the transformation of the Holy Spirit within us, we are able to know Jesus Christ on a personal basis. In Christ we are able to access the full life available to all who believe.

Believing in Jesus is believing in the abundant life. It is what he came to give us. But have we really received it? Do we believe in abundance? Are we living it? We may ask, "What are the barriers to the abundant life?" It is a matter of coming to the end of oneself. The heart believes one thing, and yet we live out another. This is the ongoing dilemma of being a follower of Jesus, but through him we are able to live another way. We can follow him, step into his footsteps, lean in when everything in us wants to run the other way, and give up what would be comfortable and easy and do what does not come natural at all. As we listen to the Holy Spirit within us and wait on Christ to give direction and counsel, we begin hearing him and knowing he is in the lead and we must surrender to his prompting. It is a wildly wonderful way to live.

God's way of life, the only authentic life, is not only in his counsel, but also in his transformation to becoming less focused on ourselves and more fixed on him. He does it without our working on it; it is truly a miracle from the God of the universe through the power of the Holy Spirit living within us. The abundant life is in the relationship with our Creator, in the person of Jesus Christ, through his Holy Spirit living within us.

A Few Scriptures on Abundance

If you then, though you are evil, know how to give good gifts to your children, how much more will your Father in heaven give the Holy Spirit to those who ask him!" (Luke 11:13)

Praise be to the God and Father of our Lord Jesus Christ, who has blessed us in the heavenly realms with every spiritual blessing in Christ. (Eph. 1:3)

And God is able to bless you abundantly, so that in all things at all times, having all that you need, you will abound in every good work. (2 Cor. 9:8)

His divine power has given us everything we need for a godly life through our knowledge of him who called us by his own glory and goodness. (2 Pet.1:3)

He who did not spare his own Son, but gave him up for us all—how will he not also, along with him, graciously give us all things? (Rom. 8:32)

Since we have now been justified by his blood, how much more shall we be saved from God's wrath through him! (Rom. 5:9)

The Process of Moving Forward in Faith or Staying Behind at the Threshold

Am I walking in faith or rejecting what God has to offer? What do I believe that would keep me from walking in faith? I remember I am to choose life and God's blessings, so what could be holding me back from fullness of joy and abundant living?

If we are not moving forward in faith, including remembering what God has already done in our lives and expecting him always to be with us, are we rejecting what he offers? Are we turning away from what he has given us and staying behind at the threshold? Where are we going if we are not leaning his way and taking a new path leading to his dream for us? Moving forward in faith means realizing that the past is gone, forgiven, and done. We are new people in Jesus Christ.

Many want to change, but they are not willing to go all the way. They want to strike out in a new direction, but they do not want change within themselves. We all have a past. God has taken care of our past through his Son's life, death, and resurrection. He is done with the people we used to be. We are new in Christ, as the apostle Paul says: "You were taught, with regard to your former way of life, to put off your old self, which is being corrupted by its deceitful desires; to be made new in the attitude of your minds; and to put on the new self, created to be like God in true righteousness and holiness" (Eph. 4:22-24).

Why would we want to hold on to what is old? Do we not trust God with the *new* he has given us? God says that we are *new* people. He has given us *new* hearts and lives, with new horizons of his choosing. As newly adopted children of God, we are on a daring adventure. When it comes to old lives and habits, God says, "Off with it. Take on the new. I am with you and I will never leave you. I will show you new things and give you new dreams. Take hold. Wear it. Dream it. I am your Father and I love you as my child. You will not be disappointed."

We want what is new, but we want to place our own conditions on it. In other words, we want control. In the end, we want to lean on our own understanding, though we are told to "Trust in the Lord with all your heart and lean not on your own understanding; in all your ways submit to him, and he will make your paths straight" (Prov. 3:5-6). Still, we don't want to take a chance and trust God.

In Scripture, God uses the analogy of a bride (the church) and groom (Jesus). We walk across the threshold to Jesus. He gives us a new name, a new family, a new life, new work, and a life of abundance in him. All this is available if we live life as God intended, life as he planned for us.

Yes in Christ Jesus

I enjoy the beauty of the deep red crepe myrtle tree in front of me when I walk. It overwhelms me with God's goodness and beauty in creation. I begin thinking of the promises we have in Jesus Christ. As the Apostle assured us, all God's promises are yes in Christ Jesus: "For the Son of God, Jesus Christ, who was preached among you by me ... was not *Yes* and *No*, but in him it has always been *Yes*" (2 Cor. 1:19). We are not rejected, we are not abandoned, and we are not lost anymore. In Christ we are found in grace; we are loved and never left alone. When we feel rejected or abandoned or alone, it does not come from him. Jesus says, *Yes*, to us. He comes to receive us, not to reject us, and he brings us hope, not despair. Jesus loves us eternally and does not condemn us.

The beauty of Christ coming for us to take us with him, even if for a little while we wait, gives us hope for the future and rest in the present. He is coming again to Earth to reign forever. Our lives here are only the beginning of our eternity, for God's plan has been always to come for us and give us a future. He is not going to leave us or stop loving us.

When we act as if we need to make ourselves "right" with God by earning our way or achieving certain goals, it means we doubt the sovereignty and promises of God through Christ. Through the willing sacrifice of the Son, the Father made us "right" with him. In his eyes, we are righteous. If we think we need to protect ourselves or hide from our sinfulness, we really do not get what God did for us in Christ. He took away our unrighteousness and our shame. He uncovered our sin and shame and replaced it with his grace. We no longer have to cover ourselves because God in his wisdom has given us a way to approach his throne with confidence through Jesus Christ. This was the divine plan before creation. All of our sin—past, present, and future—has been forgiven. Only through Jesus' atoning death on the cross is our sin forgiven. It is only through his perfect sacrifice and innocent blood that we are covered and forgiven. We did not deserve it, nor can we earn this gift of grace he bestows on us.

The promises of God are always yes in Jesus Christ. As God's children and the recipients of these promises, we are forever forgiven. Through the atoning blood of Christ, we have a shield against sin, and thus we no longer need to be covered. The Father sees us as his perfect children through the work of the Son on the cross. These are indeed good and beautiful gifts. Let us say *yes!* to the One and Only God and Father of us all in Jesus Christ!

BEYOND to the Life God Imagined for Us

If we only knew, and if we only knew and lived like we knew!

Through the Holy Spirit, God awakens us to faith. This awakening opens our hearts and minds to the great God of the universe. He then grows a yearning in us to know God and his Truth. Thus, God's Spirit pursues us with an awakening to faith, the truth that God is God, and the desire to know him. It all begins with God.

When we come to faith in God through Jesus Christ, the Holy Spirit empowers us to be more than we are and more the way God planned us to be. He makes us into new creatures with a desire to live differently and to follow and serve him. He gives us the capacity to choose life in him daily.

In remembering how God desires us to be more than we are, consider the acronym BEYOND:

God is:

Behold the Holy Spirit awakens us to faith

Eternal the Holy Spirit reveals that he is God

Yearning the Holy Spirit makes us yearn for God and his Truth

God in us:

Ordinary to outstanding the Holy Spirit empowers

Now new the Holy Spirit makes us desire new things

Determined to choose life the Holy Spirit guides us to choose his ways daily

In the beginning, when we awakened to God and chose to follow him, we may have abruptly stopped at the decision point and remained at the threshold. For many, we may know that God expunges our sin and forgives us, but we still feel we are not "right" with God. We may know in our minds we are forgiven, but we still feel we need to cover our shame. We have awakened to God's beauty in Jesus Christ, and yet we have not fully received what he has to offer. Instead of going beyond to the new life God imagines for us, we stay behind—living at the threshold.

If we were to accept in our heart of hearts that we are forgiven, we would be "new" creatures. Our perceptions of God have changed, and through the indwelling of his Holy Spirit, we have too. We move from an old perspective to a new one, although we sometimes get stuck in familiar ways and act as if we are new creatures holding onto old beliefs. We have not received the *new* as God has given it.

When we receive what God intends for our new life, we live as his redeemed children, forgiven, covered, and righteous. With heaven's help, we cross the threshold into the life the Lord has imagined for us, true living "to the full" in gratitude and worship. We are able to wear the gifts he has given to us, including the garments of salvation and the robe of his righteousness (Isa. 61:10). We awaken to God's taking us across the threshold to share his bounty and thrive as his creation in beauty and glory. We are redeemed, new, and we receive what he intends. We can go out in his splendor. With God himself in us, we are able to withstand the journey and live the life intended for the sons and daughters of God, living like we know what we know. This is living way beyond the threshold!

God Comes in Small Packages

It is certainly true that God comes in small packages—a whisper, or the simple, mundane things of the day. Scripture illustrates this truth in different ways. For example, Mary bore God's Son in a manger. Jesus cared for the single sheep that was lost from the flock. This is not to say Jesus is less majestic, or Almighty, or holy. He is surely all of these things. Though God comes to us in small packages, he is able to do far more than we can ever imagine, as the following Bible promises communicate:

> But you, Lord, are a compassionate and gracious God, slow to anger, abounding in love and faithfulness. (Ps. 86:15)

Praise be to the God and Father of our Lord Jesus Christ, who has blessed us in the heavenly realms with every spiritual blessing in Christ. (Eph. 1:3)

Now to him who is able to do immeasurably more than all we ask or imagine, according to his power that is at work within us. (Eph. 3:20)

God comes to share his abundance with us, his children. It is our inheritance. We cannot grasp it without knowing the One from whom it comes. Unless God the Holy Spirit opens our hearts and eyes, we cannot know. The relationship with the Creator of the universe through his Son is one to experience. Abundance is given through a way of life, the way of Jesus. Jesus has blessed us in the heavenly realms with every spiritual blessing.

Our Inheritance—Hope and Righteousness

Living life to the full is experiencing the hope of God as he has accomplished our being made right with him through Jesus, his Son. Hebrews 11:1 says that "faith is confidence in what we hope for and assurance about what we do not see." Hope is in the unseen but the sure victory of Jesus. Living life in God's fullness is resting in hope and God's righteousness (pure, blameless, without sin or shame), not our own.

God credits us with righteousness when we put our faith in the Son. He made us blameless with the death of his Son, who is the only pure and blameless person ever to live. He then died for our sins and was raised to give us eternal life. He resides with us through the indwelling of the Holy Spirit. Furthermore, the Holy Spirit is not the best way we can live a righteous life; it is the only way.

When we receive the righteousness the Father gives us by faith, we exercise it by believing and by being grateful for it. The knowledge that we cannot exercise our inheritance of hope and righteousness on our own helps us acknowledge we need God's righteousness. We come without knowledge, insight, or ability to believe, but God gives us this, too. He reveals our depravity and helps us to be willing to accept the Father's gift of righteousness.

Righteousness is not a thing to be grasped. In receiving the Lord's righteousness, we become like him. It is gift, pure and simple; we cannot do it on our own. God opens our eyes and hearts, and he then gives us the gift of grace to help us live a righteous life.

What does the Righteous Life Look Like?

Abraham went where God led him even when he did not know where he was heading. David, a sinner like us, cried out to God, and God called David a man after his own heart. Paul, a man who killed those who went the way of the gospel, was blinded by the light and transformed. Afterwards, he declared his joy—even in prison—in knowing and suffering for the gospel of Jesus Christ he preached and proclaimed. Peter, after denying Christ three times, continued serving and preaching the gospel, and Jesus said that upon Peter his church would be built.

Experiencing the "rightness" God gives us when we choose to follow in his footsteps, we not only discover the heart of God, we know he is much more than we could ever comprehend, and his ways to us are beyond our imagination.

God is so much bigger than is possible for us to know, and we cannot limit him. And yet, he wants us, as his children, to know him on a personal basis.

Our Lives in Christ and How We "Press On" and Grow

If we ask, God shows what he wants for our lives—to mature in the Holy Spirit and to grow in knowing Christ. What goals has he given us? What is the preparation, and what are the steps? How do we "press on?

We press on only in the power of the Holy Spirit. We choose to do so, and then the Holy Spirit gives us the strength, guidance, and direction to go the journey of faith.

Are we as close to God (Jesus) as we want to be? Are there steps to take to become closer? Here are some suggested ways for growing closer to God:

Time with God:

- Spend more time being still before God in Bible study and prayer
- Surrender—let go and let God
- Ask God to change us and change our thinking

Gratitude:

- Begin a journal of gratitude
- Start a calendar on which to track what is encountered on a daily basis (from my book *Real Struggles, Real Hope*)—recording hope/gratitude

Practicing Faith—Giving to Others:

- Give time for God to reach out to others through us
- Walk through the "open doors" to step out for God

Worship and Fellowship with Others in Church, Study, and Reaching Out

In worship and Christian fellowship, we show up and God grows us up. He takes the mustard seed of faith and makes it flourish. His Word teaches us, and he speaks to us through it. If he prompts us to step out in faith and we follow as he guides us, he produces the harvest. As the apostle Paul wrote, "I press on toward the goal to win the prize for which God has called me heavenward in Christ Jesus. All of us, then, who are mature should take such a view of things. And if on some point you think differently, that too God will make clear to you. Only let us live up to what we have already attained" (Phil. 3:14-16).

"Getting Out of the Way"

Getting out of the way of you, Lord
Take me to new places, shores
Of your choosing, to live outside
Me, looking up, you, to guide

Your truth to know, your love
To grow, your will from above
Within me, as my focus shifts
From inside me, your face lifts

To others, I see all around me
Who need you to believe, to see
You to hope, to choose life
Above all else and strife

A light shines, the veil parts
A word awakens the heart
A new spark, the soul fights
New life lives where death dies

God is good and hope is not gone
Again to remember what He has done
Waiting afresh for the next breath
Of God's newness and wealth

His presence is real, can be counted upon
God's truth, grace, and abundance - gifts to us
Waiting in some form comes and goes
As we focus our eyes upon Him

We may not know the details of this or that
But we know our Savior is coming back
He is here for the journey, that's a fact
Let's follow him for our next act

My Red Dress (Given to me by Mary at Christmas)

My red dress was a true red. The fabric was chiffon and fell softly on the body. It had a white Peter Pan collar with long sleeves of the same red color sash, which tied at the waist. Mary thought I looked lovely in it; I could tell it gave her great joy to see me wearing it. I loved the dress, especially because she gave something to wear to make me look pretty. I felt so special. But the reason I wore the dress so much was because it was such a beautiful gift, not because I felt beautiful in it.

The dress was significant in more ways than I can count. It was a new beginning. Having someone buy something for me to wear was novel. I always loved the things Mary chose, even if I didn't always think they looked good on me. They were beautiful and hand-selected, with hues made for my coloring. They were usually nicer clothes than I would have bought. They were uniquely chosen for me, and it was good being known in this way, like being adorned as someone special.

It was Christmas, twelve days after we were married. Only God would bring these things to mind of his provision all those many years ago. Mary was as happy as me for the Christmas season. She always gave the best gifts, made the best meals, and knew how to make the holidays special. I enjoyed Christmas at her table and home. It was becoming mine, too.

God was showing me his love through Mary, my new mother-in-law. He replaced the old with the new in my life. Someone knew my lack, my need, and wanted to fill it. God always knew, but he was using a person in my life to show me. God smiled as he extended his truth and grace to me. His ways are not our ways.

Red Dress Redemption

The red dress had more meaning than I knew. I didn't know what to do with such an insightful and kind gift. What do we do with gifts? Do we receive them with thanks, or do we reject them by not opening or using them? Do we love receiving gifts but never accept them as our own?

Looking back, I had been rejected so often that I probably didn't feel worthy of gifts. I thought I wouldn't look good in this dress, or that dress wouldn't fit. Or, I would think I couldn't wear that clothing with dignity because I did not feel good about myself in general. It was an unusually nice thing for Mary to do, and I loved the red dress because she gave it to me. Yet, I ultimately rejected the gift because I couldn't wear it as the gift was intended—to make me feel and look good.

Isn't this what we do with God's grace and favor? We keep wearing our old selves even though we are forgiven and stand in his grace through the accomplished work of Christ on the cross. He gives us this incredible gift, of which none are worthy, and we can't quite receive the gift he intends us to have.

I was given a new beginning into a new family. It is the same with all Christians. In Jesus, we are born into a new family when we accept Jesus as our Savior. Do we receive the blessings of Jesus, which include all of his inheritance? We know we are not worthy, but that does not mean we should not have it.

The truth is we have to put off our old selves and enter the new by the grace and work of Jesus Christ. It is a journey of faith, and we must persevere in this race because it is the race worth running.

Red Dress and Laughter

God created me with a conscientious and sensitive type of temperament. A few years ago I asked him to create in me a less serious and more humor-filled nature. I thought that if I asked, God could broaden me and transform my temperament.

A few weeks later, I was leading a Bible study group where I had been transparent about a few of my weaknesses (the serious nature not being one of them). After the session, an active participant came up to me and went on and on about what a great job I did—and how funny I was. I didn't know what I had done that was so funny, or how I had come across to her sense of humor, but I knew she was giving me a compliment. God answered my prayer that day, and I knew it. I laughed and thanked God for weeks after the meeting. I failed to see how I had been funny in any way, but God certainly has a great sense of humor.

Red Dress and Humor

My husband and I, along with our two children, were on a special trip to commemorate graduations and new educational adventures. As I have intimated, God has revealed many truths through the red dress. For one thing, he wants us to receive, wear, and use what he gives us. As one who acts and responds to life as the daughter of the King, I must act and live the life he has given. If it means leading in laughter or wearing the red dress, I am to do it as a child of the King. On this trip, many adventures reminded me that God is my father, and I am his child.

One night on the ship we went to the theater to watch a comedian doing improv. It was a formal night in the dining room, so I wore a special red dress, a classic I felt good in. We sat mid-way back from the front with nice seats and a good view. The comedian started out by asking questions of the audience. As he came out into the audience, I noticed he was coming toward our row of seats—and I was on the end. All of a sudden he was asking questions of me. He took my hand and pulled me along with him to come up on stage. I about had a cow! There I was in a comedy skit on stage in front of five hundred people. Boy, was I scared! I was laughing too … at him and at me.

Experiencing the fun and the funny, I enjoyed the laughter and the lighter side of things. All in one evening, wearing a red dress and laughing at myself, I received what God intended. He has a huge sense of humor. God is the Almighty and the One who knows us from the inside out, and still he wants to shower us with his mercy and provision. Thanks be to God from whom all blessings flow!

Being a Daughter of the King of Kings

Being a daughter of the King of kings is beyond imagination. It is what we are in Christ—sons and daughters. Then why do we not act or think as sons and daughters who are loved and given more than life itself? I don't know how to be a daughter. Actually, I am afraid of being one. It hasn't been easy. My idea of being a daughter, shaped as a small child in my family of origin, entailed being the caregiver, the responsible one, and the caretaker of the home. Most of the time, no one noticed. It was like I was invisible. In fact, I wanted to be invisible; perhaps if I were invisible, I wouldn't have to interact with others. It is only in hindsight that I have seen the larger picture of the family dysfunction.

Being God's daughter is not like this at all. Being a daughter of the King, God fills in empty places. He directs the course. He provides for his children. He knows our every need, thought, dream, or desire. And he is there to protect, guide, and deliver his daughter from harm if rescue is necessary. I know and have lived this truth the last several decades of my life. God gives us his true abundance in receiving our position in him as true daughters of the King. It is by faith that we receive our position in God and live our position in God—the abundant life, the true inheritance, and the fullness of joy in all that God has given his children.

Father God, I want to live like your daughter because I am your daughter. Teach me to trust you and live in truth, trust, and freedom as one who has your unmerited favor. I know you have given me the richest of inheritances, beyond anything I can imagine. Help me to receive your riches without hesitation as I follow you on this journey. Show me how to dare to dream your dream for my life. Guide me to choose life with every step and receive the blessing that you have for me.

In your name, Jesus, I pray.

Being a Daughter to Another Daughter

My mother needed to move out of the house I grew up in because she wasn't safe there anymore. The house was not close to anyone, and she needed help day and night. I actually prayed for years that she would come to this realization, and now she had. She called me to say she wanted to move into the Presbyterian home in our community. There was a waiting list, for it was a very popular place; it seemed everyone wanted to live out their days there. In my mother's mind, she thought she could move right in, no questions asked. That's how life had always worked for her. And so it did.

God's economy is so different from our human economy. He has enough to go around, and he meets the needs of every person. We sacrifice for one another out of our abundance in Jesus, who sacrificed his life for all others. God is owner of all and treats us like we are his best creation. We have an awesome inheritance that cannot be thrown away or discarded. Nor can it be taken away. We are the King's children, and he loves us.

We are Both Daughters of the King—My Mother and Me

No one can take away our inheritance in God, and no one can take away our honor. He holds it for us. He holds my inheritance for me, and though I don't deserve it, I want it. God is the giver of all good things. I lean in to him and anticipate all he has promised his children. I expect good things. I don't let the dishonorable things done to me or the dishonorable things I have done to others make me cynical about him and his desire for his children. I dare to dream and ask for the unimaginable, because that is who he is.

God has given me a greater inheritance than I could ever expect. He has forgiven me for my judgment and anger, and for shutting down as a daughter of the King. I tried to "make do" in dire circumstances instead of turning to him to take the burden from me and use it for his purposes. He always has a greater purpose.

Father God, help me honor you in my life, in the ups and downs, the trials and the triumphs, and the relationships that cause me to stumble. Show me how to be a daughter. I want to honor and to love each person in my life as you would have me. Give me your grace to follow through with courage and gratitude.

Enthralled by Our Beauty—Daughters of the King

Psalm 45:11 says, "Let the king be enthralled by your beauty; honor him, for he is your lord." What is this beauty God sees in us? He sees the face of Jesus when he looks at his daughters. Our beauty enthralls him when he looks at us because he sees what he created us to be. He gave us all we need to be who he created us to be. When we chose to follow him by believing in the death and resurrection of Jesus, and by the help of the Holy Spirit living in us, we may choose to be daughters of the King Jesus.

We are God's children created to do good works in his name. We are his children with a wonderful inheritance to whom he has given everything we need to do good works: "For we are God's handiwork, created in Christ Jesus to do good works, which God prepared in advance for us to do" (Eph. 2:10). God guides, protects, and gives us the strength and courage we need to live for him. And that is how our lives reflect Jesus.

His glory awakens the entire world. For this reason, God allows us the privilege of working with him for his kingdom on earth. He does not need us, but he wants us to be a part of the glory the world sees. After all, when the world sees the transformation in us, it knows that transformation comes from God, the only One who could bring about such a huge difference in us. His love and power are not equaled.

Abundant and Holy Father God

Lord, thank you for your inheritance. Give me a heart to know it and to be amazed constantly by it. Help me to see my life always as full. I know that it is; I know you have made it so. At times, I fear I lack not in things but in what it takes to do a thing. It feels that resources would make things better. But I know that all comes from you and you are the giver of every good thing. So if it is something I am to do, I ask that you provide for it. I know that you will provide the fresh thought, the dream, the action, and the resources to make it come about and that you will show me and help me to be faithful in the doing of whatever you call me to do.

Why do we ever perceive lack when we are surrounded by amazing bounty? God has given us so much materially, spiritually, emotionally, and physically. We ought always to thank him for helping us give back and live out of the fullness of him in our lives. He has abundantly supplied us with all we need for life and godliness. As we read in Second Peter 1:3, "His divine power has given us everything we need for a godly life through our knowledge of him who called us by his own glory and goodness." Another relevant Scripture is Ephesians 2:10, which teaches us that the Lord has prepared works in advance for us to do: "For we are God's handiwork, created in Christ Jesus to do good works, which God prepared in advance for us to do." Also in Paul's letter to the Ephesians, we have been given more than we imagine: "Now to him who is able to do immeasurably more than all we ask or imagine, according to his power that is at work within us" (Eph. 3:20).

The Father shows us how to respond to such bounty and grace, and helps us live out of the worship and praise of him for who he is and what he has done for us.

Father, I ask you to continue showing me who you are in secret, and taking me to the places you want me to go so you can heal me more than I imagine, and live more fully and wholly for you.
Thank you.

Ten Plus Years

God has been consistently and tremendously faithful to our family of four. We have been so blessed by the move we made nearly fifteen years ago. Both children have made good friends, done well in school, and we as a family have learned to see God's hand in our lives and to trust him. The relationships we have formed have given us great joy and wonderful connectedness to the community and to one another.

I was looking out the kitchen window and thought about the living creatures that lived in our back yard over the years. Our precious Angel, our golden retriever, was queen over her surroundings. The rabbits and squirrels knew they were living in her world. Yet they roamed around and ate in her presence because when Angel was at home, she was calm and collected. The cardinal that has been around uses our trees and fence as his own. I am simply in awe of God's creation—just in this bird's-eye view.

Then I think of the children in the neighborhood, all grown up and starting their first jobs. Some are graduating now, but it wasn't long ago when the boys were hanging from the trees as we drove into the subdivision—always a welcoming sight. Now the little ones fill up the pool across from our house in the summer. They are quite the sight on the first day of school as they gather at the bus stop right in front of our house. We have been privileged to see what God has done in the lives of those around us.

Our home these last ten years or so has been the place of teen gatherings, small and large. I remember the Panini parties our daughter had for her friends. I may be exaggerating, but I believe her high school graduation party was at least two hundred or so guests. There were students all over the floor; it was a wonderful sight. And then there are the group projects—especially the French videos made by our son and his peers. My husband has a group that meets every Friday here; they call themselves Team Oatmeal. They meet to share in one another's lives and to study God's Word. I have also been privileged to host my Bible study group here. Our home has been truly enriched by the friends who have participated in our lives.

I am extremely grateful for the spacious home God has provided for us. We are still amazed at how he moved us here—he lifted us up and set us down. Praise God from whom all blessings flow!

Transformation—Wearing what God Gives Us

I didn't want to miss the evening with my writing friends. These evenings are always inspirational and full of fun. We gather in the dining room at a beautiful table set for special guests. The delicious food is served with warmth and love by our hospitable host. We moved from story to story, each more intimate than before. We shared heartfelt struggles and questions around the table. There were words of encouragement and affirmation, moments of revelation, and, of course, much fun and laughter.

I learn so much about my sweet sisters in Christ at these transformation evenings, and also about their hearts and their hunger for God's best in their lives and relationships. I also learn much about their writing. When we meet as a writers' group, we teach each other about God's timing for our writing and not putting idols of whatever kind in our lives. Words around the table enlighten, encourage, and enrich my life. God's presence with us is palpable, and at the same time, each precious sister in Christ exhorts the truth and wisdom of the Lord.

Recently, as my turn came to share, I thought perhaps there might not be enough time to share what was on my heart. The group insisted I go on. As God would have it, I get healed again and again in the sharing of what he has done. I am humbled and privileged to tell the amazing things God has done and keeps on doing in my life. And here again, the red dress pops up as a symbol of hope, healing, and transformation as I wear God's calling. I am so thankful for my dear friends and their encouragement in my spiritual walk. I am thankful for their affirming the stories God gives me. I see God's hand more clearly each time I speak or write of his faithfulness in my life. I am especially grateful to be exhorted to allow God to work, and for me to receive and wear a divine calling.

Are You Standing at the Threshold?

I have been standing at the threshold most of my life. What do I mean? God has covered me to come over the threshold with him. He has invited me, and I have accepted his gift of a personal relationship with the God of the universe. I have peace with him. I began my journey of eternity with my Lord and Savior, Jesus Christ. He is my life. He is my hope in all the struggles of life. He has delivered me, and I have a story to tell. I am awake to the joy and the abundant life he has already offered me. Why is it still so difficult to receive what God has already given?

I keep expecting I will come to understand how God could do such a thing. God has given me a life that cannot be understood or obtained except by his immeasurable grace. It is as if I am standing at the threshold. I cannot fully grasp how and why the Father has credited me with his rightness, just as he did with his friend, Abraham: "The scripture was fulfilled that says, 'Abraham believed God, and it was credited to him as righteousness,' and he was called God's friend" (James 2:23). I live at the threshold because I want to be worthy, as Abraham was counted worthy. Yet I cannot be worthy. It is not possible unless I receive God's gift. I know this and I believe it, and I am so grateful for divine grace. But I go back. It is a journey of faith to step over the threshold and put on the clothing he has to offer. I am worthy because I am God's child. I am his child and he alone is worthy.

The new life requires that I put on God's righteousness and shed myself of the clothing of the old life. I put on the new clothing to show he is my Father and I am his child. I walk across the threshold, and he helps me to stand. The new child is a child of God, made worthy by the Lord's dying and rising to new life for you and for me.

BEYOND the Threshold

> I pray that the eyes of your heart may be enlightened in order that you may know the hope to which he has called you, the riches of his glorious inheritance in his holy people, and his incomparably great power for us who believe. That power is the same as the mighty strength he exerted when he raised Christ from the dead and seated him at his right hand in the heavenly realms. (Eph. 1:18-20)

Praise be to the God and Father of our Lord Jesus Christ! In his great mercy he has given us new birth into a living hope through the resurrection of Jesus Christ from the dead, and into an inheritance that can never perish, spoil or fade. This inheritance is kept in heaven for you, who through faith are shielded by God's power until the coming of the salvation that is ready to be revealed in the last time. (1 Pet. 1:3-5)

"Prayer for New Life"

Father God,

I want to accept my new life in full. I want to cross the threshold for all you have for me. I pray you would show me how to make each step of this journey with you at the helm.

I don't want to go back to old patterns, the old worldview, to rebellion, grumbling, striving, and worrying. I want to have a new perspective and a fresh word from you today. Help me turn from my sins and to lean in to the new me, the one you planned for me before I was born. Help me desire to delight you. Thank you for a new heart and a new life in Jesus Christ. Show me how to live like a free woman who is loved and cared for in abundance, and who is full of joy and peace.

Thank you for giving me wisdom and revelation and a heart of hope. I praise you for the things I need for the work you have planned in advance for me to do. Help me to do it in your name and for your glory. Thank you for the inheritance you have for me now and for the future. Help me to act like I have it. Help me to live each day with the power you have given me in Christ Jesus, with the Holy Spirit dwelling in me.

Praise and thanks be to God!

Thank you, Father God. I ask these things in Jesus' name and by his atoning blood.

Amen.

Ramifications of Not Receiving what God has to Offer

God intends for us to receive what he has to offer. He will not coerce us, but he does pursue us. If he has given grace as he apportioned it, will we receive it with faith? Will we step out in faith to use these gifts for the body of Christ to be unified and to become mature so we can attain to the whole measure of the fullness of Christ?

> But to each one of us grace has been given as Christ apportioned it. [8] This is why it says: "When he ascended on high, he took many captives and gave gifts to his people." (What does "he ascended" mean except that he also descended to the lower, earthly regions? He who descended is the very one who ascended higher than all the heavens, in order to fill the whole universe.) So Christ himself gave the apostles, the prophets, the evangelists, the pastors and teachers, to equip his people for works of service, so that the body of Christ may be built up until we all reach unity in the faith and in the knowledge of the Son of God and become mature, attaining to the whole measure of the fullness of Christ. Then we will no longer be infants, tossed back and forth by the waves, and blown here and there by every wind of teaching and by the cunning and craftiness of people in their deceitful scheming. (Eph. 4:7-14)

When each member of the body of Christ uses the gifts God has given, the church demonstrates the real fullness of God by living in unity and maturity.

On the other hand, we may not receive what he has to offer us. The ramifications of not receiving what God has to offer are serious. In choosing or not choosing, there are consequences on our journey of faith. The body of Christ suffers from our not choosing to believe and receive the grace and gifts God has so freely given.

What are the ramifications of not knowing and receiving what we have in God through his Son, Jesus Christ?

- o Wavering faith and unbelief

- o Increasing self-reliance; lack of trust

- o Immature belief system; not knowing him in his Word

- o Striving and burn out

- o Lack of the abundant life

- o Void that cannot be filled with other things

- o Missing out on God's intentions for his children

- o Inability to give of ourselves and losing the privilege of serving him

- o Lack of joy, peace, abundance, and rest

What are the ramifications of refusing what God has given through his Son, Jesus Christ?

- o May be a believer, but not living by truth in God's Word— still believing lies

- o Living in shame and not feeling worthy

- o Holding on to doing it ourselves

- o Trying to be worthy by pleasing, achieving, or by gaining power

Do I Get the Significance of Gilgal for This Day?

We read in Joshua 5:9 that "Then the Lord said to Joshua, 'Today I have rolled away the reproach of Egypt from you.' So the place has been called Gilgal to this day." God removed the reproach of Egypt at Gilgal when he told them to remember that he had freed them and given them a place of their own. Likewise, we have a place of our own. We are tethered to God, and in him we have God's riches. No longer are we enslaved to our former selves, to shame, and to sin. We have a new inheritance. We remember we are his.

Do we understand the significance of Gilgal for this day?

- • We are no longer living enslaved or in shame

- • We are crossing over to God instead of living in slavery

- We are letting go of the things holding us in slavery, and we will move across the threshold toward God

- We are willing to allow him to show us how to navigate the hard things so he can give us the good

- We are willing to exercise radical obedience by trusting only in him

- We are willing to see ourselves as God sees us by stepping out in faith and receiving his grace

Are we yielding to God as the Almighty conqueror by living in submission to him?

Gilgal Again—the Reproach Rolled Away and Letting Go of Shame

Honoring and doing well are high priorities, but are they higher than God? Do I want them more than I want God?

God is God, and there is no other. Instead of my shame, he has given me Jesus. I must rely on him to remind me of who I am in him and how he sees me as a child of God, forgiven and without shame. The Father receives me with open arms as a loving father who has only good things to give. He has prepared a banquet for his children that is lacking in nothing.

Are we ready to receive what God has provided? Only when we give things up, hand them over and let them go, will we be ready to live in the Promised Land of plenty with the loving and lavish Father who has given us freedom to live in his abundance. God's grace comes to us as a free gift from the Father giving up his only Son for the eternal lives of those who believe and become his children. But the price of this abundance is quite costly—radical obedience. We must give ourselves to God and trust only in him. Every moment God allows us to choose to follow him or not, and he is there to help and guide. As we surrender the shame, we move toward God and acknowledge he is the One we want to know and please, rather than ourselves. With this small step we surrender. When we surrender, God multiplies the blessing of himself in our lives. All of this leads to truly abundant living.

Not only did the Israelites cross the Jordan on dry ground, but God also gave them the land of milk and honey. He made it possible for the ones who had been obedient to cross over into the Promised Land. He no longer wanted them to live as slaves in a free land. What are we still enslaved to? What is keeping us from living in the Promised Land? What has hindered us from living the abundant life God has promised?

Why Seek God?

As God's children, we get drawn in by the world and its depravity. We fall into the trap of believing the lies of the Evil one. We wrestle not only with our failings and our unbelief, but also with our desires for more than what we have. God also wants us to have more. We have allowed the world's perspective to seep into our own. Having more is what God intended, for that is what the abundant life is all about. He has given it in his Son. Furthermore, God is able to equip us to live life "to the full" here on earth until we reach our eternal home.

Why seek God? Because God seeks us and draws us to himself. When we have more of him, we want more of him. That is the nature of the truly abundant life; with more, he gives more. Our journey on earth with God means we experience more and more of Jesus as we seek life to the full.

Being Taught by God; Being Led by God; Being Parented by God

God teaches us how to be his daughters. He is our Father God, and we are his children. He loves for us to rest in him as he shows us what he has for us. Sometimes this journey takes us through difficult times, or shows us our brokenness, but only because he has something he wants to heal in us. Sometimes God will carry us across mountains where we find we are the mountain ourselves. And sometimes he walks us through really hard times so we can learn to trust and depend on him in ways we could never have accomplished if he didn't show us who he is in the midst of it all.

God has given us his Word, and we do not need anything else, other than God himself. We don't need specific knowledge, or even the outline of things to come. We need to come to God, listen, obey, and follow where he leads.

For most of my young life I asked God the questions that came to mind, and I doubted myself and had difficulty believing him, too. If he loved me, how could I not feel his love? Why couldn't I trust anyone, including God? I wanted to believe he loved me. I just couldn't. God led me through many hard places, brought me to himself, and revealed who he is and how much he loves me. He has never left me, and he has healed my broken heart.

God is our life, and we want to be full of him. Let us pursue our Creator God, the giver of life and all good things, our Savior and Lord. The Lord God himself teaches us how to be his daughters.

Being Taught by God in His Word—Truths of His Extravagant Grace

Isaiah 50:4 says, "The Sovereign Lord has given me a well-instructed tongue, to know the word that sustains the weary. He wakens me morning by morning, wakens my ear to listen like one being instructed." We may listen like ones being taught as we come to him early in the day. We are to:

- Listen like one being taught

- Start the day

- Do not turn a deaf ear or rebel

In Psalm 32:8 informs us that "I will instruct you and teach you in the way you should go; I will counsel you with my loving eye on you." Our gracious heavenly Father loves us and makes our hearts new. With his loving eye upon us, he counsels, guides, and teaches. Our posture before our great and gracious God is to be:

- Humble

- Empty

- Ready to receive his offering

- Worshipful

- Grateful

- Available for his presence

Psalm 19:1 says that "The heavens declare the glory of God; the skies proclaim the work of his hands." God speaks and reveals himself through his creation. God may use whatever he wishes to speak or reveal himself to his human creation.

As Psalm 18:20 describes the great mercy of our Almighty and sovereign Lord. "The Lord has dealt with me according to my righteousness; according to the cleanness of my hands he has rewarded me." Because of his mercy to us, we are made right with him. Our cleanness, because of Jesus, becomes the grace by which we live. He rewards our righteousness, indeed given by him in Jesus.

What will be our response to God in light of his great truths?

- Remember, praise, and thank God that we are forgiven and covered

- Worship and thank the One and Only by which our sins are not counted against us or even remembered

- Remember and thank God that we are taught by him

- Choose to follow Jesus, who loved us first, by taking steps of faith

- Trust Jesus and enjoy his presence

What are my actions in response to his truth in his Word?

- Interaction with God all day long

- Loving his people

- Prayer for this day we have been given

Lord God,

We are awed and humbled by your mercy and love. We come to you undeserving and empty. We ask that you make us ready and willing to receive you, Jesus. Thank you.

In your name we pray,

Amen.

Abundance is God's Answer

God is the counterpart to everything we face, and he responds to our needs out of his bounty. When we are in need of relief from a stressful circumstance, or rescue from danger, God's response is always to answer with himself. He does not answer with a quick fix; rather, he comes as he is to bring us all of himself. Scripture affirms that when the Lord answers us with himself, he woos and anoints:

Job 36:16: He is wooing you from the jaws of distress to a spacious place free from restriction, to the comfort of your table laden with choice food.

Psalm 23:5: You prepare a table before me in the presence of my enemies. You anoint my head with oil; my cup overflows.

The definition of *abundance* is overflowing fullness of the heart—the full measure of all the fullness of God, the whole measure of God himself.

- He is our life, bringing us life to the full

- He is our peace

- He is our wholeness and our healing

Our response is to remember who God is and who he says he is. He promises to fill the void in us.

- When other things do not fill us

- When we are lacking

- When stressed, anxious, or fearful

- When we are in need of healing

Whether we lack, are anxious, fearful, or in need of peace or healing, God offers himself. He offers himself in place of all that hinders us, including our worry, pain, brokenness, fear, and anything making us less than he made us to be. He offers not only what we do not have, but he also gives us more than we ask or imagine. "Now to him who is able to do immeasurably more than all we ask or imagine, according to his power that is at work within us" (Eph. 3:20).

The Lord desires that we receive him in his fullness, the whole measure, life to the full, the abundant life. God offers himself where we have a void, and where we think we are full. He knows our need and how we mistakenly think we can fill it. Yet he waits for us and woos us, often with the very pain or fear that hinders us. If we let go of our human options, we see him—we know his presence even in the dark: "I will give you hidden treasures, riches stored in secret places, so that you may know that I am the Lord, the God of Israel, who summons you by name" (Isa. 45:3).

God offers himself, and when we go to him, we experience heavenly peace and healing. For a moment, we know what he means by fullness. Sometimes we linger and know the fullness of God for a bit longer. And he wants that for us. In fact, he has the table ready.

God Promises the Fullness of Jesus

God promises us the fullness of himself in Jesus. In every crevice of our being, and in the void inside, he grows us up to desire more of him, to seek him in the broken places, the empty spaces, and in the passions he placed in us before we were born. Jesus is the counterpart to everything in us that is incomplete. We need him for completion, yet the fullness of God seems impossible. But our God, the great God of the universe, is the God of the impossible.

Father God,

*I don't know how or why, but I seek you. I desire your fullness —
and even this desire gives me joy because it is from you. Change
me into the woman you have created for fullness. Father, I turn
from my old ways of thinking. Help me. Thank you for helping me
put on the new. Seeking more of you in me is a gift only you can
give. Thank you. I see your hand. Praise you, Father, for loving me
and allowing me to see you today.*

*Your love is kind and true and forever, and it is so much bigger
than I can comprehend.*

It engulfs me. In your name, Amen

Fresh New Pursuits—His of Us, His Children

God does not leave us alone in our weaknesses but allows
them to surface (okay, maybe to scream at us!) in order for us to
grow in our dependence on Christ. He then gives us his strength
and empowers us to trust him as he accomplishes his work in us.
He will not allow us to turn back to our old habits of trying to
understand. He will let us get to the end of ourselves as we
analyze, critique, and get anxious. He commands us to lean onto
him instead of our own understanding. What a sweet place it is
when we rest our minds on heaven's King!

The antidote to waiting on God is seeking him. When we are
focused on God instead of ourselves, we become more aware of
our own frailties and insufficiencies. It is not a bad thing to know
where our weaknesses lie, but it is not good to analyze them and
spend time on them to the point we become anxious or fretful.
Minds focused on God are at peace: "You will keep in perfect
peace those whose minds are steadfast, because they trust in you"
(Isa. 26:3).

There have been times when I let my mind go awry while
waiting on God. But not for long. God is good. He pursues us. He
loved us first. His timing is perfect, and we can expect to know his
love and his goodness in all things. Jeremiah 29:13 says, "You will

seek me and find me when you seek me with all your heart." Psalm 46:10 records, "Be still, and know that I am God; I will be exalted among the nations, I will be exalted in the earth." It is he whom we seek. He is the fullness, the same fullness he desires for us to pursue. The pursuit of God's fullness is a gift. He pours his love on us. Being his daughter and knowing the Father is the outcome of all outcomes—all of the Father poured out for all of us. All of him poured into us. We may have all of him.

God Can Change How We Perceive His Blessings

For this new adventure we must put on the new self, the one wearing his salvation and righteousness, including a crown of beauty, the oil of joy, and a garment of praise. After all, the sackcloth and ashes no longer suit the bride who is anticipating her groom, our Lord Jesus. We are awaiting our Sovereign Lord who has saved us, made us as white as snow (Isa. 1:18), and is transforming us into who he has made us to be. We are made anew to be new!

The Love of Christ

God is good and faithful. He does not leave us alone. He is our best teacher who teaches us about real love. God wants us to be healed and whole. Love is the answer, but our minds are not able to comprehend this love, nor will we be able to use our minds solely to receive it. But God loosens the parts of our hearts that are still hardened to his love.

God shows us that we can have faith to move mountains and know that Jesus is the hope, the anchor for our souls. But "If I speak in the tongues of men or of angels, but do not have love, I am only a resounding gong or a clanging cymbal" (1 Cor. 13:1). Proclaiming Jesus without his love would not be proclaiming his gospel at all. God, in his great love for us, heals us because he loves us. However important they are in our faith walk, it is love, not faith or hope, which is the great overriding force in the gospel.

God shows us through the Israelites in the Old Testament that he would make himself known to all the peoples of the earth through his power and his love. His parting of the Red Sea, and making the crossing of the Jordan possible on dry land, demonstrated his divine power. As a family of four we have seen the great powerful arm of God in our lives so many times. But during our crossings God has also demonstrated his great love for our family. His protection and provision are a wonderful indicator of how much he cares for us. I have returned to my old ways of earning love repeatedly, and he loves me still. He pursues us because He loves us.

What are we to do with our lives in order to know him better? Just as he showed the Israelites the land of milk and honey, the Father has demonstrated his power for the entire world to see when he makes us new creations. God gave us the victory in Jesus by conquering death for all time. I believe we have to lean on God more and allow him to develop us to be what he created us to be. How do we do that? He gives us the answer in John's gospel: "The thief comes only to steal and kill and destroy; I have come that they may have life, and have it to the full" (John 10:10). We follow after Christ to know more and more of the One who loved us so much he gave all of himself for us.

God teaches us that love is the aim, and we cannot have love without the Son. He has to pour it into us. We need the love the Father and Son have so richly given. I want to love more by the power of God, but only God can give that. As a daughter of the King, I will trust him and know he has already dreamed it. Let it be as he has said.

Beyond Gilgal

As we lean into the journey and lean into God, we move into the new land. The new land is the promise of God to lead us in the unfamiliar and to conquer what baffles and frightens us. He gives us courage and strength for today and for the moments and days ahead. It is only through trust in God that we have his Son's grace and power to fulfill the journey. Not knowing what is next, and not feeling comfortable in the new place God has gifted us, can bring on old patterns and behaviors. He knows we are vulnerable, but he has given us the tools to fight and not look back. He is at the helm, and we choose to let him lead us through it.

The invitation to God's table is always before us. We can choose life and his blessings, or we can choose death and cursings: "This day I call the heavens and the earth as witnesses against you that I have set before you life and death, blessings and curses. Now choose life, so that you and your children may live" (Deut. 30:19). Are we going to taste and see that God is good, or are we going to run away from the table he has set for us? He waits to guide us through the unfamiliar and frightening. He grows our trust in him as we choose to come to his table. Like the glimpse of beauty at the mountaintop, or the cheers of the finish line of a long race, or the last hour of a long work cycle, we know we can go the journey with him. He has been there with us, and he is going nowhere. The One who guides us overwhelms us with more than we ever asked. In fact, we begin feeling that *he* is what we seek at the table. We have come to the table at last because the One who invited us is the One who helps us complete the journey.

"Too Much Trying"

Too much trying
Too little trusting
Enjoy his passions
Gifts he gives

Whilst ridding oneself
So many faults
Forgetting our Creator
Who didn't get it wrong

Oh, for a day
When we see what he sees
Set our attention on him
To live in faith for such a time as this!

"Crossing Over"

Give me courage to
Take what God has given
Trust him to be with me
Know he will never leave me

Believe him to cross over
Follow him where he leads
Rest in my weakness
Be amazed by his strength

Keep on keeping on when
I cannot see or know
Or understand the path but
Move by his direction, not my own

God is good; his love and faithfulness
Real to me in the hard places
Wrestling and waiting in his grace
I am loved abundantly

As he carries me
I cross the chasm
To the spacious place
Where he has been all along

Open my heart, Lord
To let my walls down
Thank you whenever I'm in the difficult
Or in the joy—you are here

May I continue to cross over
The chasm that I use to separate myself
Because you took it down once for all in Jesus
The barrier gone — You gave us You in full

The walls before me all my own
You know them full well
Hide me in You to enjoy
The fullness of you inside the spacious place

Enjoying the space You give, my weakness
Made strong inside the unfamiliar, the dark made light
The pain, the broken made whole
Only as you carry me into Your rest

Based on Isaiah 64:4

"Wait"

WAIT
Know
See
Hear
God.

He IS
Waiting for us
Pursuing us
Loving us

He is God
We are His.

CHAPTER TWO

GOD CALLS US TO REMEMBER

Remember that you were slaves in Egypt and that the Lord your
God brought you out of there with a mighty hand and an
outstretched arm. (Deut. 5:15)

He went to Nazareth, where he had been brought up, and on the
Sabbath day he went into the synagogue, as was his custom. He
stood up to read, and the scroll of the prophet Isaiah was handed to
him. Unrolling it, he found the place where it is written: "The
Spirit of the Lord is on me, because he has anointed me to
proclaim good news to the poor. He has sent me to proclaim
freedom for the prisoners and recovery of sight for the blind, to set
the oppressed free, to proclaim the year of the Lord's favor." Then
he rolled up the scroll, gave it back to the attendant and sat down.
The eyes of everyone in the synagogue were fastened on him.
He began by saying to them,
"Today this scripture is fulfilled in your hearing."
(Luke 4:16-21)

God's Abundance in the Present

The sun was dazzlingly bright. Drivers were being cautious, and for that I was really grateful, because the fall morning light was making it particularly difficult to see. But luckily I could see what was just in front of me. As I drove farther, I noticed the blinding sun was not the only problem in the increasingly slow traffic. Dense fog enveloped the river ahead, and cars were crawling across the bridge. The sight was ethereal as the sun shone through the trees with a layer of fog covering everything.

Was this beautiful condition like life when I want to see in the distance, but cannot? Often I miss the moment and its dazzling beauty because I am staring off into the future, and many times worrying about it. God provided the beautiful sunlight this morning to light the path for our day. We only need light for this moment, not for the miles ahead. God will provide his light when we get to the bridge, now covered in fog. He will offer his sight to us when we cannot see. God's presence is in the present tense; it is spectacular and for the entire world to see.

What God Wants Us to Do Right Now

When do we cry out to God? How do we choose to follow him? Is it through trial or devastation? Is it through recognizing our great need that we choose to follow God? It seems that we walk with God closer and closer as we recognize our need for him in our lives. Was this the secret of the esteemed heroes of the faith? God had chosen them for significant challenges in the history of his people, and they would not be able to accomplish their tasks without God being with them. This is like our own lives; if the task is big and we need God to do it, then we must turn to him to accomplish the very thing he shows us to do. Whenever a need is great in our lives, we can turn to God for help. This is the turning point in the faith walk of very many people.

Some, but not all, of the heroes of the faith asked God for a big task. Yet God chose them. Could they have said no? How could they have said no to God? In big and small ways every day, it is true we do not surrender our wills to God. We do not turn to him with a cry for help, and we do not stop our own busyness to know our very large need for him in our day-to-day interactions and tasks. We see ourselves as self-sufficient or self-reliant, neither of which can last very long. God chose us to be his children, not so he could be a tyrant in control of us, or a taskmaster for us to serve in slavery, but instead so he could be a loving Father and a gracious and just Savior. We need him so we are not lorded over or enslaved by the things of this world. God chose us before creation to be his so he could pour out his love upon us. He gives us big things to do not because he needs us to do them, but because he has a purpose and a plan for each of us. God gives us a choice to make whether we walk with him or not, and whether we walk with him to be who we were created to be.

God has given us all of himself through Jesus Christ so we can live the abundant life. Unless we come to him, we will not know how needy we are. How can we not yield? He gives us free will to come to him or not. Yet, if we are willing to walk in relationship with Christ, we may have all the blessings God has already bestowed on us in Jesus Christ.

The heroes of the faith knew Jesus; they lived in community with him. Their lack in whatever area God had chosen them to serve was the impetus for them to turn to him and to rely on him to accomplish whatever mission God set for them. For example, Joshua knew that in order to lead his people into the Promised Land, he would have to know God's nearness and depend on him for the courage to seize the land God promised the Jewish people. God gave Joshua a significant role in the history of Israel's people. Joshua's belief in God brought blessing to him and God's people. We receive what God has already given in Jesus Christ as we turn to him and believe the promises in his Word.

In each of our heroes, it seems their belief in God yielded great blessings. God has created in us a yearning to have purpose and meaning; He gives it to us as we walk with him. He also increases our faith and even multiplies the blessing as we continue the walk of faith. We have his Word on it.

What is Redemption?

- To buy back
- To be free from distress or harm, free from captivity by payment of ransom
- Release from blame or debt
- Free from the consequences of sin
- Change for the better, reform
- Repair, restore
- Free from obligation of payment, exchange for something of value, to make good
- Atone for or to offset the bad effect or make worthwhile

The Redeemed Cross Over

"Was it not you who dried up the sea, the waters of the great deep, who made a road in the depths of the sea so that the redeemed might cross over?" (Isa. 51:10)

The God of the Bible makes it possible for his children to cross over from places they should not have gone, and from distress, blame, or debt. He makes it possible to change, repair, and restore. And he makes crossover possible with no obligation for payment in exchange for something of value.

Because Jesus is the Savior, the atonement, and the sacrifice, we are made good through the mercy and righteousness he freely offers for our redemption.

He Comes to Us

"For this is what the high and exalted One says—he who lives forever, whose name is holy: 'I live in a high and holy place, but also with the one who is contrite and lowly in spirit, to revive the spirit of the lowly and to revive the heart of the contrite.'" (Isa. 57:15)

He comes to us. He pursues us. He causes us to come to Him. It is the mystery revealed in Jesus Christ. How do we know this? We know this by his Word, his Holy Spirit, and by his history with his people.

As we study God's Word and examine the lives of those who came before us, we see the Lord's intentional pursuit of them and, ultimately, how they followed him. We ask ourselves if God is pursuing us as he did the ancients. How did they respond to God's wooing? How do we respond? How do we listen, obey, and know the Lord and his love for us through our Bible study?

We will see failure in our biblical characters' lives— hardheaded doubters turned around from fearful to confident persons. More than all of this, we will see God's love, his consistent pursuit, his mercy, his heart, his holiness, and his character.

Power Within

There is a power deep within the human heart that is greater than any other power in the world. It is from the One and Only. When the step of faith occurs and grace is received, the Holy Spirit indwells the heart of the one who believes in Jesus Christ. This power within brings the capacity to love, serve, show mercy, and act justly and powerfully in Jesus' name. Do those of us who have taken the step of faith, know, believe, and act like we have this heavenly authority and power within us?

Consider the power lines bringing power to the homes in our neighborhoods. This power makes all our houses come alive with electricity for lighting, heating, cooling, cooking, and for using all of our appliances and electronic devices. When electricity is out in bad weather, we sit in the dark and become aware of how much we depend on it for everyday life. The power of the Holy Spirit within us does not go dark or cease to exist. He is present to guide and protect, to light our way in the dark, and to give us the capacity to live as his children to represent him in this world. Without the Holy Spirit, we have no means to bring the world light and love. With him, however, we have all we need.

We may be looking in other places for love and power and everything else we need. Instead of acknowledging him and his ways, we go our own way, leaning upon our own understanding. We have received the greatest of all gifts, including the Holy Spirit indwelling our hearts. We have to determine if we are going to serve the heavenly power and authority within us, or if we will serve ourselves. Is it our Savior, or ourselves?

Sabotage or Revelation

We need to cooperate with God as he carries us toward the abundant life. We must cooperate with our compassionate and loving Father who knows what is best for us and what will bring him the glory for the entire world to see. Even though cooperating brings richer and fuller lives, many sabotage the plan God has in mind. Fortunately, God will use even our poorest judgment and weave it into something good in our lives. The apostle Paul put it this way: "We know that in all things God works for the good of those who love him, who have been called according to his purpose" (Rom. 8:28).

Have we been sabotaging God's plan? I believe the answer is yes. We don't want to do so, yet we do because there are things that seem hard, or uncomfortable, or even impossible. We substitute our plan for God's to make things easier, more comfortable, and possible. But God draws us near. He wants to meet with us in the difficult, the uncomfortable, and the painful.

I love God's revelations. He reveals himself to us by showing us his love and his heart. The truth is that God says he will do "immeasurably more than all we ask or imagine, according to his power that is at work within us" (Eph. 3:20). Our search for significance, love, success, satisfaction, and a full life are within reach through Jesus Christ. We are his, and he loves us. In his love and already determined victory we have success, satisfaction, and life to the full. God is waiting for us to join him on this journey of faith. He has been drawing us all along for the ride of our lives.

Being a Daughter

Our holy Father God has given us our roles and positions in the family and sustains us in them. A child has certain privileges inherent with the position of being a daughter or son. The parent also has certain responsibilities and privileges. The Creator established the family and its positions and privileges for his glory and our good.

Being a daughter means:

- To receive the love of the parent

- To receive the privilege of the position—to be called "a child of"

- To receive protection, guidance, and all that being a child entails

- Daughters in relationship with God the Father:

- Only grace gives us the position of being a daughter

- The role of a daughter is a spacious place

- Honor and blessing come with the position of being a daughter

- Faithful care, provision, and protection are included in being a daughter

To be daughters of our Father God, we are to receive the position he gives us. With the love and grace only the Father gives, we must respond accordingly. If we misstep, we will be loved and given grace again. We must unlearn the ways that are not the ones God has in mind. The Father guides and teaches us to be daughters and sons of the King himself. He is our Creator, our Savior, and our "Abba" (papa or daddy). Thanks be to God!

We must discard all that hinders us from being daughters of the King, which includes rebuking the father of lies and refuting all the untruths we have believed. We know the truth, and the truth has set us free. We are free to live as daughters of the King of kings and Lord of lords, Jesus Christ. In addition, there is no reason to fear this position of being a daughter. We walk across the threshold to receive him as a father, which includes all the riches of his inheritance that he has promised his children, both sons and daughters.

Receiving

God says to his daughters, "Rest your head and know my heart." What kind and gentle words those are! He is a great God, compassionate and true. As we wait to hear more, we receive affirmations of the way the Holy Spirit leads us to realize the God of the universe wants to nurture us at this juncture. Our wonderful Father God loves on us, tends to us, and shows us his amazing devotion not only in sending our Savior, but giving us real life-nurturing through his Holy Spirit who dwells within us. Another affirmation is that we have not nearly embraced all he has so graciously and mercifully given. We know in our heads he has given us life to the full in Christ Jesus, but we do not know how to live it with all of our hearts, minds, and souls.

According to one popular commentator, "God wants us to receive instead of achieve." Are we waiting to be worthy of the abundant life? God places on our hearts a desire to know him better. He shows us he wants us to lean into whatever he has for us, and then we listen and study.

God is in control. He knows our needs, and in him every need will be met. These are the blessings he has already given us, including the truth in his Word that we have every spiritual blessing: "Praise be to the God and Father of our Lord Jesus Christ, who has blessed us in the heavenly realms with every spiritual blessing in Christ" (Eph. 1:3). God shows us in his Word the great love he has for us. His embrace extends from the heavens every day all day long. As we know him and his heart better, we should embrace what he has already given. It is in the receiving that we will know life to the full.

An Epiphany

"It has been You, Great God!" As we wrestle and ponder the quiet and the still but spacious place, God has shown us great grace and compassion, and many timely provisions of his heart. He did not show us his face until we stopped fighting him in it; however, he opened our hearts to his love over and over.

As God reveals that we have been "hiding in the cleft of the rock" because we were not ready to see him, joy and peace overwhelm us. The Lord loves us so much he will not allow anything premature where we are concerned. We have his lavish love and grace all the time, but we know and see him when he gives us eyes to see—and not a moment too soon.

God draws us close. He wants us near to love, protect, and guide. He nudges, he teaches, and he matures us. He also hides us when necessary so that we will be ready and prepared to know what he wants us to know, mainly more of himself. God allows us to wait as he tucks us away to be still and close and waiting in him so we know he is all we need and nothing more. Sometimes we think we are waiting just to be waiting, but he hides us to be ready for more, to be awakened to more of God.

Chronology of the Season of Rest

WHEN HE SAYS TO "REST" IN HIM

We do not know what to do when we are told to "rest." It is all about being with God and not doing. But how do we do that? We are stressed by the concept of "resting in God" because we have to place our efforts in allowing God to be God in our lives. In our season of unrest, he tells us to let go of control and to be with him.

WHEN HE SAYS TO "KNOW" HIM — FOCUS ON HIM, NOT OURSELVES

Sometimes we take the new direction from the perspective of straightening ourselves out, or fixing ourselves. Yet, God says to know him is to focus on him, and he will direct the effort. He wants us to see him for who he is and deepen our dependence on him in and for all things. In our season of knowing God better, he tells us to know him and his heart for us.

IN GOD'S FAITHFUL CARE AND PROVISION HE SHOWED UP

He hid us in the cleft of the rock and showed us his love

He assured us of his defense and advocacy

He really wanted us to rest our heads and know his heart

HE GIVES HIS WORD REGARDING "REST" AND "KNOW"

Let the beloved of the Lord rest secure in him, for he shields him all day long, and the one the Lord loves rests between his shoulders (Deut. 33:12).

In repentance and rest is your salvation, in quietness and trust is your strength, but you would have none of it (Isa. 30:15).

Whoever dwells in the shelter of the Most High will rest in the shadow of the Almighty. I will say of the Lord, "He is my refuge and my fortress, my God, in whom I trust" (Ps. 91:1-2).

HE DOES NOT LEAVE US ALONE

The hymn, "Blessed Assurance," awakened my heart to his reminder:

Blessed assurance, Jesus is mine

O what a foretaste of glory divine

Heir of salvation, purchase of God

Born of His Spirit, washed in His blood

He gives us himself and the desire to seek him in all things and seasons.

HE ANSWERS PRAYER

> To maintain his continued relationship
>
> To grow my faith
>
> To grow my gratitude

HE HAS A PURPOSE IN ALL THINGS

> To experience his hand in retrospect and grow in a desire to know him
>
> To allow hard things/times
>
> To grow us up whether waiting in his silence or in not knowing his purpose

New Things in the Nest

God changes us in the present. Since our circumstances do not remain the same, God also changes also our perceptions. I have been struck by how many perceptions of life have changed for me. I have spent many hours thinking about the next few years and what and how I am going to spend them. This seems like an extravagant thing to be doing. Aren't we too busy or too overwhelmed to be letting our thoughts and actions propel us into these kinds of mind games? Or are they mind games at all?

I believe God is preparing us for new things. The prophet Isaiah says, "Forget the former things; do not dwell on the past. See, I am doing a new thing! Now it springs up; do you not perceive it? I am making a way in the wilderness and streams in the wasteland" (Isa. 43:18-19). For me the last few years have been fast and overwhelmingly busy with milestones and transitions. There seems to be little time for thinking about new things and making new ways. But here it is.

Isn't that what God does without our asking? He makes us ready, or he gives us the quiet when we least expect it. However, we must expect him. He is preparing us for new things. Do we not perceive him? God is growing us up to see him in the midst and to expect that he has much in the works for us as we enter this new phase with gladness.

"It's You"

Have I listened, Lord?
Your heart to mine
For your word and wisdom
Only you can provide

Heart humbling and mind mending
Your truth whispers loud
Soul awakes for more
It's you, Lord, I wait for

Time after time I call
For change in me, for newness
Instead you bring me you
Again I'm humbled and hopeful too

When I wait for stretches long
My mind goes places wrong
Grace extended and faith grows when you
Remind me to take your hand

For it is trust in you
Matters most for this journey
Taking your hand allows my heart and
Eyes to see you more, a glimpse I pray today

CHAPTER THREE

GOD CALLS US TO LISTEN

The Sovereign Lord has given me a well-instructed tongue,

to know the word that sustains the weary.

He wakens me morning by morning,

wakens my ear to listen like one being instructed.

(Isa. 50:4)

My sheep listen to my voice; I know them, and they follow me.
(John 10:27)

God's Pursuits

It should be our perspective that God's pursuits are always worthwhile. It is out of the Lord's great mercy and compassion that we are given life by him, the author and perfecter of our faith. We do not come to God on our own, and we do not initiate his pursuit of us. Christ shows us his love and acceptance when we choose to follow him. And when we follow him, we learn to love him back.

We must learn to obey his divine nudges. We must listen to his voice, not only in God's Word, but also through the working of the Holy Spirit in our lives. But the conversation, the journey, and the pursuit are all from God Almighty.

His Pursuit Grows my Pursuit of Him

Sometimes God uses really crazy times in our lives to teach us the biggest lessons. In my own case, and perhaps in others who have children, God uses the difficult circumstances in our children's lives to give us a mirror of our errant ways. More importantly, God gives us a glimpse of who he is in his kindness to us. We cannot always solve our children's problems, but we surely try at times. God is faithful, generous, gracious, and most assuredly the One and Only who shields, defends, and rescues. In the meantime, he also changes us.

There was a time when my daughter was in a real dilemma. She was at the end of her rope, and I wanted to hold on for her, not only to create a safe place to land but also to provide encouragement and comfort during a time she was striving and hurting. As God does, he provides himself. During the roughest part of her ordeal, when I was hurting so much for her, God impressed me to study his Word on the topic of joy. I learned that if I listened and stayed focused on God, I would find joy in him. My daughter came through the ordeal, not as she anticipated but more fully whole. She may not have had joy in the circumstances, but she did find she could depend on God for peace and joy. And I found joy there, too.

God wants us to see his bounty by our keeping the focus on him. Only he knows what we need, and only he knows how and when to provide it.

God's Comfort versus Being Comfortable

Do we often confuse God's desire to comfort us with our being comfortable? God is indeed our Comforter in times of grief or loss, disappointment or betrayal, and stress and pain. Yet he does not necessarily desire our lives be comfortable. In fact, he says that we will suffer, that we will go places we have not been, and that we will have days that are not as we planned. He leads, guides, and places us where he does, and all we can say about this is that he is sovereign. When we place our lives in his, he makes the way clear for us to do what he prepared in advance for us to do—even when the situation is not comfortable.

The Bible tells us the Sovereign prepares the way. He guides us in the unfamiliar; he leads and we follow, and we may not know where we are going. The following Scripture verses illustrate that he is our God of comfort in the uncomfortable:

I will lead the blind by ways they have not known, along
unfamiliar paths I will guide them; I will turn the darkness into
light before them and make the rough places smooth. These are the
things I will do; I will not forsake them.
(Isa.42:16)

Build up, build up, prepare the road! Remove the obstacles
out of the way of my people.
(Isa. 57:14)

By faith Abraham, when called to go to a place he would later
receive
as his inheritance, obeyed and went, even though he did not know
where he was going. (Heb. 11:8)

Are we in uncomfortable places in our lives? If so, let us remember that living life to the full includes, perhaps even requires, discomfort. It also requires dependence on our Creator

God in Jesus Christ, and our obedience to him who knew us before he made us and prepared works in advance for us to do. God will guide us on the adventure—to the full—and he will provide comfort as we move through the difficult parts of the journey. He knows us and loves us to all the fullness of himself: the wide and long and high and deep love of Christ is a "love that surpasses knowledge—that you may be filled to the measure of all the fullness of God" (Eph. 3:19). He indeed knows what "the ride of a lifetime" will be for each of us. He has prepared the road and marked the unfamiliar path so we can follow him. Are we going to step into it with him, even if we do not know where we are going?

A New Path

I walked a new path today, one with new views, a fresh perspective, and a hopeful outlook. When was the last time you took a new look at life, perhaps with a move, a new job, or a change in routine or life circumstance? Did it seem like a good thing? Were you expectant?

God wires us for new. He recreates us when we come to him. In fact, as we come to him, he transforms us into the creatures he designed us to be—little by little, step-by-step, and year-by-year. Knowing that God has a plan to produce in me a new person who is more like him gives me great hope.

As we keep our focus on God and lean into his grace, truth, and power, he holds us close. He heightens our awareness of his presence; we hear him in his Word, and we know him in the events in our day. He gives us the new path and the new perspective we need for this day. Peace and joy rise up, and we know he is with us. Our thoughts remain on him, and we believe him more. His love is now and forever, and he will never leave us.

By drawing near to Jesus, anyone can strike a new path. Jesus hears our cries, and he can show us the way to "new." Our part? Expect, hope, and follow him.

Walking by Faith (as Described in God's Word)

The Author of our faith created us for relationship with him. Full of mercy and truth, our creator and Savior God speaks and demonstrates who he is. The prophet Isaiah wrote, "You heavens above, rain down my righteousness; let the clouds shower it down. Let the earth open wide, let salvation spring up, let righteousness flourish with it; I, the Lord, have created it" (Isa. 45:8). As his children, our response in faith is as the psalmist put it in Psalm 28:7: "The Lord is my strength and my shield; my heart trusts in him, and he helps me. My heart leaps for joy, and with my song I praise him."

Throughout the older and newer testaments, God calls his children to know and follow him. A Song of Moses to the Israelites before he died and before they crossed into the Promised Land mentions the faithful listening and receiving the doctrine of the Lord: "Listen, you heavens, and I will speak; hear, you earth, the words of my mouth. Let my teaching fall like rain and my words descend like dew, like showers on new grass, like abundant rain on tender plants. I will proclaim the name of the Lord. Oh, praise the greatness of our God! He is the Rock, his works are perfect, and all his ways are just. A faithful God who does no wrong, upright and just is he" (Deut. 32:1-4).

Not only did God create everything, but he spoke it into existence. God is the Author of faith and words. Moses says that not only are the words of the Father to be followed, but they are also life itself. And this prophecy was fulfilled when the Israelites took the Promised Land and in the birth of our Savior, God's only Son. "They are not just idle words for you—they are your life. By them you will live long in the land you are crossing the Jordan to possess" (Deut. 32:47). In John 1:14, the Scripture tells us that Jesus is the Word incarnate: "The Word became flesh and made his dwelling among us. We have seen his glory, the glory of the one and only Son, who came from the Father, full of grace and truth."

When we follow Christ, we pay attention to his Word. It teaches, guides, corrects, and helps us to know him. His love and mercy shine forth in his character and in his promises, all recorded in Scripture. God is who he says he is, and he does what he says he does. When we trust him, he helps us know him better and believe him more. The walk of faith is God's beautiful, complex, and creative design for our journey on this earth. It is fully intended to display his glory for all the world to see, and for us to know him and his unabashed, unfailing, and never-ending love for us.

This journey, choreographed for each of us individually, comes with ups and downs and in-betweens, not because God wants us to hurt or fear, but because the world is fallen and full of evil. God promised he would use all that happens for the good of his children: "You intended to harm me, but God intended it for good to accomplish what is now being done, the saving of many lives" (Gen. 50:20). "And we know that in all things God works for the good of those who love him, who have been called according to his purpose" (Rom. 8:28).

The adventure of walking by faith was created by God for us. We choose him because he wired us to need him, our Creator, who chose us and loved us first. His promise kept in its entirety is still true: He keeps his Word always, and he will never leave us or forsake us on the journey of faith. He is by our side and knows everything about us and the walk he has planned just for us.

Friendship with God

Familiar, compassionate, intimate, confident, reverent (re-spectful), honest, loved, authentic, conversational, communicative: These words are descriptive of a relationship with a close friend— one where we have shared stories and seasons, and hardships and celebrations. We have milestones and memories, hurts and healed wounds. How do we have a close relationship with God? David taught us about this through psalms. David poured his heart out to God, and God actually called David a man after his own heart: "The Lord has sought out a man after his own heart and appointed him ruler of his people" (1 Sam. 13:14).

Scripture shows us how to be real with God. Job, for example, laid out his trials and talked to God. After Job answered some tough questions, he learned more about God's demands for obedience, more about human suffering, and more about God's complete sovereignty. Through a friendship with our Creator, God prepares us to live with him for eternity while he molds us into the persons he intended us to be in the here and now.

In order to be prepared for eternal life, we must practice. God wants a relationship with us and he makes himself accessible through his Son and Holy Spirit. When we choose to follow the Lord, he comes close to guide our journey; the more authentic and communicative we are, and as we take our lives to him, we get to know him better. God already knows where the journey leads, so our job is to trust him with it.

The Heart (The Good, the Bad, and the Ugly)

God looks at the heart. We are told that "The Lord does not look at the things people look at. People look at the outward appearance, but the Lord looks at the heart" (1 Sam. 16:7). God sees our innermost desires and our deepest needs, and he loves us unfailingly. As he pursues us with his unconditional love, he does not waver in his intention. While we are allowed the freedom whether or not to reciprocate God's love, God accepts us unhesitatingly, even with our sinful natures and selfish wants. He knows our very hearts.

What is in our hearts? Do we even know at times? If we turn ourselves around and look at the Lord, we become more the persons he sees in us—the loved and precious children of God. He is our portion; we are his treasure.

God knows the good, the bad, and the ugly of our inner natures, and that comes from his not looking at the outward appearance but at the heart. We may take the time to be attractive to those around us, and to those who judge our outward ways, but God knows the true story of the human personality. For this reason, the Father sacrificed his only Son Jesus, while we were still sinners. What might he do for us when we choose to follow him daily and faithfully?

God determines to make us holy as he is holy. He is set apart for his glory and for his purposes. We are part of something grander than we imagine. He allows us to participate in the larger story—his. He takes what is bad in our hearts and transforms it into treasure for the entire world to see. God transforms our very natures into beacons of light shining the brightness of Jesus to a poor and dark world in need of love and light. That is something only God can do.

All creation yearns for God, and when we yearn for him our hearts open to the possibility of knowing him personally. Jesus comes to dwell in them. Hearts in need of Jesus become hearts indwelled by Jesus to love and care for others who need him, too.

From the Inside Out—A Heart after God's Own

From the inside out God frees us. The gospel of John says that to the Jews who believed in the Messiah, Jesus said, "If you hold to my teaching, you are really my disciples. Then you will know the truth, and the truth will set you free" (John 8:31-32). The Word of God assumed human flesh when Jesus lived among us. He now lives within us in the person of the Holy Spirit. When we allow God into our lives, he shines his holy light. Where there is darkness, he illuminates the darkness. If we allow him into the darkest crevices of the heart, he guides us to freedom. His Truth sets us free in our inmost parts—that "secret place." As the psalmist writes, "You desired faithfulness even in the womb; you taught me wisdom in that secret place" (Ps. 51:6).

Darkness and imprisonment result when we wall ourselves off from pain or shame. We cannot free ourselves from prison, even if it is a prison of our own making. This walling off for self-protection is a barrier to freedom in Christ. If we believe the lies our culture forces on us, we cannot free ourselves from these untruths either. However, Jesus comes to bind us up from our broken places, heal us of our woundedness, give us eyes to see and hearts to know him, and set us free from all imprisonment, as the prophet Isaiah proclaims: "The Spirit of the Sovereign Lord is on me, because the Lord has anointed me to proclaim good news to the poor. He has sent me to bind up the brokenhearted, to proclaim freedom for the captives and release from darkness for the prisoners, to proclaim the year of the Lord's favor and the day of vengeance of our God, to comfort all who mourn" (Isa. 61:1-2). He shows us the Lord's way, which, in a word, is freedom. Moreover, in the midst of the pain of prison, God grants us treasures of darkness and riches stored in secret places as he calls us by name: "I will give you hidden treasures, riches stored in secret places, so that you may know that I am the Lord, the God of Israel, who summons you by name" (Isa. 45:3).

As Jesus heals us from the inside out, he restores our souls with the refreshment of his Word. His provision takes on a re-hauling from the inside out. We are no longer captive to lies, but indeed we are guided and driven by his Truth. The inside is new, and so is the outside appearance.

What about the walls we built to protect ourselves from pain? Jesus takes them down. Thanks to God the Holy Spirit, with the change inside, a new desire to trust him and to go his way thrives within us. As we do, he goes before us and opens the doors; he grows the faith within us to shield us from the Evil One along the way. We no longer need to build walls to protect ourselves, or construct gates to shut out pain or shame. We have him to guide, guard, and rescue us. He is our refuge and the freedom we seek.

God is not Angry with Us

"To me this is like the days of Noah, when I swore that the waters of Noah would never again cover the earth. So now I have sworn not to be angry with you, never to rebuke you again" (Isa. 54:9). God is not mad at us. Just as he made a covenant with the children of Israel that he would send his Son to make peace, he has now sworn never to be angry with us.

No longer angry, God has made peace with us through Jesus Christ. If he is no longer angry, then why do so many still question God's offer of grace? Partially because we know our sin; it is ever before us, as the psalmist says: "For I know my transgressions, and my sin is always before me" (Ps. 51:3). Sometimes we see God as one we have to earn approval from, or work hard to stay on his good side. But God has given us grace in the person of Jesus Christ, and we have this grace in which we now stand. "Therefore, since we have been justified through faith, we have peace with God through our Lord Jesus Christ, through whom we have gained access by faith into this grace in which we now stand. And we boast in the hope of the glory of God" (Rom. 5: 1-2).

It is difficult to believe God would give us this kind of gift. He gives us grace, unmerited favor, because he is God and he loves us—not because of anything we have done. We already please him because he sees us through the eyes of his Son, Jesus Christ. Because he does not require us to earn his favor, we are free to be and to return his love. We are worthy to receive his gifts because we are as his children. It is all about the Giver of Grace. Perhaps we bring our own relationship failures to our relationship with God. We think we have to do something to earn God's love. But the beauty of our relationship with the Creator of the universe is that he loves us and delights in us because he chooses to do so. He promises he will love us forever and will not leave us no matter what. No, God is not angry with us. "The Lord is compassionate and gracious, slow to anger, abounding in love" (Ps. 103:8).

What We Do with our Feelings

Even as we sing about sad things, the heart is full. It is soulful. It is satisfying. This is a God-given gift. And sometimes our hearts turn to joy when we sing because we know God hears us when we sing in the words of a psalm or hymn. The God who placed our emotions within us knows our every feeling. It is through communication with the Creator that we have peace and joy.

Often we want to shut down our feelings because we do not want to "go there." Perhaps this is out of a desire for control. But feelings are not bad, and they are not indicators of being out of control. They are actually communicators of what is going on inside. Turning feelings into prayers is a great way to get closer to God. In getting to know him better, we will know the truth and won't have to rely on our feelings to determine our day or the way through it.

Hope does not Disappoint Us or Put us to Shame

We don't know what God is going to do, but we know he has good things in mind for us: "For the Lord God is a sun and shield; the Lord bestows favor and honor; no good thing does he withhold from those whose walk is blameless" (Ps. 84:11). We know he loves us and wants the best for us, his children. This is true even with all the questions swirling around us—Why has healing not occurred? Why did my child not make it? Why did I lose my job?

God knows the answers. He tells us in his Word that he makes good out of it all for those who love him: "And we know that in all things God works for the good of those who love him, who have been called according to his purpose" (Rom. 8:28). How could good come from betrayal, hurt, and loss? God's Word says his love is unfailing and forever. It is the power of his love that will not disappoint us. It is the power of his love that does not put us to shame. That power of love indwells us as believers in Jesus Christ by the power of the Holy Spirit. It is this same power of love that gives us the wherewithal to stand in the midst of terrible suffering, betrayal, or loss. God does that; we cannot. But we do when we lean on the truth of Scripture, which has much to teach us about peace and hope: "Therefore, since we have been justified through faith, we have peace with God through our Lord Jesus Christ, through whom we have gained access by faith into this grace in which we now stand. And we boast in the hope of the glory of God. Not only so, but we also glory in our sufferings, because we know that suffering produces perseverance; perseverance, character; and character, hope. And hope does not put us to shame, because God's love has been poured out into our hearts through the Holy Spirit, who has been given to us" (Rom. 5:1-5). God's hope does not disappoint.

Isaiah 45:18 says, "For this is what the Lord says—he who created the heavens, he is God; he who fashioned and made the earth, he founded it; he did not create it to be empty, but formed it to be inhabited—he says: "I am the Lord and there is no other." Many love these words because they know they are true. We can feel God's nearness with these words in the darkest of hours; he shows us he is with us. This is what God teaches us in the search for truth and our quest for what has been promised—the truly abundant life. If we want to live life with nothing held back, we must first fellowship with the Lord. If we go out to live in a prescribed way, it is most assuredly an act of self-reliance. But we must live with God at the helm, who teaches us to listen and to be grounded in who he is. And who does God say he is? "I am the Lord and there is no other." If we listen and lean on him in the present, he will guide, protect, and bring about what he intends.

Our Inheritance—Our Calling

The psalmist writes, "When you ascended on high, you took many captives; you received gifts from people, even from the rebellious—that you, Lord God, might dwell there" (Ps. 68:18). In his letter to the Ephesians, the apostle Paul writes, "This is why it says: 'When he ascended on high, he took many captives and gave gifts to his people'" (Eph. 4:8). With Jesus' ascension into heaven, He gave us more. He promised he would never leave us or forsake us. He also said he would empower us to do work in his name. Jesus sent the Holy Spirit to live within each person choosing to follow him. He does not leave us to our own devices; rather, he comes closer than our own physical bodies. Through the power and the indwelling of the Holy Spirit, the Lord gave us gifts to serve the body of Christ, the church, which is the Kingdom on earth. God richly rewards his children who enter into a personal relationship with him. In addition to rescuing his children from their earthly passions, God gives each new child an eternal inheritance, as well as a gift or calling. With these gifts and the gifts of the body of Christ, we serve our broken world.

God calls his children to rise up and go the distance on this journey. Using the calling he has given, we serve this broken world and its people. Sometimes God's children wonder to what God has called them. When we are confused, God reminds us that he rescued us from the world's lies, lies we believed from the time we were quite small. What is our calling? It is to share the hope of Jesus Christ, who has given us a covering of praise instead of a spirit of despair. He has given us great joy and dancing in the place of tears, sackcloth, and ashes. Each of our callings include sharing the hope of Jesus to a fallen world, which uniquely lines up with the story God is writing on each of our lives.

When we wander from God in our thoughts, we return to striving and trying to please others. We worry we are not doing enough. This is the very problem that kept us from God in the first place. Doing things in our own power and by our own strength is part of the world's devices. But if we let go and yield to God when these things rear their ugly heads, he moves us forward to walk over the threshold as his child. From here, he propels us into the work he has for us. If we sit at his feet, he renews what brought us to him in the first place: his love for us as his children. Wanting to please God drives us to service of his people and wanting them to know him.

Jesus entered human history to live among us as God in human form. He died by the horrible death of crucifixion, only to rise three days later and then ascend to heaven to sit at the right hand of God. By his doing so, we may live with him in eternity. In addition, he gives us the huge privilege of serving his kingdom. Through the power of the Holy Spirit, we may live in unison with the Father in heaven, with Jesus by his side, and follow his lead with our lives in order to serve those around us. We have the privilege of intimacy with the Almighty—we were created for this purpose. It is the highest calling to be Jesus' child. Only God can fill this mighty need and yearning within us. Who could dream this and so much more but the Creator himself?

Trip of a Lifetime

Jesus Christ in the power of the Holy Spirit enables us to go against the grain of this world. The Holy Spirit gives us the capacity to live in Christ. Living out the love of Jesus Christ in this world cannot be done without the help of God in the power of the Holy Spirit. It is all about God, the Giver. While leaning in to the Giver, God takes us beyond the threshold of his invitation. As First Corinthians records, "What no eye has seen, what no ear has heard, and what no human mind has conceived"—the things God has prepared for those who love him" (1 Cor. 2:9). God is holy, and yet he is accessible to us, as Isaiah states: "For this is what the high and exalted One says—he who lives forever, whose name is holy: 'I live in a high and holy place, but also with the one who is contrite and lowly in spirit, to revive the spirit of the lowly and to revive the heart of the contrite" (Isa. 57:15). Beyond our imagination and expectation are his love, his power, and his hope for us and for our world. He satisfies the yearnings of a broken heart. He hears the cry of a wounded soul. And he desires the grateful songs of a joyful heart that has received his gifts of love, forgiveness, and abundance.

God does not change and he does not make mistakes. He chose well when he chose us as his children. He delights in us. We are his treasure: "For you are a people holy to the Lord your God. The Lord your God has chosen you out of all the peoples on the face of the earth to be his people, his treasured possession" (Deut. 7:6). We must cross the threshold of belief into living like we believe we are his treasured possession. If God instructs us when we haven't seriously lived like we were his chosen people, what more will he show us when we do.

God has invited us on a "trip of a lifetime," an adventure that is greater than we can imagine. It is filled with the kind of joy we have yet to experience, beauty that is greater than we have seen, and the fierce, jealous, sacrificial, unconditional, and never-ending love of the One and Only. We must remember who is driving on this trip, whose race it is, and how much he loves us and wants to share the adventure with us. Remember who he is, what he has done, how he loves us, and what he has promised us, his children. If we wait for him, hope in him, and love him, he has promised us a "trip of a lifetime."

When I became God's daughter, I knew he was my father in heaven. When I crossed the threshold as his bride, I knew his forgiveness and his tender love. But when I came to know his love for me, his child, I opened my heart to him. Now as I desire to know God better, I want to cross the threshold once again to learn all he has planned for me in this world. I want to say with my whole heart, "Here I am, Lord, send me."

"Leaning onto God"

Help me to choose to lean in
To you, to trust and to lean on
You, not my own understanding
To have courage to continue to lean

Give me new resolve to seek you
In the waiting. To be still and know you
While you pursue and love me
In the seeming silence of now

Guide me to your promises
In your word. Remind me to listen
And to expect you are there
I am never out of your care

Protect me from my old ways
Shine your light on the step
You want me to take and keep
The "new" in me obeying with your help

In awe of you and your love
To keep teaching me over and over
And to make me layer by layer
More whole into who you created me to be

Prayer for New

As your daughter, Father God, make me new today — new eyes, new heart, new ears, and new mind to know you. If you were to do this every moment of my life, and I know you are able, I would not be able to get to the end of your riches, fullness, or abundance. Help me to become more mature in my knowledge of you, Lord.

"Father, you Know me so Well"

Father, you know me so well
Help me to follow your way
Not fight you or me in how
You made me

Follow your voice in the now
Leading me always to you
Keep me aware of the lies—soft or loud
Draw me back to you and the wonder of your grace

You prepared the road
Rescued me to your spacious place
To live, grow, and serve in your house
Guide me to help your people here

Grant me a humble, willing spirit
To hear you and follow
Allow my heart to soften
For your people all around

Proclaim with your word with my life
The riches of your grace
The love and power of your Name
The wonder of you, as I live and breathe

I'm your Daughter, Father God. Now What?

I want to hear and recognize your voice, your invitation to your table, Lord. Father, you cover us through your Son, Jesus. Through your compassion and mercy, you have forgiven us. We do not need to cover ourselves or hide in the closet in shame. As your daughter, I am covered, free to be who you created me to be. And you are pleased with me.

Just as you were pleased with your friend Moses, you are pleased with us, your children. You taught him, gave him words to speak, and you hid him in the cleft of the rock. You were with Moses always wherever you sent him.

Help us recognize the invitation to your table, and help us come with confidence and without shame, for you have given it in your Son's name.

Invitation to His More

The abundant life in God is an invitation given when we become the recipients of the Lord's grace. He freely gives us eternal life, but whether we live life to the full is up to us. God has given it; the question is, "Do we want to know him "to the full?" It is our choice daily as we surrender our moments. God makes us ready to see him, and he grows us up to be ready to receive the abundant life. When Moses returned from the mountain with his face aglow, the brilliance was too much for the Israelites. They could not look directly upon the reflection of the Lord in Moses' face. Just so, we are not able to look with our earthly eyes on our holy God's brightness and light. When Moses asked to see our Father God, God allowed him only to see his shadow as he went by while Moses was in the cleft of the rock. The Lord knows our physical, mental, emotional, and spiritual state from moment to moment. He shapes us as we grow closer to him, and enables us to see him more and more in our lives. One day we will be able to see God face to face when we are present with him in heaven.

God protects us from his brilliance until we are able to receive it. We may not at times be able to handle the abundance he has for us because not only are we not ready to receive it, but we are not prepared to enjoy it. God's timing is perfect. He knows our every turn and step of faith, and he woos us and is waiting for the perfect time and place for us to come and see.

Perhaps the abundance in Him that God has waiting for us is like a table prepared by the host awaiting the guests. It is laden with the most delectable foods and there is a place set just for us. God invited us to the feast when we first opened the door to him and he became our Savior. He has been waiting for us to come and draw closer, and to taste and see that he is good: "Taste and see that the Lord is good; blessed is the one who takes refuge in him" (Ps. 34:8).

Are we ready to receive what is waiting for us at the table, and are we ready to enjoy it with him? Are we ready to taste and see that the Lord is God, and that he is good—today and forever?

Adventure into More

God has wired us for daring and bold adventures. While the world perpetuates security, safety, and comfort, God has spread the good news of the gospel through many fearless messengers who lived in danger and nevertheless preached what God sent them to preach. There were Paul, John, Peter, and James to name a few, and before them, the prophets, Isaiah, Jeremiah, and Daniel. Are these men our models? Are we fearless in our following of Jesus? Do we want to be bolder in our living out of the gospel? God has given his people a message to live out and to speak, along with the desire to tell others what he has done for us in our lives. Being part of a larger story, a piece of something very significant, is important. We want to have purpose, and God has given us purpose through Jesus Christ. In addition to our identities in him, he gives us lives that are full and abundant.

If our forefathers in the faith could speak to us now, what would they say of their lives? Would they call them full? Their stories recorded for us in the Bible are indeed full of daring and bold adventures. And not only are they full, they are authentic, with necessary brokenness and a need for God. Take Abraham, for example, a man of faith. He obeyed God, and even though he did not know where he was going, he left his own country. The New Testament tell us that "By faith Abraham, when called to go to a place he would later receive as his inheritance, obeyed and went, even though he did not know where he was going" (Heb. 11:8). Not only did God promise Abraham the land, and the many blessings of a great nation, he also gave Abraham and Sarah the promised child, a son, but not until they were very old. If we look at Moses' life, we see a young man saved by his mother when the Egyptians were carrying out a plan to kill all the Hebrew babies. In a miraculous turn of events, Moses was raised by his mother in the Pharaoh's house. He lived among royalty, but he was no stranger to the desert, as God prepared him to lead the Jewish people out of slavery into the land promised them. The story of Moses is another story of love, promise, and redemption. Not only did God use Moses in the lives of the Israelites, he used Moses' life itself to reveal God's purpose for us individually, as we are part of his huge plan for all humankind. David's life from a shepherd boy to the king of Israel depicts the life of a servant of God with many failures and successes—but always a life packed full of daring and bold adventures. He had a huge heart for God, but David made many errors of judgment. He ran from Saul and committed adultery with Bathsheba, and yet God used him in powerful ways. While David was yet a shepherd boy, God chose him to be the king of all Israel.

We were chosen before the creation of the world. Do we know what we were chosen for? Are we ready for the adventure of a lifetime? God himself is at the door with an offer of abundant life. Open wide and let him lead.

What do We Want?

How do we obtain the things we want, such as love, significance, and power? Only through God will we be satisfied with the fulfillment of these quests. We may look for them the world over and we may find the world component we think will fill the desire for them, but it will be a counterfeit. God has wired us to need him. He has the love, greatness, and power we seek.

To his children here on earth and into eternity, God has promised he loves us forever and he will not leave us or forsake us. He has also promised us his greatness and power. Why would we search for it anywhere else? We become comfortable and complacent with our worldview and our own comforts. We think we are satisfied with our lives—until we are not. Then we search by crying out to God.

God wants us to seek him, trust him, and lean on him for all we want and need. He is waiting for us to call on him, and he does not withhold any good thing from us. God will not force us to come, nor will he force us to choose him over worldly perspectives. At every turn, we have to choose—life or death, blessings or curses: "This day I call the heavens and the earth as witnesses against you that I have set before you life and death, blessings and curses. Now choose life, so that you and your children may live" (Deut. 30:19).

God's love, significance, and power come from living a life surrendered to the Deity. It is a paradox that God's love is greater than we dream or imagine, and yet it came at the cost of his own Son's sacrificial death on the cross for the sins of the world. Another paradox is that we have significance and power as children of God through the Son the Father sacrificed on the cross. If we seek God we will have all we need. But we have to let go of our demands in order to have what we need or want in him. We cannot control our own lives, but we can turn to the Creator of the universe with our lives. He is the author and creator, Savior and sustainer, Sovereign Lord and Almighty God of all, the author of truth, love, greatness, and power.

Crossing over the Threshold of Life in Faith to Life to the Full in Him

Are we crossing the threshold to the new life God has offered us? Or, like the Israelites, are we afraid of the Promised Land because of all the giants there? What hinders our view of the Father's bountiful provision? What stops our receiving it? The hindrance is ourselves—our standing still and not crossing over the threshold. Perhaps it is a spiritual battle. John 10:10 says, "The thief comes only to steal and kill and destroy; I have come that they may have life, and have it to the full." The Evil One came to destroy, but God came to give us life to the full. We will face many battles in life, yet they all belong to God. He is the ammunition we need to cross over the threshold. God gives the armor and the faith to proceed. One hindrance is fear of what is on the other side. God says we are not to fear, that he is with us, and that his love conquers all fear. When angels appear in Scripture and tell us to "fear not," this mean they have good news. We remember that the things we face with God ultimately bring us the most joy.

Could it be the desire for comfort over all else causes us to stay stuck? Does being comfortable fit into God's paradigm? God wants to comfort us, but stepping out in faith is not always comfortable. He gives us adventure, romance, and great things to conquer, but could it be we lack the desire to move out in faith or to cross over? God creates in us a desire for him and a desire for life to the full. Earthly desires seemingly bring comfort or abundance, but they only add dissatisfaction and the illusion of a plentiful life, like achievement, success, significance, power, beauty, and money. If any one of these is the destination, it will only bring trouble and destruction. But the ones God gives us bring fulfillment, satisfaction, and eternal reward.

Venturing Across the Threshold to Life to the Full

> We must ask God for his perspective

> We must lean into God with trust and prayer

> We must expect God to show up

> We must make the first step in faith across the threshold to observe how God prevails

> We must remember his provision in the past

We must know that struggles and pain will come but that God is enough

We must acknowledge we are not in control, and if we let go and lean on God, we will have the ride of our lives

We are always crossing over from one spacious place to another, getting closer to God. It is in the closeness to him, as we surrender more and more, that we find "life to the full."

NOW What?

Life changes. With new surroundings and new life stages, sometimes things feel a bit "off." We try to solve things, alleviate them, and analyze them. Yet God stays the same. God has truly delivered us from the anguish of the past, and yet we still want to control things as well as our feelings about them.

God teaches that we cannot hold on to the past and at the same time step out in faith with him and hold on to our old selves, the ones who doubted and condemned. God allows our circumstances to show us the holes in our beliefs. We are his children, and he is our Creator, Savior, Guide, Comforter, and Judge. We cannot take on any of these roles—not if we are to be his daughters. A daughter feels. She may be sad, disappointed, or aggrieved. She may talk to God about her anguish. She may sit at his feet, cry it out, be comforted, and talk to him about it all.

Too often we want to get past things without the usual steps, to skip over the part where the parent helps console the child. Somewhere in the subconscious, we fear what will happen. We hold on to the hurt of the parent being absent or not being able to comfort the child. Because we don't want to be disappointed again, or because we don't want to live out the grief we already felt, we avoid it altogether.

Avoidance is one of our old behaviors. When we avoid pain; we become our own saviors, comforters, and guides, and we are terrible at it. We condemn, rationalize, or run away from the pain. But God wants us to trust him with the pain. We run because are scared; God pursues us in the pain to love us more. It is interesting that the very thing we need most is what we run away from. God allows our disappointments in order to show us that he is the parent we yearn for and that we are his dearly loved children, who he comes to comfort and hold in their pain and disappointment. This is how the journey of being a daughter of the King often begins.

Journey to the Table

Most of us think of faith journeys as overarching affairs with monumental spiritual victories. While God gives these kinds of victories, more often he takes great pains with our lives and works out all the details in a sort of slow motion. The testimonies we tell of these journeys full of joys and struggles are not high adventure so much as slow moving and life-transforming years with our Father God, who remains with us and who is willing to shape us moment-by-moment over time.

So it is with waiting on God. When we finally turn our waiting over to him, we get a glimpse of God. He knew it all along, but we needed to grow in our waiting in order to see him. That is how life goes so often, waiting on and wrestling with God teaches us through his Word. He is the riches we learn about. The Great "I Am" comes fully alive, new, fresh, the One for whom we search.

God dwells within us. With his Holy Spirit, we know the deep things of God's heart. His Spirit within us searches and knows him deeply within in the pain or the wrestling or the waiting. But he comes down in his holiness and majesty and strength and kindness to us in our greatest need and when we least expect it. Deep within, we enjoy him and his rest. He remains as he surely was, and is, and is to come.

Chapter Four

God Calls Us to Trust

The Lord is my light and my salvation—whom shall I fear?
The Lord is the stronghold of my life— of whom shall I be afraid?
… One thing I ask from the Lord, this only do I seek: that I may
dwell in the house of the Lord all the days of my life, to gaze on
the beauty of the Lord and to seek him in his temple…. I remain
confident of this: I will see the goodness of the Lord in the land of
the living. Wait for the Lord; be strong and take heart
and wait for the Lord. (Ps. 27:1; 4-5; 13-14)

Then Jesus declared, "I am the bread of life. Whoever comes to me
will never go hungry, and whoever believes in me will never be
thirsty. But as I told you, you have seen me and still you do not
believe. All those the Father gives me will come to me, and
whoever comes to me I will never drive away. For I have come
down from heaven not to do my will but to do the will of him who
sent me. And this is the will of him who sent me, that I shall lose
none of all those he has given me, but raise them up at the last day.
For my Father's will is that everyone who looks to the Son and
believes in him shall have eternal life, and I will raise them up at
the last day." (John 6:35-40)

God Plants the Seeds

In God's economy, there is so much more. Even though the psalmist writes, "The Lord is my light and my salvation—whom shall I fear? The Lord is the stronghold of my life—of whom shall I be afraid?" I was at times fearful and afraid. My fear of having children was real and tucked away inside of me. Of course, my real fear in having children was that they would not know the love of a mother, because I had not received or felt the love of my mother. What if they had the same feelings of abandonment, or shame, or rejection that I did? But in God's economy, there is more. It has been miraculous that our children know a mother's love and the love of their earthly and heavenly Father.

God wants us to be his daughters. He has planted the seed in us to know him as our Father—our protector, guide, provider, comforter, teacher, and the one who encourages, inspires, and fills us with himself in unfathomable ways. Being God's daughters results in the journey of walking with him and listening to him as daughters who need to know him in order to live as he has planned. Are we in need of knowing our Father in heaven in this way? Yes *if* we are to hear our Father and know his love and plan for us to have life to the full.

As God sows seed in our lives and grows us up in his time, we have the privilege of knowing him. He knows our deepest desires, and also our most painful struggles. And he loves us more. We know God in his fullness when trusting him as he works his purposes out. His harvest of plenty is all around us.

Trusting in Him—Portion, Plenty, Spacious, Free, Abundant

God is the creator of our portion. He says it is plentiful, spacious, free, and abundant. "You prepare a table before me in the presence of my enemies. You anoint my head with oil; my cup overflows" (Ps. 23:5). God anoints us in the presence of our enemies, including sometimes the enemies of health or even ourselves, to the comforts of his blessings: "He is wooing you from the jaws of distress to a spacious place free from restriction, to the comfort of your table laden with choice food" (Job 36:16).

Does God's abundance include rest? We seem to go through motions not designed for us, and God needs to get our attention in order to teach us and calm us to his sovereignty. Jesus tells us, "My yoke is easy and my burden is light" (Matt. 11:30). So why do we take on things that are difficult and heavy? Jesus is the burden-bearer and the One in control of all things.

In Christ's pursuing love, God wants us to know his heart. Knowing his heart transforms ours. The abundant life is knowing and experiencing the heart of God. He has a great love for us, the kind of love we know nothing about, the kind of love that is wider and deeper and higher than any love we have ever experienced. As the apostle Paul wrote, "I pray that out of his glorious riches he may strengthen you with power through his Spirit in your inner being, so that Christ may dwell in your hearts through faith. And I pray that you, being rooted and established in love, may have power, together with all the Lord's holy people, to grasp how wide and long and high and deep is the love of Christ" (Eph. 3:16-18). Through the work of the Holy Spirit in our lives, Christ enables us to know him and the love he has for us. When we cry out to him, he pours this love into us. If our hearts are open, we will know the Giver as our Father God who gave his only Son so that we may know him, the Creator of the universe and the Father of us all.

Being still is contrary to what our world tells us will give us our portion—plenty, spacious, free, and abundant. But if our goal is to know God, then we have to get quiet and listen to him, as Psalm 46:10 says: "Be still, and know that I am God; I will be exalted among the nations, I will be exalted in the earth." He is the One in whom we must trust, not for a season, but a lifetime.

Throwing Down the Hurt

I was recently reminded again that I am a people pleaser. I am dreadfully aware of my need to please. It seemed I had made progress in this area some time ago, but I am once again in the throes of it. The ugly head of rejection still looms large. Old habits return when I have enough interaction with those who bring out the worst in me and when I have spent more than enough time back in trenches with my old self. I am still a people pleaser.

The only way for this entanglement to go away is to throw it off intentionally, to seize the habit and cease it. "Therefore, since we are surrounded by such a great cloud of witnesses, let us throw off everything that hinders and the sin that so easily entangles. And let us run with perseverance the race marked out for us, fixing our eyes on Jesus, the pioneer and perfecter of faith. For the joy set before him he endured the cross, scorning its shame, and sat down at the right hand of the throne of God" (Heb. 12:1-2). Running the race with perseverance is not easy. If it were, I would have done it long ago. Yet, if I turn to God with it, fixing my eyes on Jesus, the striving and trying to control the situation by pleasing would change.

The cycle goes like this: I have been rejected, or I fear being rejected again. I have an interaction with someone I associate with the rejection. I choose to do something I think would assuage any future rejection. Thus, I perform a pleasing act. It is not a conscious cycle, but after evaluation of recent events, this is the way I interact.

Today I have asked God to help me to let go of the rejection—to throw down the hurt that has hurt me in the past. I must not fear future rejection; God is with me and will give me the strength I need. If I fix my eyes on him, faith is possible and fear gets smaller and smaller, until it becomes virtually nil.

God helps us on this new path by giving us the faith to expect and to know that we do not have to fear anything. He is the One upon whom we will fix our gaze, not on ourselves in protection, or on others in pleasing. And when we go out in faith, we will please him. He requires us to receive his way, to please him and not others, and to travel his path in faith, not in fear. If we throw our hats in the race with perseverance, to throw down all that hinders us, we remain tethered to him who guides and leads us on the journey.

God invites us to this new path of letting go of the fear of rejection and of control by pleasing others. We accept his invitation with faith because he leads the way and he goes with us. As he heals us of unbelief, and replaces it with faith, we remain in awe that he allows us more and more grace.

Dear Lord,

Help me to be humble to receive what you have already given

in this area of my life—grace. Guide me to lean into the faith you have given and I have yet to receive. Thank you for providing me with strength to throw off the hurt of the rejection, which so easily entangles me to sin in trying to control the circumstances.

Thank you for allowing me a fresh start with this old problem in my life.

You are the God of newness and invitations.

Thank you!

Hiding (Where and From What)

Set me free from my prison that I may praise your name.

Then the righteous will gather about me
because of your goodness to me (Ps. 142:7)

Hiding becomes a way of life for some. David hid in caves from his enemies as they tried to find and kill him. Psalm 42:7 is a plea to God to free David from his life of hiding. Even if we are not fleeing from our enemies, we may still be hiding out, hiding from, or imprisoned by something. Do we desire freedom? Are we in hiding, or in chains, or both?

I wrote a book about a little girl (my former self) who is now a grown woman who was trapped in her hallway closet of despair, fear, anger, and sadness (*Real Struggles, Real Hope: A Journey to Truth, Trust, and Freedom*, 2013). I hid from the real world because I could not live up to what I thought it wanted from me. Trying to make myself more valuable, I achieved, pleased, and made myself into what I thought would make me feel loved and significant. None of these things worked, yet God was working in my life.

No longer do I feel trapped in this life. I want the life to the full that the Lord has promised. He has transformed me out of many of my old habits and he has also given me perseverance in the race he set out for me. His hope has changed me into his daughter who knows his unfailing love.

Are there places still void of God's love and power in my life? In other words, are there parts of me that want to remain hidden? Where could I still be hiding? From what am I hiding? I believe God has healed many pieces of me, but he is still allowing things to surface that I must surrender to him—either for him to take away or refine, or for him to transform and to heal. As he continues in his timing, I am amazed how he peels away the onion of my life where I have been hardened by my own decisions to protect myself and not lean totally onto him when I am hurt or afraid.

Rejection in the form of harsh words, or rejection by non-inclusion, or feeling invisible because of rejection are each ways we become hurt, disappointed, angry, or fearful. We want to hide from rejection and from people knowing we have been rejected. But God knows. And God cares deeply. He is distressed by whatever distresses us, as the prophet Isaiah wrote: "In all their distress he too was distressed, and the angel of his presence saved them. In his love and mercy he redeemed them; he lifted them up and carried them all the days of old" (Isa. 63:9).

As the writer of Hebrews tells us, we need to throw down all hindrances to our faith. "Therefore, since we are surrounded by such a great cloud of witnesses, let us throw off everything that hinders and the sin that so easily entangles. And let us run with perseverance the race marked out for us, fixing our eyes on Jesus, the pioneer and perfecter of faith. For the joy set before him he endured the cross, scorning its shame, and sat down at the right hand of the throne of God" (Heb. 12:1-2). Like all sin, the hurt from rejection becomes entangled. A single hurt grows and grows as one lets it fester. As we are rejected, we must give God the hurt. None of us cause rejection to occur; in fact, it is out of our control. Neither can we change that it *did* occur. God says to throw down the thing that hinders our trust in him. We must cast off the rejection that hurts, and we must cast it off onto God. Our casting this care onto God, or throwing this hindrance down, we will also increase our faith.

The hurt cannot grow inside of us if we throw it down. It is so easy to allow the hurt not only to remain but also to increase as we ponder it and try understanding why it occurred. We can try doing something different so it does not happen again. Striving to control the rejection and the hurt, protecting ourselves when we hurt, and trying to understand why it happened, are not what God has in mind for us. Instead, he tells us to trust him in all things—even when we hurt. If we throw down what hurts and allow God to appropriate the hurt, perhaps our propensity to hide will recede. Hiding from hurt does not allow us to know God more; it takes us away from him. If we choose God, we must also choose not to hide. The hurt from rejection may still occur, but choosing to trust God with it when it occurs will allow us to know him better and depend on him on our walk of faith.

Are we hiding from something? Do we feel imprisoned? Go to God. Allow him in the place that remains hidden—he will make it into a spacious place.

"Only God"

Extends mercy
Washes away all my sin
Creates in me a pure heart
Gives me grace to follow him

Replaces my sin with his kindness
Grows the faith in me when I go with him
Loves me in the midst of my failure
And when I choose another way

Pursues me intentionally
As his own and for his plan and glory
Reminds me of his love and choice
To make me his daughter

Gives us life and provides the means
To have life to the full
Through the walk of faith
His love and abundance along the way

Knows our every need and want
And gives us immeasurably more than
We imagine for all the world to see
He is God and there is no other

Living without Walls

Do we have something in life imprisoning us or keeping us from fully embracing our lives—perhaps it could be fear, or worry, or anxiety? In what do we place our hopes or dreams? God says that in him we are free to be who he has created us to be. Then why is it we are not free? When we set our focus on our living God, and when we live in a relationship with him through Jesus Christ, we know him, his love, and his truth. It is then we are set free to live life to the full.

There are many reasons for fear and anxiety and living an imprisoned life. Some are made by the world we live in, and some we inflict upon ourselves. And yet, Jesus said, "If you hold to my teaching, you are really my disciples. Then you will know the truth, and the truth will set you free" (John 8:31-32). It is through a relationship with Jesus Christ that we know the truth and that we can be set truly free.

When we are in dire circumstances, we cry out to the One who created us to ask for relief, change, or rescue. The freedom we receive from the One who made us, however, does not depend on our circumstances at the moment. He can certainly rescue and transform us, and he can even change our circumstances. But he may not. He may use our current situation to help us become more dependent on him, to know him better, and to trust him more. There is no substitute for this relationship. No circumstance, remedy, or transformation can become the hope to which he has called us. As Paul prayed, "I pray that the eyes of your heart may be enlightened in order that you may know the hope to which he has called you, the riches of his glorious inheritance in his holy people" (Eph. 1:18).

God in Jesus Christ is our hope. We can turn to him and find he has already been pursuing us with wild and captivating love. With him we may live without our own devices, without substitutes for him, and without walls to protect ourselves. We may freely come to him and live as his own. After all, it is how he designed it.

Comfort Only God Gives

My heart is not proud, Lord, my eyes are not haughty; I do not concern myself with great matters or things too wonderful for me. But I have calmed and quieted myself, I am like a weaned child with its mother; like a weaned child I am content. (Ps. 131:1-2)

Praise be to the Lord, for he has heard my cry for mercy. The Lord is my strength and my shield; my heart trusts in him, and he helps me. My heart leaps for joy, and with my song I praise him. (Ps. 28:6-7)

In you our ancestors put their trust; they trusted and you delivered them. To you they cried out and were saved; in you they trusted and were not put to shame. (Ps. 22:4-5)

For this is what the Lord says: "I will extend peace to her like a river, and the wealth of nations like a flooding stream; you will nurse and be carried on her arm and dandled on her knees. As a mother comforts her child, so will I comfort you; and you will be comforted over Jerusalem." (Isa. 66:12-13)

The message God gives through our struggles has to do with his comfort, treasure, hope, love, revelation, care, grace, presence, fullness, bounty, and goodness. Also, it has to do with his name, glory, handiwork, truth, mercy, abundance, joy, and inheritance. The Lord hears our cries and comforts us as a mother comforts her child.

Comfort is not something easily given. The kind of comfort the psalmist talks about is the comfort only God gives. To speak words of compassion and empathy to those who are hurting is difficult for us at times. Yet, giving comfort in ways God has comforted us is what he guides us to do. We would rather not focus on the serious side of life. We would rather laugh and tell wonderful tales. Leaving the real comforting to God is our way to avoid such difficult matters.

God knows all of our hardships, and he has wired us to need him for them. He knew before we were born that one of the struggles we would face would be the lack of comfort in our childhood and growing up years. He knew we would have to depend on him for it. I myself looked high and low for the soothing I lacked during my formative years, yet I always came back empty. God is not empty, and neither is he far from us. He is near and knowing and he pursues us wherever we are.

God pursued me even in my mother's womb, and that is true of everyone. He knew I would need his comfort not only before I was born but everywhere and at all times from the time I was born until the time I die. God is good, and his plan and purposes are for our good and his glory. I found the comfort I sought in him. He is the arms I seek, the chest I rest upon, and the everlasting love I desire. He made all of us to require his presence above all else.

God comes to meet us right where we are, in the darkest night and the place we think the pain is too large for us to handle. He presents himself to us as the One who understands our pain, and the One who knows us and how difficult it is. He comes to give us comfort, to give us himself. It is in this place God calls us. He knows our name and where we have been. He also knows the lengths to which we would go in order to release ourselves from the pain. When he shows us who he is and what he has done, we must choose to acknowledge him. The comfort becomes the salve on our deep need, and we know it must be him. But we have to choose him in this place of need. When we do, he rests upon us just as we enter his rest.

I have found the deepest comfort in God, a comfort that goes beyond that of a weaned child at its mother's breast. "But I have calmed and quieted myself, I am like a weaned child with its mother; like a weaned child I am content" (Ps. 131:2). This comfort is the presence of God in the midst of real struggle. He comes to us, a holy God, perfect, merciful, and just. He joins us in the pit to rescue us—not only to lift us up or walk us through, but also to give us his comfort and rest amidst dire suffering and pain.

I am in awe of my heavenly Father, who comforts me in pain and in life during good times and bad. He is my rest and my honor; He is the treasure I seek and the One I want to know more and more. He hides me in the comfort of his arms, making me safe and secure. It is the heavenly Father who comes to save and shield all of us. He is waiting for us, and he has come to comfort us.

Taking Possession of It—Walking by Faith

God commanded Joshua to enter the land the Lord God provided for the Israelites and take possession of it. God had promised the land to Joshua's ancestor, Abraham, when he told him he would bless him and make his name great. After hearing his children's cries, God gave Moses the leadership to bring the enslaved Israelites out of Egypt into the land he promised them. But when the Israelites, under the leadership of Moses, came near and scoped out the Promised Land, they became fearful of what they saw. Even so, in his kindness God provided for them as they wandered in the wilderness until they were ready to enter the land he had originally given their ancestors.

In Christ we have received God's promise of salvation. It is ours and we can take possession of it. We have all of God in the person of Jesus Christ; he has already given all of himself. In order to have all of him, we must walk by faith and "take possession of the land." By crossing into the Promised Land, those led by Joshua crossed over by faith in the Lord God—the same God who gave guidance in the form of a pillar of cloud by day and a pillar of fire by night in the wilderness. This is the same One who rained down manna from heaven daily as God's chosen people wandered.

The same Lord God who dealt with Joshua and Moses has given himself to us. When we receive him and begin walking by faith, we have all of him. Do we live like we have taken possession of him? Do we really know what we have received when we have possessed all of him? It is clear the Israelites did not know what they had received from God with the gift of the Promised Land. They were commanded to conquer their enemies in the land: "I will give you every place where you set your foot, as I promised Moses. Your territory will extend from the desert to Lebanon, and from the great river, the Euphrates—all the Hittite country—to the Mediterranean Sea in the west. No one will be able to stand against you all the days of your life" (Josh. 1:3-5). God told them he would be with them and would never leave them. He said, "As I was with Moses, so I will be with you; I will never leave you nor forsake you" (Josh. 1:5). They were told not to be afraid. As we walk with the Lord, do we acknowledge he is with us and will never leave us? Do we walk by faith over the difficulties, the unexpected, and the disappointing? Do we depend on the Lord to help us conquer our unbelief, our fears, and other enemies?

As we learn to trust God and lean in for his help, we know him better and experience more of him. As we cross over from dependence on ourselves and lives lived by sight, we take possession of the very thing he has already given us—himself. It is by walking with him that we learn to walk with him. This becomes a faith journey to more of God and less of ourselves. As we seek him in all things, we see he has been pursuing us from the beginning. As we surrender, we receive God in full.

Receiving all that God has given us in Christ is a difficult matter for most of us, even if it seems so simple. The command for the Israelites to enter the land God gave them and take possession of it seemed simple as well. But that turned out not to be easy at all. Walking by faith requires training on how to receive what God has already given. The Israelites, trained in the wilderness and by their experience taking the Promised Land, learned how to walk by faith and take possession of what God wanted them to have. Receiving and owning what God has already bestowed on us is elusive at times. Yet it is the most rewarding and satisfying journey we will ever take. And we will not journey alone!

Believing and Receiving

To believe in Jesus Christ is to lean wholly upon him rather than upon our own understanding. It is to trust him with all matters, and to follow him with all of one's heart, as we are told in the book of Proverbs: "Trust in the Lord with all your heart and lean not on your own understanding; in all your ways submit to him, and he will make your paths straight" (Prov. 3:5-6). When we take the step of belief, God gives us the capacity to follow. With each step of faith, God grows the measure of faith in us. He multiplies the courage, passion, and yearning for God's best. Is receiving God's fullness in proportion to the steps of faith we take? Is receiving God's fullness in proportion to leaning in God's direction and trusting him with our whole heart?

God certainly implies the interaction of receiving and believing in his Word. Our trust in him brings huge rewards into our lives. Also, as we receive what he gives us, he gives with more abundance. It is as if God were saying that if we receive the faith he alone has given, then he will give us more. In other words, we cannot receive all God has to give. Yet, if we receive what he offers, he will in turn multiply his gifts to us. This is life in its fullness as he planned for us.

One of the premises of walking by faith is that, as we do, God bestows life to the full—abundant life. When we veer off the walk of faith, we limit God and eliminate the abundant resources he had in mind to give us. His love and mercy are unfailing. We cannot deplete his love for us, for he loves without caution and without condition. However, he gives us the choice to love him back. It is our prerogative to accept or reject him. If we do reject the Lord and the faith he has given, there is no sense in which we will qualify for the abundant life.

Believing in Christ with all our hearts, and living in such a way as to proclaim our faith, we will have more of him and more of the life abundant. On the other hand, God does not require us to live this way. He wants to pour himself out in our lives, yet he will not force us to choose this way.

What would we receive from God if we were to let go of all we hold too tightly? The answer is more of God. And when we have more of God, we have a fuller and more abundant life, a life of walking by faith and receiving what he planned before the creation of the world. His plan is perfect. The Father sees us as he sees his Son Jesus. He has already given us all of himself; may we receive more of God by believing him and living like we do.

Replacements

God gives so much more to his children than the world gives, and this is demonstrated through the significant losses in our lives. Losses in our earthly lives are significant, but God's bounty far exceeds our lack. We have new lives and new stories to share because of his love for us.

Thank you, Jesus,
for your replacements, your rebuilding what has been broken,
your restoration and healing in me and others in my family system.
Help me to see your hand in many more ways and experiences.
Show me how to receive what you are giving and have given me.

Guide me in how to receive the honor that my shame says was
stolen from me. I know that in you I have no shame.
But it rears its ugly head at times.
I don't want to live like that anymore.
You have given me honor and an inheritance;
help me to live like it is true.

*Help me to know that what has been taken away was allowed by
you so that I may know your inheritance and not that of this
world's. Help my unbelief and grow my faith in you
to blossom in ways unexpected.
Help me to see your design in the secret
and love you and serve you more, Lord.*

*I didn't know that I could bear the pain of family suffering but you
did. I was able to do it because you were there and you allowed me
to face it and go through it with you by my side—before me,
with me, and behind me.*

*I didn't know that I could lose family members and still live, but
you did. I made it through with you. I didn't know that I could face
the shame and write about it, but you did. I am healed of family
shame and trauma and a history of lies and unbelief.
You knew that you would do it and I know that it is true.*

*I ask for healing for the secret places that keep me from your
fullness and receiving what you have already given. Bring the
sorrow and shame to light—only that which is hindering me from
your grace and mercy. Help me to allow you to heal me as only
you can do and as you have done before.*

Thank you!

The Abundant Life, Complete Joy, and Every Spiritual Blessing

In the first chapter of the book of Ephesians, Paul writes,
"Praise be to the God and Father of our Lord Jesus Christ, who has
blessed us in the heavenly realms with every spiritual blessing in
Christ. For he chose us in him before the creation of the world to
be holy and blameless in his sight" (Eph. 1:3-4). It is by the
Father's grace that he gives us Jesus. It is also by the Father's
grace that we choose to follow the Son. It follows then that it is by
God's grace that we have what he chooses to give us. As we
continue seeking God, we want him to change our view so we can
see him and know his heart behind the abundant life, complete joy,

and every spiritual gift he has already given. Perhaps it is in the gift of a new heart—a new stance to know God's grace—that he opens our hearts and eyes to all the wonderful things we have been gifted. We want to open up to them, to open them up, and to be open to whatever God has for us. Do we behold the gifts the Father has given us? Do we thank him for his bounty, but then go back to our own devices for living our lives? God gives us power and authority in Jesus, the love to serve others, and divine truth and grace to live out his purposes.

We cannot live life from our own perspective and expect to experience God's abundance. To experience that, we must depend on him in every way. He "has blessed us in the heavenly realms with every spiritual blessing in Christ" (Eph. 1:3). What more do we need? God gives us life, free will, the capacity to choose to follow him, and new eyes and hearts to grasp the beauty and bounty of his love and grace.

Our prayer as we seek Father God:

Lord,
give us the eyes and heart not only to behold these gifts,
but having received them, the humility and desire to live boldly for
your purposes today and everyday.

Reasons to Trust God

His mercy is great; his love is unfailing

I have been saved by the grace of God through faith in Jesus Christ

I was made alive in Jesus Christ even when I was dead in my sin

I am clothed in Christ

I have the Holy Spirit within

I have the mind of Christ

My body is the temple of the Holy Spirit

I am clothed in the armor of God

God goes before, with, within, and behind me

God is with me; he will never leave me or forsake me

He has raised me up and seated me with Christ Jesus in the heavenly realms

I am an heir of Jesus Christ; I have a glorious inheritance

I have every spiritual blessing in the heavenly realms in Christ Jesus. He chose me before creation and has made me holy and blameless in his sight

He has opened my heart to the hope to which I am called in Christ Jesus

He has given me wisdom and revelation so that I may know him better

He has given me power—incomparable power, the same as resurrection power

He has made me one with him and with his chosen people

I am no longer a foreigner or stranger, but a member of God's household

He has given me access with all his children to the Father through his Holy Spirit

I am being joined with his holy people to rise to be a dwelling for God in his Spirit

True Worship

"Then your light will break forth like the dawn, and your healing will quickly appear; then your righteousness will go before you, and the glory of the Lord will be your rear guard" (Isa. 58:8). True worship from knowing God compels us to share his abundance with others. When we know the Lord's heart, we know him. Our healing will quickly appear when we are open to receiving it. And when his glory shines in our new and healed hearts, the world knows him as he brings in the harvest.

By our knowing God and his heart for us, we want to reach out through his heart in us and with his healing in, for, and through us. Then he shines in us and makes the whole world know him, his harvest.

God Fills Our Emptiness

When we open the door of our lives for God to enter, he comes in and gives us what is needed to fill the empty places. Where we were once void of that which completes us, we now have the God of the universe. His fullness is greater than we ever imagined. God shares his great love for us through his Son. As we enter into this relationship with our great Creator, our own hearts grow. If and when we want more he gives us more and fills our emptiness.

As we grow in our knowledge of the Savior, he shows us our broken places and creates in us the desire to be whole by his healing. When we receive what he offers, he mightily heals. We were once alone, lonely, and altogether dissatisfied with life. Then God so mercifully and graciously revealed our need to be filled with his compassion and truth.

As the Savior heals us, we have the privilege of sharing in the glory of his being known. He wants the world to know him, and he uses us to show them who he is. He doesn't have to do things quite this way, but that is how he does it in the divine economy. The mighty and holy One equips us with himself to share our brokenness and his healing. He is our rear guard for all of life, the beginning of our faith, and the sustainer of our souls. He enables us to accept what he has to offer, and he equips us to run the race of life. He shines his light in the world so that the world will know him; that is how he brings in the harvest. It all begins with the Savior, flows from him, and returns to him. He comes to bring us faith, true worship, and the privilege of knowing and seeing heaven's harvest.

Then your light will break forth like the dawn,
and your healing will quickly appear;
then your righteousness will go before you,
and the glory of the Lord
will be your rear guard (Isa. 58:8).

The Red Dress Symbolism of God's Abundant Gifts

God's abundant gifts are hope, love, healing, joy, true calling, wearing of the new self, and Christ's adornment. God gives us himself and makes us new. We answer his new calling on our lives and receive it by serving others. In doing so, Christ equips us to wear his garments.

Jesus knows our woundedness. He heals our broken hearts and gives us new lives of purpose and hope. He gives us stories to share his truth and grace. In fact, it is in telling others what he has done that he heals over and over again. And over and over again we see his faithfulness, goodness, and desire to give grace upon grace as we share the story of hope with others.

Mary, my mother-in-law-to-be, spoke kind and generous words of affirmation and encouragement as we talked before the wedding. At the time, I didn't know whether she knew about my mother's rejection of me, or of my woundedness. She saw the inappropriateness of my mother wearing a red dress on my wedding day (the story is earlier in this book, and is taken from my first book, *Real Struggles, Real Hope*). As I shared earlier, some few weeks later, just after we were married, Mary gave me a red dress. I always loved the dress, mainly because she gave it to me. It was such an act of love. She clothed me as a daughter who needed dressing and adornment.

For me, this story is a beautiful reminder that God comes in and clothes us with his adornment. We are children of the King, and he dresses us in garments of his pleasure. Mary gave me a garment of her pleasure; I did not get its significance until later. God wants us to wear his adornment for his glory today and every day.

Healing through God's Word

"He sent out his word and healed them; he rescued them from the grave" (Ps. 107:20). We should be amazed at God's timing. He takes our broken places and continues working with them. After all, he is the master potter. It is astonishing that God has this desire to make us into something he can use, and it is also astonishing that he continues working and transforming us into what he had in mind from the beginning of time. God's desire to transform us into something is an inside-out process—that is, we get to be involved from the inside out. He starts deep within, working with the brokenness, and works toward healing and wholeness.

As God meets us in our brokenness and our desire for help, he shows us his presence. We don't know what he has planned or what he will do, but in his presence, we get a glimpse of his nature while he gives us the capacity to believe he can and will help us. In the broken and hidden places of our lives, God turns the most hurtful and disappointing experiences into beautiful pictures demonstrating his love, compassion, and hope for the future. The Lord has done much through our betrayals and disappointments, by taking away a layer of earthly wounds and replacing them with a deep and strong layer of his healing truth.

On the last meeting of my "Real Struggles, Real Hope" study group, I brought out pictures of my family of origin. One study group member made some really astute comments about my family, especially my mother. Then she shared her difficult relationship with her own mother. As she looked at my husband's family in the wedding pictures, she remarked about his mother, my mother-in-law. As I listened to her and agreed with what she was saying, I heard myself say, "She was so gracious and loving. She gave me a red dress soon after we were married. It was such a special gift, something to make me feel pretty. I wore it often, and it pleased her so much." Then not thinking about the words but hearing them come out of my mouth, I said, "Did she do it on purpose? Did she give me the red dress on purpose because my mother wore a red dress on my wedding day?"

I remembered what my mother-in-law said to me on my wedding day. She was with me in the bride's room as I waited to enter the back of the sanctuary to walk down the aisle. She kept telling me how lovely I was, and that I was "the loveliest bride" she had ever seen. That was part of the way God brought me healing. My book, *Real Struggles, Real Hope*, was borne out of God's healing. Again, God comes to heal and to bring wholeness. His word heals us. In the telling of his healing, the Lord heals over and over again. He allows us the opportunity to participate in it with him. From the inside out, God takes the broken places and makes them whole for the world to see. He is God, and there is no other.

We are His Friends and His Chosen Ones

Our Father in heaven chose us, and he sent his Son Jesus to rescue us. Instead of calling us servants, he calls us, friends. He chose us before we chose God. He chose us first, but we have the responsibility to choose him in return. We may run to him with awe, reverence, worship, gratitude, and joy. Or we may turn away from him in shame and rebellion, as if we are not worthy to be his chosen ones. Which indeed, we are not. But our Father God in Jesus Christ made us worthy because he himself is worthy.

> As the Father has loved me, so have I loved you. Now remain in my love. If you keep my commands, you will remain in my love, just as I have kept my Father's commands and remain in his love. I have told you this so that my joy may be in you and that your joy may be complete. My command is this: Love each other as I have loved you. Greater love has no one than this: to lay down one's life for one's friends. You are my friends if you do what I command. I no longer call you servants, because a servant does not know his master's business. Instead, I have called you friends, for everything that I learned from my Father I have made known to you. You did not choose me, but I chose you and appointed you so that you might go and bear fruit—fruit that will last—and so that whatever you ask in my name the Father will give you. This is my command: Love each other. (John 15:9-17)

Do these words invite us to choose Jesus? God loved us and called us before we even knew him, and actually he chose and appointed us before we were born. We will never earn this relationship by virtue of anything we say or do. The Father earned it for us through his Son. When we seek him because he has first invited us in, he comes alongside and teaches, guides, protects, and draws us closer. He wants us to have a deep and close relationship with him.

Through a close relationship with the Lord, we may have rich prayer lives. He teaches us how to pray and to want to pray for his will over our lives.

> When you pray, go into your room,
> close the door and pray to your Father, who is unseen.
> Then your Father,
> who sees what is done in secret,
> will reward you.
> And when you pray, do not keep on babbling like pagans,
> for they think they will be heard because of their many words.
> Do not be like them, for your Father knows what you need
> before you ask him.
> This, then, is how you should pray:
> Our Father in heaven,
> hallowed be your name,
> your kingdom come,
> your will be done,
> on earth as it is in heaven.
> Give us today our daily bread.
> And forgive us our debts,
> as we also have forgiven our debtors.
> And lead us not into temptation,
> but deliver us from the evil one. (Matt. 6:6-13)

When we pray the Lord's Prayer, we pray for "your kingdom come, your will be done, on earth as it is in heaven." Do we realize how much of God's heart we may have this side of heaven? Do we know how much he may reign in our hearts and lives, and that this is all possible through the Holy Spirit? If we are his friends and his chosen ones, do we not have what we need to draw down the Kingdom into our very hearts, souls, and lives?

As God's friends, we now have the power to command heaven and earth. We can bring heaven to earth. Jesus came to earth once, and he will surely come again, as he said he would. But in the meantime, the Lord has given us himself and the power of the Almighty in heaven here on earth. As friends of the Savior and the Almighty, He chose us to be his allies on earth, and the bearers of the divine name for the entire world to see. He chose us and calls us his friends, not his servants. What more do we need to go out and proclaim the goodness of the gospel news and the greatness of our God?

To Know God

What does it mean to know God? Are we willing to suffer, die, and be conformed to his likeness? To know God means choosing and following him. In this relationship, God meets us where we are. At each step along the way, we determine whether we will follow his lead. Following means surrendering ourselves to the Almighty Savior and the Creator Father God, who gave his own Son to die in our stead so we may live with him everlastingly in the kingdom of God. As we surrender our lives, we come to know our Father in heaven. He lives within, and he goes before us and with us, and he always follows to protect us and grow us up— and to bring in the results of his work. What is his work in maturing us? It is our transformation for his glory and his plan, as he predestined it.

The apostle Paul said that to know Christ is akin to suffering: "I want to know Christ—yes, to know the power of his resurrection and participation in his sufferings, becoming like him in his death" (Phil. 3:10). We will have struggles, some struggles of our own doing, some allowed by God, but all used by God for our good if we are his followers. We suffer because we are his children, because we live in a fallen world, and because sometimes we are just unwise. But God uses all the struggles in our lives to bring about his glory and his good in and for us for the world to know Christ. "And we know that in all things God works for the good of those who love him, who have been called according to his purpose" (Rom. 8:28).

To know God means being conformed to the divine image as we develop into his mature followers. Becoming mature in the knowledge of God requires time and the surrender of ourselves to our One and Only. One day, when we enter eternity, we will know him when we see him because we will look like him: "Dear friends, now we are children of God, and what we will be has not yet been made known. But we know that when Christ appears, we shall be like him, for we shall see him as he is" (1 John 3:2).

When we know God, we know love, grace, and hope. And we know his Word and his power. To follow him and suffer in his name requires God's power. When we know the depth of his love, we know in part what he endured for us. When we live our lives for him and in his presence, we will be changed. We will wake up one day and realize that God is our life, and he is what we yearn for. He is life, and he represents life to the full.

First Things First

Knowing God's fullness is knowing the love he has for us in his Son. God's love and mercy is an indescribable gift. He gives us his fullness when we follow him and when we experience his fullness as we step out in faith to follow him and hold on to his hope when we struggle. Most Christians do not experience the fullness God has for us because not only do we not know what it means, but also because we don't expect to have it on this side of eternity. Yet, God gives us the fullness of himself in Jesus.

We sometimes believe we can't fathom God's love for us, and, not only that, but we believe we lack the necessary know-how to receive it. But Scripture assures us this is not so. Through God's

Spirit and fellowship with his people, we can grasp his love and attain to the measure of all the fullness of God:

> For this reason I kneel before the Father, from whom every family in heaven and on earth derives its name. I pray that out of his glorious riches he may strengthen you with power through his Spirit in your inner being, so that Christ may dwell in your hearts through faith. And I pray that you, being rooted and established in love, may have power, together with all the Lord's holy people, to grasp how wide and long and high and deep is the love of Christ, and to know this love that surpasses knowledge—that you may be filled to the measure of all the fullness of God. (Eph. 3:14-19)

The fullness of God is a mysterious gift from the hands of the One who loves us so much he sacrificed his only Son for us.

First things first, we must know the love God has for us. Knowing and experiencing heaven's love is a lifetime journey as well as a moment-by-moment pursuit—God's pursuit of us. God is in charge of the journey; we must choose to go with him each step of the way. To experience the love he has for us, we must encounter the One who is Love. And then we must decide to love him back. A love story unfolds where we expect to experience life's fullness on this earth and in heaven.

The story begins with God's love. As we step out in faith and follow him in hope, we experience his love over and over. The fullness of God cannot be grasped without knowing and experiencing the love he has for us. He desires to show life in full in ways we may never understand. Therefore, we must first trust Jesus in order to reciprocate his love. He multiplies our decision to follow him and grows our choice into the fullness of life in Christ.

The paradox of the gift of our very Creator and Sovereign Lord, the One who gives his only Son to those who are not worthy of the smallest gift but to whom he gives the fullness of God, is also his Son Jesus. We cannot fathom the Almighty's creation and his indescribable gift. How can we grasp the Father's fullness? Our amazing Father God gives us the way to Himself through his Holy Spirit. In the midst of our very lives, he is present to love, live, guide, protect, rescue, and bring us back into a right relationship with himself. The Father will lead us if we ask him to lead us, and he will show us how to receive and live his fullness—the truly full life he has given us in his Son, Jesus Christ.

God's Love

God's love changes things for his children. Sometimes we take responsibility for things that are not our responsibility. God in Jesus Christ is the gap, the bridge. He is in charge. There are situations when there is nothing we can do—or not do—that will alleviate the matter. God wants us to release the matter to him by praying about it and handing it over. If we take on things outside our realm of responsibility or control, we must seek forgiveness. It is difficult to discern when another's burdens are helped by our efforts, or if our efforts are even what God has in mind for them. He is bigger than all difficult circumstances put together, including all of our efforts to help. He is also much bigger than all of the ways that keep us from him, including ourselves. He is love and he is power.

Father God,

We put on your Holy Spirit, and with your power in us, forgive ourselves for the many ways we have not let go of past hurts, particularly the hurting we have done toward ourselves. Please give us the strength and grace to forgive ourselves.

We are in awe of the mercy you have richly given. We thank you that you are far greater than we imagine and that we can turn to you. You give us the power, grace, and strength to do the very thing that you have commanded us to do.

We ask you, in Jesus' name, to help us to let go of unforgiveness, to let go of ourselves to you, and to allow you to heal our desires to get it right—instead of accepting your mercy and grace.

Your mercy is so much better and bigger than we deserve; yet, you give it.

Help us by your power to take it and move on.

Thank You, Lord Jesus!!

God teaches us about love and how to love. But first, he teaches us to love even ourselves. Why is it so difficult? In gratitude for his teaching, let us trust him and in his name, let us put on love.

Jesus' love showed us how love is contrary to what we think and know. God helps us to live paradoxically and gives us the power and grace to give others love in the manner that reflects him. We first have to allow God's love to fill us before we can be the vessels of his love. Is there something within us which blocks his filling us with his love? Perhaps we find it difficult to receive his blessings? Or we may find it hard to forgive ourselves. God is waiting for us to put on his forgiveness and move on in his work to pour his love out on his children.

God's Armor

God's armor is made just for us, and he knows the battles we will face. His armor protects and shields us from the evil spiritual forces surrounding us:

> For our struggle is not against flesh and blood, but against the rulers, against the authorities, against the powers of this dark world and against the spiritual forces of evil in the heavenly realms. Therefore put on the full armor of God, so that when the day of evil comes, you may be able to stand your ground, and after you have done everything, to stand. Stand firm then, with the belt of truth buckled around your waist, with the breastplate of righteousness in place, and with your feet fitted with the readiness that comes from the gospel of peace. In addition to all this, take up the shield of faith, with which you can extinguish all the flaming arrows of the evil one. Take the helmet of salvation and the sword of the Spirit, which is the word of God. And pray in the Spirit on all occasions with all kinds of prayers and requests. With this in mind, be alert and always keep on praying for all the Lord's people. (Eph. 6:12-18)

Every battle is the Lord's; we wear the armor he provides. If we acknowledge who God is and if we know the truth, we will still encounter battles in life. God has not promised us that we will not. But he has promised they are his battles and that he will prevail. Sometimes the victory does not look like what we expected, but the Lord always wins. He has already conquered all through the life, death, and resurrection of Jesus Christ.

Wearing God's armor is necessary. Just as we put on clothes for the day, we must acknowledge our need for the Lord's protection on a daily basis, for his guidance, truth, and grace for this day. We need him. He goes before us, with us, and after us. Why would we ever think his armor is not enough for us, or that God's armor is not necessary? We have an illusion that life is what we see, but he tells us that we cannot see. So much of what God has for us is unseen. Therefore, he protects us and shields us from what we cannot see, just as he allows us to see when we need to see what will grow us up to be who he created us to be. When he reveals something profound, the blessing is exhilarating. His protection from the unseen and the unknown shield us in this very way.

Focus and Artwork

Why do we tend to focus on the hard stuff? Analytical thinkers want to set things in order, to make things right. God is in charge—sovereign over his entire creation. In reality, there is little we can set aright. Our ways and our thoughts are not God's. His ways and thoughts are higher than ours:

> Then you will call, and the Lord will answer; you will cry for help, and he will say: Here am I. "If you do away with the yoke of oppression, with the pointing finger and malicious talk, and if you spend yourselves in behalf of the hungry and satisfy the needs of the oppressed, then your light will rise in the darkness, and your night will become like the noonday. The Lord will guide you always; he will satisfy your needs in a sun-scorched land and will strengthen your frame. You will be like a well-watered garden, like a spring whose waters never fail. (Isa. 58:9-11)

If we allow him to work in the situation, we receive his peace and his rest: "My heart is not proud, Lord, my eyes are not haughty; I do not concern myself with great matters or things too wonderful for me. But I have calmed and quieted myself, I am like a weaned child with its mother; like a weaned child I am content. Israel, put your hope in the Lord both now and forevermore" (Ps. 131).

Many things are too difficult for me. Being an analytical thinker, I usually have the idea that I can work something out if I work on it hard enough and long enough. I heard an artist describe his creative work in the forest, and the imagery has stuck in my mind's eye. Above the canopy of the trees, you can see the order and the beauty of God's creation. Down in the trees, it looks messy and tangled. Only God can make something beautiful out of our messes and troubles. As we allow him to work in our lives, as intricate, confusing, and troubled as they are, he not only sees the big picture but he is in charge of it. God will weave a masterpiece of our messes and struggles in his time.

If we seek God's face and let our analysis rest, he gives us his order and many other wonderful things to think about—like his canopy, his beautiful creation, and his face. Let us always praise the Lord for his creation and his work-in-progress. The work-in-progress is us.

Our Advocate

We cannot defend ourselves to our heavenly Father God, who is holy and just. But because of his rich mercy, we have an advocate in Jesus Christ, who knew no sin but died for our sin in our place and rose again so that we would be righteous in God's sight and live eternally with him at the right hand of the Father.

Why do we continue defending ourselves when we cannot? Trying to make things right, working to earn our way, and coming up with works to make ourselves better are just a few ways we attempt to defend our sin. But there is no defending our sin for we are wicked and morally corrupt. We may come to him to defend us, but there is no other way for this defense of lives so full of sin.

No one comes to him without faith, and faith cannot occur unless he summons us. Our one defense is his righteousness—the rightness with God that only comes through Jesus dying for our sins and paying the price once and for all.

The only defense we have is the right relationship with God through our Savior. We cannot make ourselves right with our holy and just and almighty Father in heaven without his Son, our Savior. And furthermore, we not only have an advocate sitting at the Father's right hand in heaven, but we have the Holy Spirit, our anchor and advocate, living inside of us and making it possible for us to believe and showing us how to live.

I heard a minister talking about how we try defending ourselves to others who think we are in the wrong. This struck a chord with me. God is our defender; he is our advocate. There is not another advocate on the face of the earth who could do it better. We are sinners and only through his defense can we be made right with God and with others. We must take the whole thing to our Advocate and leave it there. There is no other defense. Only he can make my relationship with him and my relationships with others right. He is my defense; there is no other.

A Advocate in Jesus
D Defends through Jesus
V Victory in Christ Jesus
O Only way in Jesus
C Children of God
A Authority of God through Jesus
T Truth of God in Jesus
E Eternal life through Jesus, Son of God

Being the Daughter of the Triune God Who Is:

Authority of The Almighty Creator, Savior, and Father God
Advocacy of The One and Only Son and Savior, Jesus Christ
Assurance of The Hope and Salvation, The Holy Spirit

By the authority of our Almighty Creator, Savior, and Father God, we have an Advocate who defends us. Because we cannot save ourselves by working, by earning it, or by living good lives, God sent his Son to rescue us from our sin. By his design before the creation of the world, he created us to be holy and blameless, as the apostle Paul has said: "For he chose us in him before the creation of the world to be holy and blameless in his sight" (Eph. 1:4). Scripture is very clear that only God's own righteousness can make us holy and blameless, and only he can save us. Out of his rich mercy, God gave us the way through his Son's death to become right with him.

Jesus, then, is our Advocate, sitting at God's right hand and interceding on our behalf. Not only did he die for us, but he also lives in us and for us for all eternity. The Savior is the only defense we need, and the assurance of our only hope and salvation is the Holy Spirit.

When Jesus left the earth following his resurrection, he ascended to heaven to return to our Father. Victorious over Satan and his army, Jesus took us captive and freed us from sin's grip. He not only defeated the Enemy, but he also gave us a reminder, a teacher, and a comforter to assure us that he remains with us and will never leave us. Through the Holy Spirit we have the capacity to believe him, to walk with him, and to serve him. In addition, Jesus gave us gifts to use for serving others, for building up the body of Christ, and for the maturing of the body of believers to all the fullness of Christ. "This is why it says: 'When he ascended on high, he took many captives and gave gifts to his people'" (Eph. 4:8).

By the authority, the advocacy, and the assurance of Jesus Christ, we may live in rest and peace with our Father in heaven. His plan encompasses all of creation for all time, including his purposes for us. Through Jesus Christ, we have the hope and rest now and for eternity.

When we follow Christ, we no longer need to defend ourselves. Jesus is our Advocate in salvation and the model for how we live out our salvation. We do not have to worry about living right, making the right choices, or being good. It is not only something we do not have the capacity to do; it is also something God cannot and will not accept. He made the way of salvation through his Son, Jesus. He provides.

The Son's defense of God's daughters and sons is huge, for we need defending even against ourselves. But "there is now no condemnation for those who are in Christ Jesus" (Rom. 8:1). God is greater than our conscience; he knows our motives, and he has given us the way through Jesus to know him and his love and mercy toward us. "If our hearts condemn us, we know that God is greater than our hearts, and he knows everything. Dear friends, if our hearts do not condemn us, we have confidence before God" (1 John 3:20-21). The Holy Spirit assures us of this defense and of our hope and salvation. Our part is to choose him and to know him, the giver of all good things, starting with his authority, advocacy, and assurance.

Jesus—Our Sure Defense

Our advocate and defender made the way for us. We may approach God with confidence and freedom through the perfect sacrifice of the one and only Son. "Therefore, brothers and sisters, since we have confidence to enter the Most Holy Place by the blood of Jesus, by a new and living way opened for us through the curtain, that is, his body" (Heb. 10:19-20). We are no longer accused and found guilty, and no longer bound by shame or the law in order to make peace with God. Our sure defense and one and only way is Jesus.

He is our foundation, the lens through which we choose life. He is the path we take. With him we can persevere through the fire. In him we know the light and we experience the treasures of darkness where he calls us by name: "I will give you hidden treasures, riches stored in secret places, so that you may know that I am the Lord, the God of Israel, who summons you by name" (Isa. 45:3). Only through Jesus do we know hope, that which carries us when we no longer have the wherewithal to take the first step on the journey.

God administers our first breath and he directs our path when we do not know the way. When we admit we do not know what we think we know, we will experience God, the lover and sustainer of our souls, and the One who loves us and knows us and plans for our lives.

Not only does he have the best for us, if we have chosen him to be the Lord of our lives, but he also weaves whatever we experience, however painful or chosen unwisely, into that which is more beautiful and fulfilling than we could have asked or dreamed. We cannot fail because the Lord takes our life experiences and does something good with them. He is God, and there is no other.

Faith, Hope, and Love

We trust God for faith and hope, but somehow we try doing love on our own. Yet we need God most of all for *love,* to love others, really to love them. We usually feel good about this area of our lives most of the time, but aside from relying on our feelings, which we should not do, the truth is that we are doing a miserable job at loving people. The reason is, of course, that we must rely on God to help us do it. He is the source of all love, our Father God who created us and loves us unfailingly. How could we love without his love filling us first and showing us how to love?

When we read Paul's words in First Corinthians chapter thirteen, where he says "If I speak in the tongues of men or of angels, but do not have love, I am only a resounding gong or a clanging cymbal" (13:1), we know it is true that we need God to love. There is an axiom that seems pertinent: "Love isn't love until you give it away." If we do not love another with the love that God has given us, then we must not have love.

The love God has given us is truer than any other thing on the planet. I believe in Jesus and the life he has given me through his death and resurrection. God has given me the faith to believe. I have hope in him, and he has shown me his hope like no other. But his love is more than life, more than words, and more than we can fathom:

For this reason I kneel before the Father, from whom every family in heaven and on earth derives its name. I pray that out of his glorious riches he may strengthen you with power through his Spirit in your inner being, so that Christ may dwell in your hearts through faith. And I pray that you, being rooted and established in love, may have power, together with all the Lord's holy people, to grasp how wide and long and high and deep is the love of Christ, and to know this love that surpasses knowledge—that you may be filled to the measure of all the fullness of God. Now to him who is able to do immeasurably more than all we ask or imagine, according to his power that is at work within us, to him be glory in the church and in Christ Jesus throughout all generations, for ever and ever! Amen. (Eph. 3:14-21)

As Paul prays in Ephesians 3:14-21, the love of Christ is wide, long, high, and deep, and it surpasses knowledge. We can know it through faith in Christ Jesus; we can grasp it, and he will show it to us through and with his people.

We need the Lord for the strength necessary to both believe and grasp his love. Both his power and his love are available to us through faith. If we choose to make the step of faith in him, he gives us the faith for the journey where faith, hope, and love, abide, but the greatest of these is love.

Our Father God—His Heart, His Healing and His Harvest

I heard a voice say to me, "Rest your head and know My Heart." I knew this voice—it was the gentle and gracious presence of my Father God. With this realization, I relaxed into his strong and loving arms, and I put my head upon his shoulder. I remember thinking there is nothing like God's rest for the weary soul.

As I allowed my mind to wander and analyzed this season, I began thinking that I had perhaps misheard what God spoke to me. But I reclaimed his truth and it resounded in my heart and mind— God really loves me as his daughter. I believe him. And yet, I asked myself, "Why is there such resistance in me to know his heart?"

After several months of waiting and wrestling with God, he has once again shown me his heart. My shame is not bigger than his grace. He repeatedly gives me more grace than I deserve. My brokenness keeps me from receiving the very thing that would heal me—his heart full of his everlasting love. God reveals himself through his Word. He comes to bind us up and heal us, free us, and release us from the darkness, as the prophet Isaiah foretold:

> The Spirit of the Sovereign Lord is on me, because the Lord has anointed me to proclaim good news to the poor. He has sent me to bind up the brokenhearted, to proclaim freedom for the captives and release from darkness for the prisoners, to proclaim the year of the Lord's favor and the day of vengeance of our God, to comfort all who mourn. (Isa. 61:1-2)

God awakens us to his heart. As we come to rest in him, he shows us again his heart through his healing power. This power that dwells within us through the Holy Spirit transforms us into those knowing his heart and displaying his character and beauty. It is not from ourselves that we know this kind of love from our Father's heart. But we will know him when we see him. And we have the privilege of sharing in it with him. We will never get to the end of God's heart, for it is truly infinite and everlasting. In his heart and through his heart, we have the abundant life. The thrill of this is not only for this life but also for the one hereafter.

CHAPTER FIVE

GOD CALLS US TO REMAIN

Show me your ways, Lord, teach me your paths. Guide me in your truth and teach me, for you are God my Savior, and my hope is in you all day long. Remember, Lord, your great mercy and love, for they are from of old. Do not remember the sins of my youth and my rebellious ways; according to your love remember me, for you, Lord, are good.

Good and upright is the Lord; therefore he instructs sinners in his ways. He guides the humble in what is right and teaches them his way. All the ways of the Lord are loving and faithful toward those who keep the demands of his covenant. For the sake of your name, Lord, forgive my iniquity, though it is great. (Ps. 25:4-11)

I am the vine; you are the branches. If you remain in me and I in you, you will bear much fruit; apart from me you can do nothing. If you do not remain in me, you are like a branch that is thrown away and withers; such branches are picked up, thrown into the fire and burned. If you remain in me and my words remain in you, ask whatever you wish, and it will be done for you. (John 15:5-7)

Experiencing God as He Invites Us to the Table

As we experience God's presence and his invitation to stay near (to listen, follow closely, and stay on his course), we come to know him who pursues us and does not force himself on us. He invites us to live with him and remain with him. God in his Son Jesus, with the Holy Spirit within us, allows us the choice to stay near, to follow closely, and to obey his course. Staying close to Jesus is tantamount to experiencing more of him.

Jesus has come so we may experience his compassion and abounding love. When we live close and follow, we know him better with each step we take. Every moment we trust Jesus more than we lean on our own understanding we experience more of him. Each time we ask the Lord for guidance instead of relying on ourselves means we experience more of him.

The table where he reveals his true identity is one where he meets us as we are, loves us the way we are, and shows us mercy immeasurably more than we can fathom. In return, we do not offer him a thing at all. He is the Creator and the One answering and completing all of our needs. Indeed, the place where he meets us is a sacred, hallowed, and spacious one.

The Father's Table

God has invited us all to his bountiful table. It is ready, and our Host is waiting. Do we try escaping God? Do we want what is offered? Do we push away from the table because we think we can find something better elsewhere? Or do we reject the bounty because we feel unworthy of his supply of extraordinary and wonderful things?

When we approach the Father's table, we find the most delicious treats. Even so, after quickly tasting the treats, we often leave the table and forget what we received. We run again toward emptiness: Everything not coming from God brings only emptiness. He is the One and Only who can fill the very void inside that pleads to be filled with him and his abundance.

Sometimes if we stay long enough at the table in the Father's presence, he gently encourages us to eat foods we have never tasted, or talk with him about things we have never shared. It is nice to be close and try new things some of the time, but often we leave the table early so we don't open the partitions of our lives that are shut down or off limits. If we taste the bitter or the sour, we are ready to leave the table. But when we allow him to offer us more, we see him more clearly and know how much he loves us.

The Father teaches us the most when we stay with him at the table. That is where we grow in our trust. He opens our eyes and our hearts to his heart, and he clears away the fears we have associated with many things that have been closed off. He shows us what he has planned for us in the bounty of his table. But the most amazing treasure at the table is the abundance of our Lord himself. He is there, and he is the bountiful gift—a treasure beyond measure for all our senses.

Father:

God, help us to stay close to you so we can drink in your beauty and eat of your bounty by knowing you.

Thank you, dear Lord Jesus.

Waiting on the Lord—a New Perspective

We need a new perspective on the matter of waiting on the Lord. We tend to think *we* are doing the waiting. Perhaps we wait to receive an outpouring from him, or we wait to be in a relationship with him. But we should turn this around. We are not the ones who are waiting. God waits on us. It is all in his timing. His rhythm is what counts. *He* is the one waiting upon us so that he can give us what we need for his purposes and his glory.

Rest—Relinquish and Receive

Are we willing to admit our disappointments? Will we relinquish them to our Almighty Savior, our refuge, comfort, and strength? Will God help us let them go? Not only will he give us the courage to lay them down, he will also guide us to replace the void they leave in the heart.

As we study the life, relationships, failures, and triumphs of David, we find in the Psalms that David knew how to give his disappointments to God. With expressions of anger, disappointment, remorse, and anguish of the soul, David shows how we must relinquish our own sadness or disappointment in order to receive God's help. It is in the relinquishing that we make room for divine hope and help. It is in stepping out and admitting we are disappointed with God, or a person close to us, or our life journey, or the dashing of a dream, that we relinquish its hold on us. When we do not acknowledge our disappointments and take them to God, we are deprived not only of living in freedom, but also of filling the space God desires to occupy within our hearts. When disappointment is left unattended, it becomes a wall barricading ourselves off from further disappointment. In other words, we erect barriers for self-protection. The lie in this type of behavior is that we are safe only if we take care of it ourselves. The truth is that the One and Only is our refuge, protection, comfort, and strength.

The rest David sought and received, and the kind of rest we search for, may be found only in God. It is the rest God provides through the relinquishment of our hopes and dreams. Rest comes when we receive Christ—his hopes and dreams in their stead.

The Greatness of the Gift He has Given Us

There are times when God's Word is unsettling. We ask, "What does it mean? What are you saying, Lord?" When Jesus taught the crowds in parables, many asked him to interpret the meaning for them. Sometimes when we read the parables, we miss the basic meaning until someone interprets for us. Otherwise, we just don't get it.

In the story of David and his descendants, there is so much manipulation, shrewdness, and trickery that it is difficult to discern who is on David's side. What does God want us to learn from

Scripture? Certainly the Bible displays the sinful nature of humankind, as well as the consequences of generational sin in David's descendants. It is not only difficult to read, but it is like a mirror of how self-focused and driven by our own desires we can be.

A person in the lineage of Jesus would be one who keeps God's laws and learns from his or her mistakes. While we see God's mercy in David's life, we also see his continued failure to live by God's laws. And it is no different for us. We need God's mercy.

God cannot be put in a box with a bow on top. He is grander and more merciful than we dream or imagine. God's mercy shines ever so brightly for his children in their depravity. The fact is that we must remain in conversation with God in order to know him better. His desire for us to know him and to know he loves us and will never leave us, woven through his love letter to us in the Bible, becomes more and more apparent as he writes his Word on our hearts. As we seek him out to answer questions on our journeys as children of God, not only do we see our sin—and even more the greatness of the gift he has given us in Jesus Christ—but we also see the One we seek.

God's Care—a Spacious Place

God cares about place. He is intentional in everything that concerns us: where we live, where we work, where we go, into whose family we are born, to which school we go, to which church we belong—all of these things matter to God. He uses all of our circumstances, our dreams, and our goals to pursue us in ways drawing us closer. The Father wants us to come to believe in him and to believe him for the sacrifice made by the Son on our behalf. In order for us to live the life he has dreamed for us, he goes the extra mile.

God's care is a spacious place. Through him we go from one spacious place to another even more spacious place. Because we can never get to the end of God, we can draw near to him just as he has already drawn near to us. God is present and he wants us to be present. He tells us he will not turn us over to the Evil One, but he will rescue us and set us in a spacious place: "You have not given me into the hands of the enemy but have set my feet in a spacious place" (Ps. 31:8). The covenant God made with Abraham was to give the chosen people the land where they could be God's people and flourish in the land of milk and honey. God led them to the chosen place. As Abraham obeyed, God made him into the man he was created to be. God promised Abraham and his descendants that he carried forth in his Son, Jesus. If we follow Jesus, we will live with him on this side of heaven and also with him in eternity. We always have a place in him.

When we seek God above all else, we grow up in him. When our hope is in him, we will be transformed by our interconnection. We will become like him in our attitudes, hearts, desires, and willingness to serve the people he loves. Our place in God is one of rest, hope, transformation, and abundance. He is the One for whom we long and belong. He is our spacious place.

Waking up with God

"Waking up with God"

When I awake and know you are there
I can rise and move in your care
Only then does the day go toward
Your love and truth to guide forward

"Walking with Him Today"

With you I acknowledge I cannot
Go it alone but in step with you I can
Talk it through and make a way
Where I did not think so today

"Going to Sleep with God"

When the day is done I lay
Down to rest my head
God takes me in his loving arms
Quiets my heart to sleep he takes

Good along the Way—God Shows His Love

On my morning walk, I ran into a woman I had not seen in a very long while. I used to run into her more regularly, and we would smile and say hello to one another. Her smile was always welcoming, and her gaze was shy. There was a familiarity in our common routine.

This morning she was in her garden, alongside the path I walked. I called out to her as she leaned over attentively to her thriving plants. She straightened up and in her usual way she smiled and welcomed me enthusiastically. It was good to see her. She asked if I would like some tomatoes, to which I answered affirmatively. As she ran back to her house to get a bag, I stood and reflected on how I had not planned to go on this path today.

My friend handed me a plastic bag with a couple of heirloom tomatoes and a Chinese cucumber. It was a wonderful gesture of friendship, arranged by a Father who loves to converse with his creation. I want to converse with God often, so I will not miss him and so I will notice the things he does for me—through others, in circumstances, and in the words and actions of the people along the way. But how often does God show up where I fail to recognize him? How often do his gifts pass me by unnoticed?

In our walking by faith in him, he blesses us with his kindness and his gifts. God often uses the kindness of others to bring us back into focus on him. I set out on a walk this morning, just to get the chore done for today. Instead, God gave me a glimpse of himself along the way.

Simultaneous Steps or Syncopation: Waiting on the Lord

Are we waiting on the Lord, or is he waiting on us? We tend to think we are waiting on God when time seems to stand still, or when things are not happening as quickly as we think they should. But perhaps God is waiting upon us in that he is making us ready for what he planned all along. In fact, God waits upon us all the time. He is a pursuer, a compassionate and kind heavenly Father who wants us to know him and how much he loves us.

Because we are watching for something else at times, we can miss the Lord's love. We cannot imagine the extent of God's love for us. As we study his Word and his promises, we begin understanding what he has for us. When we sit still and listen to what he is saying to us in Scripture, and then remember what he has already done for us, we know he loves us, entirely and without reservation—so much so that it is difficult to receive this kind of love.

The journey of human life is about the transformation we make as children of God when we come to know him and how much he loves us. As we take in God's amazing love for us, we become the very children he has created to live in freedom with him forever. Indeed, we have this waiting thing all wrong. God is waiting on us to receive that which he has already and completely given. He is pursuing us to get it, to take it in, and then holding us to sit in his presence to live freely and wholly with him.

We must actively embrace our heavenly Father. Are we in step with him, and are our steps in simultaneous rhythm or syncopated rhythm? The Holy Spirit marks us with the ability to walk in step with our Creator. We walk by faith, not by sight, and we follow his lead moment-by-moment and day-by-day. On this earth, our heavenly Father has enabled us to keep in step. It gives us so much joy to think of the things our Creator God has given to us—his creation in nature, words, music, rhythm, and so many other wonderful things. Rhythm is an especially imaginative thing; without it, there would be an overabundance of mundane moments. God gave us rhythm to make music and living more fun and wonderful. Are we in step with our Creator God? With his creation? Are we in step with the journey he has placed in front of us? What are we waiting for?

Only God Soothes and Comforts

Outcomes, even when they are ones for which we hope, cannot soothe us. Only God soothes and comforts us when life happens. We think we know what makes us happy, or fulfilled, or satisfied. We imagine what life holds for us. Sometimes, our hopes and dreams come crashing down by unforeseen circumstances. Yet God is still holding us, and he is still holding our dreams. It is what he does best. He is the holder of all of our wildest imaginings and our deepest hopes. He is the Creator of each one of us, and also of each one of our desires.

God says he "is able to do immeasurably more than all we ask or imagine, according to his power [the Holy Spirit] that is at work within us" (Eph. 3:20). The power is his, and he has given it to us. And with the yielding of our dreams and hopes, he gives us the power to allow him to place within us dreams and hopes greater than we have asked or imagined. Of course we may ask him, and indeed, we should ask him. According to Paul's letter to the Ephesians, by the Holy Spirit's power in us, God gives better, greater, and more than we ask or imagine.

In order to hope or dream, we must turn first to the Creator of hopes and dreams. He knows what we seek, for he made us in his image. But human answers, outcomes, hopes, and dreams will not suffice; only God's dreams will. His are greater, and he does not disappoint.

When an answer comes, or an outcome changes the horizon, perhaps we are looking for the wrong thing. Maybe we are moving in the right direction, but God is waiting for us to see that he is the author of all that is good, and that he is the holder of all we desire and seek. He pursues us. He waits us out until we come and cry out to him. And when we turn toward him, he comes. The dreams he has for us are too big for us to miss, and he does not want us to miss a single one. When we hurt over an answer or an outcome, however, he hurts with us. He is there to comfort, provide, and listen to our petitions and hurts. He knows our every thought and whisper. He knows us by name and answers us when we call. He wants us to know him and the love he has for us.

When we think we have missed out, we must cry out to him. Perhaps we have not missed out with an answer, or missed out on an outcome, but we may have missed him. He is waiting. He loves us enough to wait and he loves us enough not to let us have a lesser answer or a lesser outcome.

No Analysis—Walking by Faith

There is no study or consternation in the walk by faith; that is why it is called "walking by faith." Only God knows what is to come, what the future holds. We study God's Word in order to know him better. We are told to trust Him with what is to come. Therefore, to walk by faith is to hold onto God. He leads the way, and we follow. We will not see what is going to happen, but we will trust that God knows the way and carries out his good plans for his good purposes.

An advisor to my daughter, a medical resident in her first year after medical school, told her that she should not analyze her performance. I think this is a good and wise thing for all of us not to do. When we analyze each step of the journey beforehand, or take too much into account in retrospect, we are living either in the past or the future, neither of which helps us. Walking by faith is like that—we cannot analyze the options, lest we depend on our own understanding. And if we take a schoolbook analysis over our previous steps, we may only look back with the eyes of the present, which cannot help us in our understanding. In fact, understanding is not what the walk of faith is. It is a hindrance, not a help.

God lives with us in the present. He is our guide, and we can trust him to guide us in the way he has for us. We may only do it in the present. His presence is our guide in the present. We live only in the present, so his guidance and lead are in this moment. He wants a relationship with us and he wants us to know him and his love for us. If God is not analyzing our behavior, why should we?

Waiting on the Lord

LOVE Waits

God loves us—God WAITS:

W	walking
	writing
A	abiding

I	intercedes
	intervenes
T	trust
	tests
S	simultaneous
	syncopated

God waits in his rhythm. I think I am walking, writing, waiting. But *he* is. I think I am abiding. *He* is. God intercedes, intervenes; yet, I think I am interceding with him. God tests me; I think I am trusting him. Simultaneously, God is doing all, and we are being equipped to do and to carry out his purposes as we walk in faith. Perhaps when we look at it, it appears we are in syncopated rhythm with him. I love syncopation, and, wonderfully, God made it too. When God looks at our walk of faith, he sees it as one simultaneous motion—a rhythm just as perfect for him as it is for us. And when the beat is syncopated, he made it that way, too.

Walking by Faith—Remain in Him

The gospel of John, chapter fifteen, says we are to remain tethered to our Savior and Lord. We cannot do anything without him. In addition, it says we will not bear fruit, meaning doing anything for God and his people, if we do not stay attached to him. We are merely branches needing the nourishment from the source. Furthermore, God takes all the excess and non-essential parts and cuts them away, and he also takes the good parts and prunes them to make the branches more able to produce fruit. We are not in control of how God grows us or makes us better able to serve him in this world. We decide, however, if we remain close to him. We are only one step away at any given time; we are only as close as we want to be. For those who walk by faith, growing closer to God with each choice made daily, is how we trust in God. If we say our hearts trust in God, we must remain in him. And if we want our hearts to trust him, we must stay close. He is our guide to remain, and he helps us do so.

We see God at work through the lens of the Holy Spirit. It is also through his help that we observe him in our lives—we know him and experience him. The Holy Spirit cuts through the noise of all that is around us and helps us discern God's voice and truth. The mind of Christ, which is ours when our minds are controlled by the Holy Spirit, helps us give our thoughts over to him to guide us into all truth and thereby cut away damaging and harmful thinking patterns in our daily lives. When we remain close to God by allowing the work of the Holy Spirit in our lives, we become transformed in our hearts as powerful examples of God's love and truth.

How do we remain close to God? First, we must *look* for him. He is always present, but he tells us in Scripture to search for him. Our eyes and hearts must expect to see him by looking for him. We must also *listen* to God. If we want to hear his voice, it stands to reason we must practice listening for it. As we read Scripture, we actively listen to what it teaches us. God is alive and active in his Word in our lives. Third, we have to *leave* all with him. Now at first this sounds like a cop-out—a way to forego and forget all the hard stuff. But it is much more than that. When we learn to forgo our difficulties and our intercessions for others with God, we learn to trust him with them. Not only do we learn to trust, we develop a relationship where we know that it is he for whom we look, to whom we listen, and to whom we carry our burdens. We go to him to leave our sins and regrets, as well as our leanings that are not of him. We also go to him for changing our ways and acknowledging that we know he is God and that we need him and his saving grace. And we must approach him about all things: each transgression, intercession, desire, dream, and conversation. We leave it all with our Creator God, the Almighty and the Savior of our souls. Our method to remain close to the One and Only who has saved us and who has great things in store for each of us, is simply to look, listen, and leave it all with the Father.

Walking by faith is the act of taking a step of trust in the One who holds it all—our lives, the journey, and eternity. It is always a first step with him, because he multiplies himself within us as we trust him on the wild, wonderful, close-up, and personal trek God has designed for us as we remain tethered to him.

Walking with God

Life is an active process; living requires action, even if it is just breathing. God supplies the breath, just as he supplies the capacity through the Holy Spirit to tack with him on the journey he has set out for us.

Walking with God is also an active process in the present. No one can walk yesterday or tomorrow. We cannot follow God yesterday or tomorrow; we must seek after him today. He desires we seek him today, not to wait until tomorrow. He loves us just as we are in this moment.

God is an abundantly loving, gracious, giving, merciful, and compassionate Father. Are we living like we believe that to be true? We stand at the threshold. How do we live what God has promised? Living like we believe God is living a life that attracts others to him. Behavior that fails to match what one believes— typically called unbelief—repels others to him. Could it be we hold onto the past while living in the present? We want to believe God, but we are still holding on to old desires and habits. We fear the new because that means things will change, including us. The trouble is, we are comfortable the way things are.

Present in God's Presence

Living life to the full is the abundance of God, which comes to us in God's presence. Living life in its fullness is experienced in the present by God's presence in us through the indwelling of the Holy Spirit. The gospel of John tells us that "the thief comes only to steal and kill and destroy; I have come that they may have life, and have it to the full" (John 10:10). When we know life to the full, we share in God's perspective; we are present in God's presence. Increasingly, we grow to know him more, for he is our life.

We cannot experience true rest or true joy yesterday or tomorrow. But we can remember what God has done and find rest and joy for today. God in the now is a reminder that he is our daily bread. He wants us to gather it for now, not for yesterday or tomorrow. He provided manna for the Israelites enough for the day. He is certainly enough for this day!

If we are working through things on our own, either about the past or in the future, we may miss God. Though laughter is an "in the moment" thing, we can laugh about things from our past. In the moment, laughter is good medicine. It is true about any experience; it is in the moment that the real thing happens. We do not want to miss the real, the authenticity of God in our lives. He allows experiences to change us, to change us into knowing him better, and to make us ultimately into who he designed us to be.

Being His Daughter at the Table

As daughters and sons of God, we must humble ourselves and surrender our lives to our Almighty Creator and Savior. It is an appropriate response to our holy and heavenly Father. In order to know him and enjoy his nearness, we must receive his Holy Spirit into our lives. The place he gives us at his table is an honored one that allows for us, his children, to be who he created us to be. With the Holy Spirit in control of our lives, we must follow where the Lord goes. When we lean into him and trust him, we will have life, joy, and gratitude in our hearts for today and for the future. He will cause us to remember who he is and what he has done for us, and we can expect him to be with us always. These are his promises to his forever children.

The Father loves us as we are. He knows our very nature, and he sacrificed his only Son in our stead. Since God loves us just as we are, we must come to him just as we are—brokenhearted and sinful. He accepts us in our brokenness, sinfulness, and unbelief. It is only through Jesus Christ that we have our sins forgiven and covered by his grace. We must receive what our Savior has given the way a child receives—by humbling themselves and surrendering.

As we allow our Father God to be our Father, he loves us, teaches us, disciplines and corrects us, and gives us good gifts. As we receive his love, he pours more and more of himself into us. As daughters and sons, we humble ourselves to our Father and surrender.

To be/receive all he is:

- Get to know him

- Receive rest

- Enjoy his nearness and loveliness

    o Go where he takes us (the appropriate child's posture):

- Lean in/Trust

- Gratitude

- Choose life, joy

- Expect

- Remember

Allow ourselves as daughters and sons to be:

o Broken

o Waiting

o Still (an attitude of the mind) with effort toward God (in quiet and in movement)

o Accept how one feels with trust and belief in God and his truth

o Expecting, not avoiding, but looking forward (today may be the day)

Let the Father protect and provide (God Almighty, our Savior, and Loving Father):

- Teach

- Lead

- Love/show affection

- Discipline/correct

- Pour Himself into you

Give good gifts through Jesus, which we must receive:

- o Grace, sin atoned, covered, forgiven
- o Capacity for change, transformation
- o Ability to desire Jesus, trust Jesus, and live intentionally in him
- o Meaningful relationship with him and others
- o Joy, peace, satisfaction, hope, faith, and rest
- o Capacity to look forward
- o Ability to persevere
- o Choose life and God's blessings
- o Capacity to run the race and throw down hindrances
- o Eternity with him

Our heavenly Father will be our Father for eternity. He never dies, and he never abandons us. He gives us perfect guidance, perfect love, perfect answers, and perfect discipline. His *affection* for us is shown in our being chosen before the creation of the world, and given every blessing with grace freely lavished on us. We were predestined to be holy and blameless in his sight through his only Son, Jesus, who died so we might live in and with him forever. He made us *alive* when we were dead in our sins. He raised us up to sit with him and beside Jesus in heaven.

> Praise be to the God and Father of our Lord Jesus Christ, who has blessed us in the heavenly realms with every spiritual blessing in Christ. For he chose us in him before the creation of the world to be holy and blameless in his sight. In love he predestined us for adoption to sonship through Jesus Christ, in accordance with his pleasure and will—to the praise of his glorious grace, which he has freely given us in the One he loves. In him we have redemption through his blood, the forgiveness of sins, in accordance with the riches of God's grace that he lavished on us. With all wisdom and understanding, he made known to us the mystery of his will

according to his good pleasure, which he purposed in Christ, to be put into effect when the times reach their fulfillment—to bring unity to all things in heaven and on earth under Christ. In him we were also chosen, having been predestined according to the plan of him who works out everything in conformity with the purpose of his will, in order that we, who were the first to put our hope in Christ, might be for the praise of his glory. And you also were included in Christ when you heard the message of truth, the gospel of your salvation. When you believed, you were marked in him with a seal, the promised Holy Spirit, who is a deposit guaranteeing our inheritance until the redemption of those who are God's possession—to the praise of his glory. (Eph. 1:3-14)

God gives us faith to persevere, to throw down our hindrances, and to fix our eyes on Him. Our faith also helps us receive his discipline: "Therefore, since we are surrounded by such a great cloud of witnesses, let us throw off everything that hinders and the sin that so easily entangles. And let us run with perseverance the race marked out for us, fixing our eyes on Jesus, the pioneer and perfecter of faith. For the joy set before him he endured the cross, scorning its shame, and sat down at the right hand of the throne of God. Consider him who endured such opposition from sinners, so that you will not grow weary and lose heart" (Heb. 12:1-3). God refines us through the hard things, such as being imprisoned. By his power we are transformed and we become more mature in our grasping who God is and how he loves us. "Instead of your shame you will receive a double portion, and instead of disgrace you will rejoice in your inheritance. And so you will inherit a double portion in your land, and everlasting joy will be yours" (Isa. 61:7). We will become part of the "great cloud of witnesses" in heaven. "Therefore, since we are surrounded by such a great cloud of witnesses, let us throw off everything that hinders and the sin that so easily entangles. And let us run with perseverance the race marked out for us" (Heb. 12:1).

What We Lack may be Found in God

What we lack may be found in God. The giver of all good things who does not withhold anything good from his children meets every need. God is the counterpart to anything we have missed in our lives. In addition, he will not disappoint. He is our hope, our rescue, our strong arm, and our very present help. This is why we can cry out to him. He is waiting for us; in fact, he has been there all along. He will not push or barge in or demand our attention, but he is drawing us near. We can call on him while he may be found.

We all have lack or need. When we seek God in this condition, we find that in Christ Jesus we have everything we need and more. With Christ we do not run out of options. We may run away from God, but we will not find what we are looking for without Christ. We must run into the arms of the One who holds us.

When we feel we lack what we need, we sometimes try to fix it on our own. The shape of the void is the puzzle piece only God can complete. Old habits change as God transforms a life. Sometimes we don't know what we are running from, and that is why we should be suspicious of feelings. He is all we need, and we must trust him with it.

We only get the surface of God's abounding love for us. Yet, he has given it and wants us to receive it. By trusting Christ, we know our great God. The more we confess our need, the more God meets that need. He listens. He comes. He quiets us in our search, for he is what we seek. If we are still, we will hear God speak to us through his Word. He gives us courage when we are weak. He provides fully, even when we are empty.

Who God Is and What He has Done—Abundance

When we focus on God and what he has done, our faith perspective changes. There is no more trying to achieve or proving we are worthy enough on our own. That can never happen because we cannot and we are not. But God is.

Our relationship with God is life receiving and life transforming. God transforms our lives with his truth and grace. As we seek to be with him, remain in him, and follow his lead, he will guide us into his truth. As his mighty hand saves, guides, protects, and changes us, we become vessels of divine love, mercy, and truth.

With each step of faith we lean into the heart of Jesus. He shows us more of himself and we become surer of who he is and surer of who we are in our faith. Because Jesus takes our very weaknesses and uses them for his better purposes, he becomes the focus of our journey. His good is abundant and merciful because it makes it possible for our lives to have purpose. We have the privilege of being part of this salvation story. His glory and our good are his trademarks. On offer is abundant living to the full because of Christ's fullness poured into us.

The Son's life overflows in our lives. The world knows him by the Holy Spirit they see in us. The mountain of circumstance keeps us from his overflowing love in our lives, and thus obscures the world's identifying Christ in us. Often, we ourselves are the mountain, the obstacle to what God has in mind. He has a path, and we are on it, but we keep getting in his way. He makes the unfamiliar known step by step, especially when we cannot see or know the next step ahead. He is smoothing over the obstacles if we would just get out of the way and allow him to do it. We must internalize God's Word and allow it to change us as we learn and study the Bible. We are the barrier to his outpouring, and we forget with whom we go.

Father God,

Grant me the capacity to know you in ways I have not yet known.

Help me get out of your way in my life. I do not want to be the daughter who knows your Word but misses you in the process.

You are my compassionate, gracious, and giving Father God.

Thank you for loving me so much that you gave yourself to me.

Please transform me to know you better.

Amen.

God's Help for Living the Abundant Life

Living life to the full can only be done with God's helpful guidance. We cannot trust him on our own; we even have to have his help to believe and trust. Isaiah 32:15 says we will need God's help "till the Spirit is poured on us from on high, and the desert becomes a fertile field, and the fertile field seems like a forest." Unless the Lord gives us the capacity to surrender to him, we cannot. So it is with all of life. He is our guide, protector, helper, comforter, and refuge when we need rest, and he is our deliverer when we need rescue. There are no needs he cannot meet. We must look to him for all. Therefore, we put our faith in him and keep our focus on him for everything. We must take the necessary steps and follow his leading, however difficult or unclear the next step is.

Life cannot be lived while looking back, but we may remember the Lord's provision and presence over our lives. We must depend on him in the present, and find his abundance while living in it. We also must expect his abundance for tomorrow. He says we must forget the past and be conscious of him in the present. He is making a way for us: "Forget the former things; do not dwell on the past. See, I am doing a new thing! Now it springs up; do you not perceive it? I am making a way in the wilderness and streams in the wasteland" (Isa. 43:18-19).

Hope in him and expect to see his goodness. God gives us the abundant life for all seasons, not just in the good times. While going through the difficult times, we can hope and we can expect to see his goodness. With his help, we remember the goodness of God, and we see God's hand, even in the painful and hard stuff. We must trust him for his provision. Even if we cannot see it, we may depend on his abundance. In faith we can trust him and thank him for his provision.

God's help extends from our first step of faith through his Son Jesus, until we see him face to face. He gives us his Word, the Word made flesh in Jesus. "The Word became flesh and made his dwelling among us. We have seen his glory, the glory of the one and only Son, who came from the Father, full of grace and truth"

(John 1:14). He moves us to believe, and then he helps us live the very life he promised. Never does the Son expect us to live lives on our own. He continues to be our guide and he does not want us to miss him or what he has promised—a life to the full.

Big Things

What are we holding onto from the past and what are we not facing in the present? Whatever the answer, they are big things, and we cannot run from them if we expect to be healed and whole. We have to bring them to the forefront and ask for God's help. Through God's mighty power, we can place our efforts on trusting him and his work in our lives:

> Finally, be strong in the Lord and in his mighty power. Put on the full armor of God, so that you can take your stand against the devil's schemes. For our struggle is not against flesh and blood, but against the rulers, against the authorities, against the powers of this dark world and against the spiritual forces of evil in the heavenly realms. Therefore put on the full armor of God, so that when the day of evil comes, you may be able to stand your ground, and after you have done everything, to stand. Stand firm then, with the belt of truth buckled around your waist, with the breastplate of righteousness in place, and with your feet fitted with the readiness that comes from the gospel of peace. In addition to all this, take up the shield of faith, with which you can extinguish all the flaming arrows of the evil one. Take the helmet of salvation and the sword of the Spirit, which is the word of God. (Eph. 6:10-17)

The Scripture says to "Trust in the Lord with all your heart and lean not on your own understanding; in all your ways submit to him, and he will make your paths straight" (Prov. 3:5-6). In addition, Scripture informs us that God will direct our paths. His path is not one of fear, but of compassion and never-failing love. He has a purpose for his children. God's purpose for us can never be thwarted.

"I know that you can do all things; no purpose of yours can be thwarted. You asked, 'Who is this that obscures my plans without knowledge?' Surely I spoke of things I did not understand, things too wonderful for me to know. "You said, 'Listen now, and I will speak; I will question you, and you shall answer me.' My ears had heard of you but now my eyes have seen you. Therefore I despise myself and repent in dust and ashes." (Job 42: 2-6)

God is sovereign over all aspects of our lives. He is good, and he is faithful. We lean on our own understanding when we worry or obsess over our lives, especially over our children's lives. It is a false understanding, because we do not have all the pieces of heaven's puzzle, or of God's purpose for us and our families. God's love is greater than we can imagine, and his thoughts and desires for us are greater than we can dream. Why not hold onto his hope and desire and purpose for all of our lives?

We must reach up and out to God to help us stand on his promises, one of which is that we have a hope and a future. He releases us from the bent-over position to one of standing straight and being wholly dependent on him for our lives and our children's lives.

God's Greatness—Mystery Revealed through Trust

Understanding a problem or crisis is not what usually brings answers. Actually, it may even make the problem worse. The Bible says, "Trust in the Lord with all your heart and lean not on your own understanding; in all your ways submit to him, and he will make your paths straight" (Prov. 3:5-6). It is in our trusting that we walk through the struggle or live in dire circumstances. Our understanding, however, does not give us the wherewithal to go through something difficult. Relying on our own devices to solve something is a hindrance to our faith and our relationship with God. God is good and faithful. We may not be able to see what he is doing when we are in a dark period, but he is at work. "God is our refuge and strength, an ever-present help in trouble" (Ps. 46:1). He is at work as our refuge and strength for every day, including the difficult days. When we turn ourselves to him, we have access to his peace in the middle of a storm in our lives.

The good news is that we do not have to understand in order to trust God. He does not require that we know what he is doing. In fact, we cannot know. God is incomprehensible, and his thoughts and ways are not our thoughts and ways: "For my thoughts are not your thoughts, neither are your ways my ways," declares the Lord. "As the heavens are higher than the earth, so are my ways higher than your ways and my thoughts than your thoughts" (Isa. 55:8-9). God reveals himself to us in the person of Jesus Christ, and he also makes himself known when we are walking through the hard times. When we seek him, we find our holy Lord and Savior who loves us unfailingly and who will never leave us or desert us. As we continue to call on him, he grows our trust.

Jesus accepts us and loves us right where we are, which is somewhere in between trying to understand him *in* our lives and trusting him *with* our lives. What God has planned for us, what he is doing, and how he gets us there is a great mystery. Understanding all of this is not the thrilling part, but it is in the living of it and leaning on him that we will have the ride of our lives. We don't need to understand the Lord; we need to know him. As we know him through trusting him, we will trust him more—this is another great mystery of God.

Walking through the hard times brings us closer to knowing God. We will know him in our suffering. Philippians 3:10 reads, "I want to know Christ—yes, to know the power of his resurrection and participation in his sufferings, becoming like him in his death." Jesus suffered and knows our suffering, and when we participate in his sufferings, he gives us the comfort and strength we need to persevere. The hidden treasure in the dark places is God revealing himself to us. Isaiah 45:3 says that "I will give you hidden treasures, riches stored in secret places, so that you may know that I am the Lord, the God of Israel, who summons you by name." We know he has called us by name because we see his hand on our lives—especially when we do not understand why we are in fact in the difficult place.

Trusting is like a tether; we are constrained to God by our choosing him to be Savior and Lord of our life. We can still resist him and insist on our own understanding of life and hardship. But through trust, we can lean into him, the holy One who makes himself accessible, to comfort and strengthen and guide us through the good days and the bad. "For this is what the high and exalted One says—he who lives forever, whose name is holy: 'I live in a high and holy place, but also with the one who is contrite and lowly in spirit, to revive the spirit of the lowly and to revive the heart of the contrite" (Isa. 57:15). Trusting is the right path. He is the holy One and offers himself to us in our brokenness. We do not comprehend it, but it is powerful, good, and true. God loves us and even in our worst moments he saves us so we can live in his abundant goodness. He is trustworthy. To be tethered to the Almighty, the compassionate One, full of grace and truth, is to live. Trusting the One we do not understand, except to know he is holy and yet our refuge and strength, reveals God's greatness beyond restraint.

Rest in Whatever Is

Rest in whatever is. Accept it. Embrace it. Lean into God with it. Rest when God is saying to you, "Stop your labor. I have it. Trust me with what I am doing." Rest when you expect God is present and he is working. There is no rest without him, and there is no trust without him, either.

God allows the storm for us to know what his rest and peace in him really means. Personally, I want to reject the storm. I want to run from it, or work hard to make it go away. But this is not the way of God. He wants to make his presence known to us inside the storm. The world's way is avoidance, shutting down, or making our own way in it. But if we choose the world's way, we will not know the Almighty One who is full of grace and truth.

If we follow God's way, he will make himself known in ways we will not expect. He grows us up by his work in our lives. If we acknowledge that the storm in our life is under him as we are, and we take the step of faith and obedience, he will grow us up in our relationship and in our hope and knowledge of him.

God changes us by his Word and his words in our lives. His direction, guidance, wisdom, and will are not necessarily ways we have known before. But when we receive and follow them, with each tiny step toward him, he grows more trust and faith in him in us. We look to the Lord, and the blessing of looking to him increases. His long arm, loving embrace, and always faithful presence grow our desire for him more because he fills us and completes us. He really does "get" us. He knows our listening and our tiny steps. We feel his Spirit deep within us when our hearts say, "He did this for me."

When we know we cannot know Jesus or trust him or rest in him without his help, we come to understand he is doing it all. He is doing this for us. With the abundant life God gives us in this relationship, he allows us to be part of his work. We are his vessels for his treasure— the transformed life in Christ Jesus. Not only will we find our rest and peace in him, but we also will most assuredly find the treasure, God himself in Christ Jesus. We enjoy all of him and live by his design, in unity with him—the abundant life in Christ.

Being His Daughter—His Pursuit

God teaches how to be his daughters by his lovingkindness and his pursuit of us. God is our Father. He enjoys his children and has an abundance of love for us. God as our Father is of ultimate significance in our relationship with him. How do we embrace all the benefits of being his daughters—nurture, affection, and encouragement, to name a few? Living fully as a daughter to God our Father is necessary for our Christian growth.

In reverence and awe of the gift of being God's daughters, we humbly wait on him. Listening. Expecting. Gratitude. Praying for his presence. Asking for a revelation. Observing signs of heaven's goodness. Accepting what is. Knowing him more. Always hoping in him. Choosing him.

We are the recipients of God's truth, grace, and love. This means we are not even in charge of being daughters to him. We can only love Him back. His blessings are abundant, and we receive and embrace them in gratitude. In addition, we are the recipients of his leadership as daughters to their father; we must surrender and embrace it humbly and with obedience. Each time we receive what he has to offer, he increases our faith. Then, with each step we take, he entrusts us with more faith.

Every season is a gradual learning curve, but it is life giving. With gentleness and love the Father opens eyes to deep flaws. In the gaping hole of flaws now removed by grace, we embrace the nurture and affection of our Father's great love. We come empty to Father God when it comes to knowing how to be a daughter, but we come in wonderful expectation of his teaching. We are not just a daughter to him, but we are *his* daughters. It is a great pursuit, his for us. How great is the Father's love!

The Generosity of God

God gives us grace when we do not deserve it. It is free, and it is abundant. He gave his only son so that we may have eternity with him. And this is not all. He adopts us as sons and daughters with the full inheritance of his own Son. He gives us new lives and as often as we need it and ask for it, which is often, he gives us a clean slate to begin again with him at the center.

God does not withhold from us; he is the giver of all good things. He generously

loves and meets us where we are. He knows our cry even before we do, and he answers with his loving-kindness every time. It is God's character to be generous with his children, whom he loves unconditionally and without fail.

God's abounding love fills us up if we allow him into our hearts and lives. He generously takes our cares and concerns and gives us rest and peace when anxiety, grief, and betrayal overtake us. He gives us the comfort and strength we need to give comfort and encouragement to others.

God is abounding in his honor and favor on us. We do not have to earn it, for he gives it when he calls us his children. With his honor and favor, he gives us the privilege of working beside him. He comes with us all the while leading and guiding us to the persons in great need of him. When we care for them, we serve them as his hands and feet, and in some cases, his very words. The joy that comes with serving is another generosity from God.

God multiplies our faith when we most need it. He takes our tiny steps and turns them into the kind of faith that moves mountains. With every ounce of himself, God gives. He transforms us into the persons he created us to be with each piece of our lives. He takes the very small things we do and helps us see the transformation he has made. The transformation comes from a generous heavenly Father who has only his best for his children. His best is beyond anything we have on earth, and heaven will contain much more. The abundant life is God's generosity to us.

As a Daughter of Our Father God

From an early age I vacillated between wanting to trust people and knowing in my heart of hearts that what I felt was indeed true. It is a slippery slope for a child. I know that God gives discernment, as he did even when I was a little girl. He wanted me to know he was guarding me and giving me good instincts. But all I knew were distrust in the situation and my own tyrannical judgment of the distrusting thoughts and desires.

God is good, gracious, and compassionate in this area of my life, as he is in all others. He offers his insight, protection, and healing. With each revelation from the Father, I embrace his truth with more trust that it is true because it is from him. He is generous and merciful and he helps us in this faith journey to know we have discerned.

God delights in revealing Truth to us, whether it is his presence prompting us to notice something in our path, or a thought the Holy Spirit has placed on our mind with perfect timing for a specific need or prayer we have asked him about. It isn't the thing itself that is the most extravagant treasure, although it is certainly a huge gift, but it is God himself, letting us know he has heard us. He knows us. He gets us. He loves us and wants us to know him in the biggest and smallest things. He is God, full of compassion, grace, and truth.

Discernment is one of the gifts our Father God gives us as his sons and daughters. It is one of the many spiritual blessings from the heavenly realms. Embracing what he gives us is a step of faith or trust in him. If we believe him, we must receive what he offers. Acting on what he has given is also a step of faith; in fact, it is a step of obedience to our Creator, Savior, and Lord.

It is also an act of submission to an Almighty God that we hear, receive, and act on his discernment given to us. He is God, and there is no other. He is compassionate, slow to anger, and full of mercy. He is also holy and just. We have the free will to choose whether or not we surrender ourselves to him and his Truth, and also whether we trust him. But he tells us to remember that he is our life and that if we love him, we will follow and surrender to his Truth. His discernment is a huge privilege and a challenge to love, honor, and obey the Lord of our lives. Deuteronomy 30:19-20 says that God is our life and that we must choose to love him, listen to his voice, and hold fast to him, and we will live lives of blessings as will our children—also his sons and daughters.

> This day I call the heavens and the earth as witnesses against you that I have set before you life and death, blessings and curses. Now choose life, so that you and your children may live and that you may love the Lord your God, listen to his voice, and hold fast to him. For the Lord is your life, and he will give you many years in the land he swore to give to your fathers, Abraham, Isaac and Jacob.

What a legacy to pass on to our children—great hope from our great God. So it is with discernment that we must choose to receive his love and love him back, listen to his voice, and hold fast to him and what he tells us. He is our life, and it is good.

Being God's Daughter is Not a Natural Thing

Being God's daughter should be a natural thing; after all, I am already someone's daughter. Daughterhood, however, does not come easy to me. I must commit myself to it, or at least fend off the natural reactions of avoidance, fear, and running away. I don't think of myself as rebellious, but in this I must be. This is not good for my relationship with God, or for me.

My prayer is that I would be a daughter to God in the way he created me to be. He knows the hardships I have had in the past in being a daughter in my family of origin. Indeed he knows how he has rescued me from the lies I believed. If there are untruths in my beliefs on being a daughter, I want him to reveal them to me and replace them with his truths. I want to be his daughter in all ways, to acknowledge that he is my Father God, to know him, to love him back, and to receive all he has for me in this special, one and only relationship. More than anything, I want to surrender all I have thought, known, or reacted to in the past and lay it at his feet for him to transform it into his intention for our relationship. I want to worship him as a daughter of the King, in spirit and in truth. I don't want anything to get in the way of it—including any hindrances I have held and am still holding.

Father God,

Help me to throw down all that hinders my relationship with you,
especially the special one I have in being your daughter.

You have rescued me from lies and unbelief.
You have healed my brokenness.

You have set me free to live in a spacious place —
one designed by you especially for me.

You are now healing me in this aspect of our relationship.

You have more in store for me and I want to take hold of it for your
glory. Help me to grow and to be and to do all that you ask
and have planned.

Father God, I am so grateful for your healing and your rescue and
your many blessings of love, family, and friends.
It is more than I ever believed I would have.

In you, I have more than I ever dreamed.

I have found that you are an abundant God in every way.

Thank you for your presence in my life. I praise you for your loving kindness and your sovereignty over all.
Your compassion and mercy astound me.

Your grace is beyond my comprehension. Indeed, You love me and You want me to be your daughter.

God's abundant grace is never ending. I want to take his leading and embrace his revelation that I am broken in this area of being a daughter. I want to prayerfully listen and take hold of his Word to me. I am asking that he write these truths on my heart and help me believe him with fervor and acts of obedience. He is a faithful God, and I know that is true because he has already shown me his faithfulness in numerous ways. I am going to thank him ahead of time for his work in my life. His change in me will not only benefit me in knowing my Father God better, and on a whole new level, but it will also be a privilege working with him as he grows me up to serve others in this new capacity.

Aspects of the Abundant Life

The abundant life is gathered daily. It is in the living with and walking with God that we know what he has promised. We cannot know—nor will we know—until we make the step of faith that says, "I desire to follow you, Jesus. I want you to be Lord of my life."

Jesus gives us the promised Holy Spirit to help us live and follow him. But it is in the heeding of and the listening to God's voice in the Holy Spirit that we have the capacity to choose him all day long. It is in him that we find peace and contentment.

I believe life lived to the full is the one Jesus lived. He was sent by his Father to live with us and to die for our sins. He told us what the Father sent him to teach. He demonstrated what the abundant life is—one where we are rich in mercy for each other, one where we take the disappointments, hurts, and struggles and learn to grow more dependent on him and his comfort and guidance, one where we love even our enemies because we have the love of Christ Jesus in us, and one where we measure our days by the time we spend being guided by our Father in heaven in whatever we think, say, or do.

We gather our daily bread from him, and he provides abundantly each day. We look to him for every spiritual blessing he has already given. We come to his throne of grace because we crave time spent with him. We know his promises are true, and we rest in them in his Word. His Word guides us and his love is abounding. We know we don't deserve it, but we relish it and hold it in our hearts until they are overflowing with the love we want to pour out on others. We live in abundance because our Great God is abundantly faithful, loving, and true to all he has said in his Word. We look to him for all things, and he is there to provide fully, in abundance.

Fullness of God—Scripture References

In Rest Psalm 91

In Work Psalm 90

In Provision Psalm 81:10; Job 36:26

In Joy Psalm 84:12; Psalm 126

In Being Known Psalm 139

In Strength Psalm 84:5-7

In Comfort Psalm 46:10; Psalm 45:10-11

In Mercy Psalm 51

In Laughter Job 8:21; Psalm 126:2

Living in Abundance—Receiving and Becoming

Life to the full is the life in which we become who God created us to be. When God makes a promise to His children, He keeps it. When we decide to follow Him, we receive His promised Holy

Spirit. In receiving His Spirit, we have the capacity to know Him and His love for us, to grow in faith, and to become like Him. God's design is for us to become like His Son, Jesus Christ. We come to know our true selves as we become more and more like the Son. As we study and obey God's written revelation, follow Jesus' example, surrender by the filling of his Spirit, and love and serve God's people in this world, we know him more and more, and we become more like him.

"For those God foreknew he also predestined to be conformed to the image of his Son, that he might be the firstborn among many brothers and sisters." (Rom. 8:29)

"Dear friends, now we are children of God, and what we will be has not yet been made known. But we know that when Christ appears, we shall be like him, for we shall see him as he is." (1 John 3:2)

God has promised he will rebuild and restore what was lost. When we become his children by faith in his Son, Jesus, we know his love for us. He guides, teaches, and counsels us in the way he has planned. God shows us how he has loved us in the past and reminds us about what he has done for us as his children. We can hope and expect in him because we know he never goes back on a promise. He promises us new life with new hearts, and restored and rebuilt dreams and lives.

Living life to the full means recovering what was lost to us. God's Word assures us that "The Son of Man has come to seek and save that which was lost" (Luke 19:10 NASB). Jesus came to save all that was lost, not just all the people, but all that was lost. Jesus came to save that which was lost to us in addition to his saving us. What an amazing promise from the giver of all good things! It reminds us of Isaiah 61 when the prophet declares that what was taken will be recovered in double portion for the believer. "Instead of your shame you will receive a double portion, and instead of disgrace you will rejoice in your inheritance. And so you will inherit a double portion in your land, and everlasting joy will be yours" (Isa. 61:7). Jesus came to fulfill the promise of that prophecy. What have you lost? What has been taken or lost can be recovered in your life in Jesus Christ.

"Seeking His Heart—Meeting Him in the Present"

Matching mine to his
Dark parts opened to his light
Healing power—covers shame
Every dark corner out

Poured out worries, distress, disappointments
Crying out for his help, rescue
Laying down the hurts, betrayals
Giving, entrusting dreams, hopes to him

Sharing the day, mundane and deep
His presence goes with you
Lovingly guiding you onto his path
One of heart treasure, transforming and true

He takes our tiny steps with our hearts
Multiples the distance from little feet
To changes, large, hearts unfolding—to his
Seeing his face and we know him—he is our Father

Heart to Heart

In Scripture, we learn that David was a man after God's own heart. "After removing Saul, he made David their king. 'I have found David son of Jesse, a man after my own heart; he will do everything I want him to do'" (Acts 13:22). David was considered a man after God's own heart because God said he was "a man after my own heart; he will do everything I want him to do." An obvious question is how could God call David a man after his own heart when he committed so many and such terrible sins, including adultery and murder? I believe God wants us to be after his heart. He cherishes our "heart to heart" relationship with him, and that is exactly what David had with God: a heart to heart relationship. The psalmist, shepherd, giant slayer, adulterer, youngest son of Jesse, king, but most importantly, child of God who met with God and sang to him.

David worshipped the Lord with abandon; he begged for his rescue and praised God for his deliverance. He poured out his heart, even when it made him sound hopeless or even greedy. He knew God loved and heard him. He also had great reverence for the most high and holy God of the universe. Yet David cried out to God because he knew him and talked to him about everything. When he strayed from God's path, he came back in repentance. God makes it possible for us to stay close to him and to be in relationship with him. David wanted more than life itself a relationship with the Creator God, the Father and Savior of the world.

To have a heart to heart relationship with the Lord Jesus Christ is life to the full. God pours himself into his children in order for them to know him, to live freely and abundantly with him, and so the world may know him. It actually sounds completely impossible that the God of the universe wants a heart to heart relationship with each person on the earth. But with God, it is possible. He allows us to see what seems humanly impossible, so when he makes it happen, we know the impossible becomes possible only through him. And so it is with our heart to heart relationship with Him.

God pours out his love and pursues us with his loving-kindness, the riches of his glorious grace. Because of his great love for us, he gives us the gift of grace—through the life, death, and resurrection of his only Son, Jesus, through whom we may be saved. With one step of faith, we become children of God, and have the remarkable and amazing opportunity of a heart to heart relationship with the Creator. The blessings from this relationship are more than one can count. He lavishes himself on us. We are his family and we are part of the household of God, with Jesus as the chief cornerstone. The family of God has a glorious inheritance, not only on this earth, but eternally. We are called, "the riches of his glorious inheritance in his holy people" (Eph. 1:18). We are God's holy people; not only has he given us every spiritual blessing in the heavenly realms in Christ Jesus, but he has also raised us up and seated us with Jesus in the heavenly realms. We are God's possession and his handiwork.

Not only do we belong to God, but he has also given us the privilege of working with and serving him while we are here in this life. Through his Holy Spirit dwelling within us, he makes his power available—the incomparable power that "raised Christ from the dead and seated him at his right hand in the heavenly realms" (Eph. 1:20). This same power is available for all who believe. He made us to be holy and blameless in his sight, and he gives us the capacity to grasp the divine love that surpasses knowledge and fills us to the measure of the fullness of God himself. Indeed, he has given us the boundless riches of Christ and a relationship with God himself through Jesus Christ.

The Daily Trenches of Life to the Full

TO REMEMBER (it is all about him)

While God has wired me to be introspective, his plan for my life entails my sharing his story with others. When I depend on him, I am invigorated by the work he gives me to do. In my great need to analyze, God allows my weakness, which he turns into strength and uses for his purposes. I can count on him to go before me, to go with me, and to go behind me. He is the One for whom the work is accomplished, and he will bring the harvest as he is the harvest itself.

TO EMBRACE (he is right)

God has made us "right" before him in Jesus. While God has wired me to like order and getting things done well, he does not want my pride or my need for getting things right to come before my relationship with him. I must lean in to how he wants me to embrace him for "rightness."

TO ALLOW HIS REWIRING (obey him)

God changes me into the daughter he has created me to be. When things get difficult and I am overwhelmed with life, he does a work—providing I allow him. He does the work for me, giving me the words and the strength. I must allow him to show me what pleases him, and then I must do it.

To Expect (expect him to show up)

Why do I wrestle so with the trenches? I know from past experience that God meets me in the mundane things in life. I experience his love and his hope, and I know him better. If we ask him to help us in our unbelief, we can expect him to show up, refine us, and keep us from unbelief.

Each According to His Need

What life to the full means is unique for each individual: each according to his or her need. God is good, and his mercies are new every morning. If we show up, he is there to meet our needs. His compassion never fails because he is faithful to his children. He is our portion and our abundance.

> I remember my affliction and my wandering, the bitterness and the gall. I well remember them, and my soul is downcast within me. Yet this I call to mind and therefore I have hope: Because of the Lord's great love we are not consumed, for his compassions never fail. They are new every morning; great is your faithfulness. I say to myself, "The Lord is my portion; therefore I will wait for him." (Lam. 3:19-24)

Our portions change through the seasons of life, but God does not change. He always shows up because he never leaves us. He knows our lot, our troubles, and our great need during every season of life. He does not turn away or leave us with our problems. He wants a relationship with us, and he wants our dependency on him. We are not self-sufficient, and we are not able to carry the loads of this world. God knows our frame, and he wants to carry the burdens for us. He wired us to need him, to need a relationship with him. Out of this relationship comes his abundance to us.

We are in great need of the Lord every day, but sometimes we go about the day like we can do it on our own. God says to pour out our troubles to him, even though he already knows them, along with the answers and outcomes. He hears us before we call on him, according the prophet Isaiah: "Before they call I will answer; while they are still speaking I will hear" (65:24). Showing God our brokenness and allowing him in the place where it hurts is dear to his heart. He comes in our darkest hour, in our greatest need. But he is also there in the smallest of details. Nothing is hidden from him, and he knows the desires and details of every living thing. He clothes and feeds all who depend on him in his creation, down to the tiniest of all aspects.

Why would we try hiding anything from God when he already knows everything? Is it because we don't want to confess it to ourselves? If we don't think of it or talk of it, maybe it will go away. Of course the surest way to make a small problem a large one is to neglect it in this way. God is in the business of growing his children up, but sometimes we are in the business of letting secrets grow.

God loves to replace shame with honor. He has already done it by the blood of his Son. As God's children, we have honor that no one can take away. We may not feel the honor if we allow ourselves to be fearful and prideful, and at the same time ashamed of the dark recesses of our thoughts and minds. Yet God desires for us a life full of him. He brings light to our darkest shadows and healing to the broken places in our hearts, minds, souls, and bodies. When we allow him in the strongholds of shame, sadness, and struggle, we experience the treasure of God in his fullness.

When after many years I faced the pain of my youth and the struggle of my adulthood, I cried out in despair. In my despair, he was there. He had been there all along. When I look back, I see the ways the Lord took care of me by bringing people into my life, by whispering of his love and affirmations, and by his presence in the darkness during those years. I still could not see the issues at hand in my relationships, in the problems of my family of origin, or the pain I just thought I was saddled with for the rest of my life. It was too difficult, too painful to let be true. But God does not let us go. He allowed me little by little to glimpse his truth amidst my struggle. He convicted me to bring the pain into his light, and he made a way through it for me. I began knowing his truth instead of the lies I believed for most of my life. He was there and met me at every turn with an abundance of compassion and gentleness I had never known. God is compassionate. He is our portion, and he is faithful. My need was his desire to love me, hold me, and bring me home to him. He brought me home to his truth, his love, and most of all, to himself.

God loves us. When I received the truth that God loves me personally, my world changed. He was taking care of my soul, my heart, and my pain. God expressed himself in abundance. He gave his love and poured out his blessings on me with a fervor I am still in awe of. He knows our every need.

Great God,

Allow me to glimpse your great mercy as I know you are showing me this day. Your abundant compassion and gentleness have paved the way for so many things in my life. Grow my gratitude in proportion to your abundance.

Lord God,

Keep me humble and broken to hear your voice and to know your great love in my life. Keep fear and pride from making me hold on to the dark places and help me bring them to your light so you can heal and provide out of your great compassion and abundance. Thank you, dear Father.

"God Answers Me in Love"

God answers me in love
From on high he stoops low
To carry me to himself above
Cherishes and guides because

He loved me first
My response to his plan, I thirst
But I try to fill it with other
Empty, dry, I cry for cover

Covering he does well
Taking my shame, he quells
The fear, pain, distress
Filling me with hope, peace

Change my wandering heart, Lord
Staying close, not to forge
Out into my own sights, plights
But turning my focus to you aright

With you I have new desires, new eyes
To go the distance, clinging on high
Letting go of me to lean into you
Joy and peace come in view

Perspective—at the Table

We need more of Christ, more redemption, grace, courage, love, truth, and hope. We have high aspirations for our lives. But though we want to achieve, when we decide to follow Jesus, we must:

o   Humble ourselves/submit and surrender

o   Lean on him/put our whole weight upon Jesus

o   Depend on him and trust him

o   Appear low to ourselves

o   See God on high

We are brought high from our low status through our relationship with the Son. Seeing God on high is reflected in Isaiah 40:22, which says, "He sits enthroned above the circle of the earth, and its people are like grasshoppers. He stretches out the heavens like a canopy, and spreads them out like a tent to live in."

Living life to the full includes changing our perspective from the view "on high" to one from "on low." God descends so we can know him. He loves us in our lowly state from his high one: "For this is what the high and exalted One says—he who lives forever, whose name is holy: 'I live in a high and holy place, but also with the one who is contrite and lowly in spirit, to revive the spirit of the lowly and to revive the heart of the contrite'" (Isa. 57:15).

When we come to the end of ourselves, we recognize our need for the one who lives on high. When God changes our view of ourselves in light of the view of his majesty, we have new eyes to see him and new hearts to know him—to know more of the fullness of God himself. The seemingly sad struggles that bring us to the end of ourselves encourage us to see through the Holy Spirit that our lives are filled with plenty and abundance.

Embracing What Is

- Embracing what is means not fretting over yesterday or worrying about tomorrow

- Embracing what is means receiving God's presence in the present

- Embracing what is means getting out of the way and stop being obstacles

- Embracing what is means God is showing us he is the Lord every day

If we accept and embrace what is, not fretting over or grieving about yesterday, or wondering and worrying about tomorrow, then we are able to receive God's presence in the present. We must also turn our focus on God instead of the situation we are in. In doing so, we must get out of the way of heaven's work in our lives, whether that means changing our perspective or transforming us to be more like the Lord. Our trusting him to be who he is and to do what he says he will do removes the persistent worry over yesterday as well as tomorrow.

If we remember what God has already done in our lives and in the lives of those around us, including our family and friends, we have ample evidence of who he is and what he has done. Through whatever is going on in our lives or in the lives of those we love, God's hand may be seen. We choose to see him through faith, for that is where he shows us who he is and demonstrates that he is who he says he is.

The day-in-and-day-out of life in the Lord Jesus is like nothing else. He guides us through difficult passages to show us God's heart. He even draws us to him to rest so he can prepare us for what is next. Even though we do not always talk with him about what is troubling us, he knows us and loves us. He does not force us into fellowship with him, but he draws us close. When we confide in him, he covers us and reveals how much he treasures us. As the psalmist divulges, "The Lord confides in those who fear him; he makes his covenant known to them" (Ps. 25:14).

God's heart for us is vast; he loves us even when we do not love him back. He confides in us; when we confide in him, we know him better and better. We will never know him as completely as he knows us, but we will keep growing up in him as we entwine ourselves around his person and his message. Embracing God daily changes our perspective to one full of hope and courage for whatever circumstance in which we find ourselves. Receiving God's presence in the present is living life to the full.

God's Extravagant Lessons Concerning Abundance

Emptiness is a good thing because it is the beginning of recognizing what we cannot do for ourselves. Coming to God empty is the only way. We do not bring anything to our relationship with God. He created us, and he knows everything about us, including what we might choose to bring him today. He most assuredly wants us to come to him, and the grandest news of all is that when we come to him he accepts that as our offering. We have nothing God needs or wants, other than for us to approach him. He has already given the life and the means by which we can come to him in Jesus Christ. And he has given the grace for access to our high and holy God himself, the Creator of the universe.

Whether or not we come to God empty-handed is not the question. We know his great love and compassion for us. He is the generous, loving, and compassionate God who covers us on both ends. Not only did he give us life, but he also gave us the gift of life with him—life to be received so we may have life to the full.

Have we received him in full? If we try bringing something or trying to achieve something—or even attempting to live a full life on our own—we will come up empty. He is life itself, the giver of life and all good things.

What do we give him then in return? We give him ourselves, with all of our puniness, faults, weaknesses, fears, doubts, and anxiety. In all ways he knows and loves us, including the things we think are pretty decent about us. But we first have to come in our broken states, full of emptiness, nothing to offer the great and compassionate God the Father. We must confess our lowliness and brokenness, a posture that allows God to move in where we have let go. He frees us as we speak of our need for him in our lives. He gives us life where before there was only death.

Being Made New

God creates us anew when we lay down the old, let go of what we want, and die to ourselves. In fact, we are made new when we lay ourselves down to him. He is trustworthy and faithful, and he knows we cannot understand even with new knowledge. Yet it is not necessary to understand God so much as to trust him. If we ask him for newness, he will give it. But it will cost something. We have to lay the old down. He shows us himself—not in the answers to the "whys" but in our leaning on him in complete surrender. He comes to reveal his love and the life he has for us—a life full of himself. Are we ready to be made new?

Living Fits

The mindset of lack and fear is filled with lies. God's Word tells us that perfect love has no fear and that he loves us perfectly and without fail. In addition, God will not withhold any good thing from his children. The book of Psalms puts it this way: "For the Lord God is a sun and shield; the Lord bestows favor and honor; no good thing does he withhold from those whose walk is blameless" (Ps. 84:11).

God says he has given us life and blessings. If we were to leave this mindset of fear and lack behind, we would truly live as he has created us to do. God says that "living" fits us, so much so that he has given us souls to live with him for eternity. On earth he wants us to live with eternity in mind. In Deuteronomy 30:19, Moses tells the Israelites to choose life instead of death, and to choose God's blessings instead of curses. "This day I call the heavens and the earth as witnesses against you that I have set before you life and death, blessings and curses. Now choose life, so that you and your children may live." If we believe that God is our life, the mindset of fear and lack has no place in our thinking or living.

God desires that we truly live. He has given us his gift of life, which is a measure to all the fullness of God. He has not given us something that does not fit us.

The New Fits

We no longer fit in our old ways. The *new* fits. His *new* fits us. God has renewed the attitude of our minds; we were created to be like him in righteousness and holiness, as we read in Ephesians 4:24 where Paul tells us to "put on the new self, created to be like God in true righteousness and holiness."

If the *new* life fits us, why do we try making the old fit into the *new*? God has given us a new spirit and the capacity for his desires within us. We trample all over his new way of life while clumsily going about the new with the old in mind? What keeps us from acting upon his gift of newness? Part of the answer is our human frailty, but a larger part of the answer lies in our unbelief. We have a small view of who God is and how much he has done for us.

Again, what constrains our view is the old. Our old ways are comfortable and familiar; they seem secure and safe, but they are not. Only God provides safety. He guides us in the unfamiliar; only he is our security. How do we change the old mindset? God grows the tiny step of faith we make when we surrender to him the old ways and lean into him in the new way of life—the one he had in mind before creation.

His new fits—one step at a time.

Expectation of Healing and Wholeness at His Table

Expecting God's interceding into our lives in order for us to live it out in full is an essential part of our spiritual walk. Sometimes God interrupts us with things we do not want, such as an illness, a death, a job change, a move, and other types of painful or stressful events. Other times, he becomes more real to us even though we know he has been there all along. God draws us closer during difficult situations that seem to go on forever. Even though it is contrary to how we humans think, God allows us any one of these things in order to move us closer to his plan for our lives. He loves us and wants more for us than we can even dream. He lets us choose whether or not we are close to him, and he allows us to cry out to him when our troubles overwhelm us.

We may be disappointed in life events and even in our closest relationships. There are times we can even be disappointed in God. If we call on him and ask for divine guidance and comfort, however, he is always available. We expect God to give us life as he promised, and this life includes sorrow and joy, good days and bad, and times we hear him and moments we cannot. But God will not have failed us. He uses each moment of our days and weaves them into a tapestry of a life transformed into a beautiful masterpiece. We become the people he designed us to be. During the process, even in the times when the Evil One attempts to steal, kill, and destroy, God's victory remains. We become victors and mighty warriors with full, rich lives in the One who heals and makes whole.

Healing and Being a Daughter

God fills us with his presence and affirms his love for us. If we lean on him and trust him, he will show us the way. We must receive his parenting and let it make a total claim on our lives.

Being daughters of the Father, we are recipients of his truth, grace, and love. We receive his parenting, his generosity, and his guidance:

- His parenting

- His nurture and affection

- His training, as in being taught by him

- His encouragement, affirmation, and anointing on our lives

- His generosity and good things

- Inheritance

- Good gifts

- Provision

- His guidance and direction, his presence, and his purpose

- Revelation

- Drawing us close; his pursuit of us

- Correction; discipline

Dear Father,

Please help us receive you and your promises today as your daughters, and remove all the baggage and hurt we bring with us.

We want to be clean of hindrance. Grant us healing and wholeness in this area, and help us to receive your parenting.

Thank you, Lord.

Allowing God to Take What Hinders out of the Hurt

Being hurt over and over by those who said they loved me, I became a monitor of hurts. I did not trust easily. Over time, I developed a hard exterior and did not want to get close to anyone. I also developed a rule that I would not hurt anyone. For me, it became an idol not to hurt anyone.

In her study on the book of James, evangelical speaker and author Beth Moore has written on "taking the hindrance out of the hurt." Her message has been revolutionary in my life. God heals hurts and takes what hinders us out of the hurts. He has healed me in many of my hurting places. Urging me onto the next step, he takes the hindrance out of hurting words and betrayals. He conforms me from a hurt person who has been healed into one who by God's power shares healing words with others. The hindrance thrown down by his strength and grace becomes the new perseverance to share his power and promise of hope and healing. The red dress mentioned earlier as a symbol of betrayal and hurt becomes the red dress transformed by the truth and grace of God into his promise of joy—a life turned into worship and praise where there was mourning and despair.

Jesus has given us all of himself. Then what keeps us from all of him? We must remember to fix our eyes on the Messiah Jesus, "the pioneer and perfecter of faith. For the joy set before him he endured the cross, scorning its shame, and sat down at the right hand of the throne of God" (Heb. 12:2). Jesus endured the cross by throwing down all of its hindrances and he died a horrible death in order that we may run the race and know he has gone before us. If we cry out, he will answer with his unfailing and faithful love.

Living in What God Gives

When the Israelites were given the land God promised them, Joshua led and instructed the people to confidently receive the land that was their inheritance. God told Joshua to be strong and courageous, and Joshua did as God commanded him to do. Likewise, God gives us gifts we are to receive and use. As we live with them and use them, we are to remember who gave them to us.

God spoke to Moses in the burning bush and told him he was on holy ground. The text in the book of Exodus reads this way: "Moses thought, 'I will go over and see this strange sight—why the bush does not burn up.' When the Lord saw that he had gone over to look, God called to him from within the bush, 'Moses! Moses!' And Moses said, 'Here I am.' 'Do not come any closer,' God said. 'Take off your sandals, for the place where you are standing is holy ground.'" (Exod. 3:3-5). God's ground with us is also holy. He meets us wherever we are and he rescues us and takes us to a more spacious place. He goes with us wherever he commands us to go. Living in the more spacious place with God requires that we receive what he has given us.

The unsearchable riches in Christ Jesus proclaimed beautifully by the apostle Paul in his letter to the Ephesians boldly demonstrates the love God has for us. He writes, "He made known to us the mystery of his will according to his good pleasure, which he purposed in Christ" (Eph. 1:9). As Paul uses the words "good pleasure," we see that God desired to do what he did for us in the sacrificial death of his Son for the sins of the world. He loved us so much he gave us his grace. It was something he planned all along, and it happened before he created anything. In addition, he freely gave us this grace. God chose in his love and power to give us love, power, unity, and peace. He not only included us in his household, but he also seated us beside his Son in the heavenly realms.

The gifts in Christ Jesus that Paul details in Ephesians are plentiful and actually more than we are able to grasp. The apostle describes who we are in Christ and what we have been given. And what have we been given?—every spiritual blessing in the heavenly realms. "Praise be to the God and Father of our Lord Jesus Christ, who has blessed us in the heavenly realms with every spiritual blessing in Christ" (Eph. 1:3). Not only are we God's children, but we were also chosen to be holy and blameless before the creation of the world: "For he chose us in him before the creation of the world to be holy and blameless in his sight" (Eph. 1:4). The gift of grace is not offered because of our own works, but it is a free gift from God. He made us to do works for him and prepared them in advance. Christians are God's children, and we have every gift from on high because of Jesus, who came so that we may have eternal life.

Paul describes the love God has for us as something to be grasped in unity with all God's people. He writes for us to "Make every effort to keep the unity of the Spirit through the bond of peace" (Eph. 4:3). He has brought us into a relationship with him and with others in order to keep the unity of the Spirit. We may know him to the measure of all his fullness. Through Jesus Christ, and as we step out in faith, God grows us up by his Word and by his love and power.

If we are to live in what God gives, there are responsibilities. Paul urges us to "follow God's example, therefore, as dearly loved children" (Eph. 5:1). We are to be humble, patient, loving, and keeping the unity of the Spirit as we live lives worthy of God's calling. We each have spiritual gifts to serve the entire body of Christ. These gifts have been apportioned so the church, the body of Christ, may be built up and reach maturity in the fullness of Christ. Living as children of the light, we are to find out what pleases God so we can live as the wise and make the most of every opportunity. We are to be filled with his Spirit in living lives of worship, praise, and gratitude.

Paul instructs us to live in Christian households with reverence and submission to one another, just as we would to Christ. He tells us how to live in God's power when we "put on the full armor of God, so that you can take your stand against the devil's schemes" (Eph. 6:11). He says putting on the armor of God is necessary for us to fight the devil's schemes: "Our struggle is not against flesh and blood, but against the rulers, against the authorities, against the powers of this dark world and against the spiritual forces of evil in the heavenly realms" (Eph. 6:12). Paul gives the final instruction for God's children: live in worship, praise, and gratitude of our Father God and the Lord Jesus Christ. Pray on all occasions with all types of prayer and requests so we may live the lives God has given us in the authority and power of Christ Jesus, who lives within us.

God's Table is Set When We Know our Great Need

Our great need brings down God's great love. We know it because he has done it before. He pours out his rich mercy and kindness, and we know it deep within. It is what we cry out for and that for which the need in us yearns. We ask him to bring us back, to hold us close.

This is the table our Father in heaven has set—the place where we meet him. He pours out his great love and mercy and quenches our thirst. He gives us his bread of life to satisfy our great hunger for him. And he remains with us to continue filling us.

AND WHEN WE WANT MORE ...

Not only is the table set for us when we know our great need, but it is also set for us when we are yearning for more. The Lord is the One and Only who fills us when we are empty, when we are weary and depleted from battle, or when we are just not satisfied. If we open the door to him, he comes and rejuvenates us with the bounty and variety he offers, including rest, delight, good things to taste and see, fellowship, intimacy, and adventure. We are invited to full participation with the Lord at God's table.

AND WHEN WE LEAST EXPECT IT...

Sometimes we just want to rest, or have a change of pace, or participate in some fun. God is intentional in how he has wired us. He knows us at our very core because he created us. He created us for adventure, for the need for rest, for purpose, and mainly he created us for himself. At the center of things, we need God, and we will find the other things when we move toward him. When we choose life in Christ, he shows us just what we came for—when we least expect it.

AND WHEN WE EXPECT IT ...

When we know the promises of God, we learn to expect him at any and all times. God has said, "Never will I leave you; never will I forsake you" (Heb. 13:5). We accept this at face value as God stretches out his hand to lead us toward purpose, adventure, and rest.

The Riches of God Himself

At God's table we are blessed with the riches of God himself. He serves us with kindness and his good pleasure. As he delights that we are with him, he invites us to come closer, to accept his offer of so many good things. Psalm 81:10 reads, "I am the Lord your God, who brought you up out of Egypt. Open wide your mouth and I will fill it." The psalmist also writes, "For the Lord God is a sun and shield; the Lord bestows favor and honor; no good thing does he withhold from those whose walk is blameless" Ps. 84:11). What does the Lord offer us at his table of plenty? He embodies all we hunger and thirst for. There is nothing he withholds from his children that would be the counterpart to their need; moreover, he is the counterpart to every need we have. When God gives us what we are longing for, it is perfect. He is the perfect Father, guide, help, comforter, teacher, and friend. He is our perfect Savior. What are the abundant riches in Christ Jesus that are served to us at the table of our Father God and Lord Jesus Christ? Each of the riches is poured out upon the family of God during their lives through the Holy Spirit dwelling in them. At the table, we find:

- Jesus loves us as his children
  - Planned before creation
  - Holy and blameless
  - Grace as a gift
  - Inheritance
- Jesus teaches us
  - The plan for peace through Christ
  - The plan for unity through the gospel of Christ
  - The plan for the church
- Jesus encourages us
  - How wide and long and high and deep is the love of Christ
  - Wisdom and revelation
  - Hope

- Jesus empowers us
  - Incomparable resurrection power for we who believe
  - Seated in heaven beside Jesus
  - To stand, put on the full armor of God
- Jesus shows us how to live
  - Put on the new attitude of your mind as you were taught in Jesus
  - As children of the light
  - Mature children
- Jesus shows us how to be in relationship
  - Submit one to another
  - Serve knowing that God rewards us
  - There is no favoritism in him

Jesus shows us how to live in unity—one faith, one Lord over all.

At the Table of Your Presence, Lord

Dear Lord,

May we not leave the table until we have heard what you have to say. You invited us here to hear you, to know you, and to experience what you have for us.

We know that it is good.

Lord, sometimes we cannot take in the good because of the shame we carry, or because of our unbelief that you have something good for us. We want to sit in your presence and receive what you have to offer.

*Give us the desire to sit still with you, to breathe in you,
and to allow you to love us in this moment.*

*We want to open the gifts you have so carefully wrapped for us.
They are beautiful and more than we imagine, and yet, we run
before we see them.*

Allow us the quiet within to know the wrappings of your blessings.

*We know our Father God has good things in store for us. Help us
to want them when you offer them and to take them with gratitude
instead of with guilt, shame, or an unreceptive spirit.*

*We want to open up and offer our whole hearts in response to the
good you have placed in front of us at the table of your presence,
Father God.*

*What have you placed in front of us that we are running from? Or
what have you offered us that we are stumbling over?*

*Open wide our hearts, minds, ears, and eyes to perceive you as our
loving Father God, Creator, Savior, Sustainer,
and Author of our lives.*

*Reveal to us things we can only know through you. Help us see and
experience the bounty placed before us. It is too overwhelming to
see and receive, but we desire that you grow within us a way to
receive it with more faith, more gratitude,
and more closeness to you.*

*As we draw near to the table, Lord, help us to approach you with
freedom and confidence. You have made the way for us.
You cause us to come,*

and you give us faith to stay.

*As you have tethered us to you, teach us to hear and grow as we
come and stay longer each time at the table with you.*

This we pray at the table of your presence, Lord.

"By His Mighty Power"

Only by your mighty power
You calm the stormy seas of my heart
Focus my mind on thee
Only you extend grace and impart faith

For my first step to your table
Full of bounty, beauty, and love
In your presence, you open my senses
You bring down walls by your mighty power

Your love is not to be distinguished
From your power, immovable, unrelenting
Unchangeable, Father God, only you
Move us to move toward you

Might you move me onward
In your mighty power to go without
Fear, but with love and power, yours
To the table set by you for all of yours

Seasons of God's Offering—Part 1

During the seasons of our lives at the table of our Lord Jesus Christ, he allows many things for his glory and our ultimate good. He uses them all for our transformation into his likeness. "Dear friends," writes John, "now we are children of God, and what we will be has not yet been made known. But we know that when Christ appears, we shall be like him, for we shall see him as he is" (1 John 3:2). What love is this that Jesus would make us like him?

Much of what transforms us happens through hard things and suffering:

- Transition, life change

- Pain, loss

- Remembering

- Hiding

- Waiting

- Out on a mission

- Wanting more

During these seasons, God offers us his heart, his healing, and his harvest. He wants us to know him through his showing up during these hard times with his love, healing, and transformation. Here are some questions we might ask ourselves during these seasons:

- Do I want to know God?

- Am I receiving what he has to offer? Or am I running away from his table?

- Am I leaning in or leaning out?

  o Am I throwing down the hindrances and lies keeping me from believing God at his Word?

  o Am I in fellowship with other believers in his Word and contributing to the unity of believers by grasping his love in this season and holding onto him tightly?

  o Am I relying on God and the power of the fellowship of believers, or am I standing alone?

Seasons of God's Offering—Part 2

- Transition and change

God offers his comfort if we make ourselves available to him. He also builds in us dependence on him through more faith. He can use this time to prepare us for new things. In the process, we receive divine love, mercy, and courage through the power of the Holy Spirit. "The Lord is my shepherd, I lack nothing. He makes me lie down in green pastures, he leads me beside quiet waters, he refreshes my soul. He guides me along the right paths for his name's sake. Even though I walk through the darkest valley, I will fear no evil, for you are with me; your rod and your staff, they comfort me. You prepare a table before me in the presence of my enemies. You anoint my head with oil; my cup overflows. Surely your goodness and love will follow me all the days of my life, and I will dwell in the house of the Lord forever" (Psalm 23).

- Pain and loss

God offers comfort through our loss and our pain. He also turns our tears into joy: "When the Lord restored the fortunes of Zion, we were like those who dreamed. Our mouths were filled with laughter, our tongues with songs of joy. Then it was said among the nations, 'The Lord has done great things for them.' The Lord has done great things for us, and we are filled with joy" (Ps. 126:1-3). God pours out compassion on us and gives us strength to persevere through the tough times and the courage to walk through it with him at our side. "Do not fear, for I have redeemed you; I have summoned you by name; you are mine. When you pass through the waters, I will be with you; and when you pass through the rivers, they will not sweep over you. When you walk through the fire, you will not be burned; the flames will not set you ablaze. For I am the Lord your God" (Isa. 43:1-3).

- Remembering

God shows us how he has been with us and walked through our journeys—and never left our sides. He also reveals to us who he is and what he has done. We are strengthened by the memories and the gratitude we have for him. "He who pours contempt on nobles made them wander in a trackless waste. But he lifted the needy out of their affliction and increased their families like flocks. The upright see and rejoice" (Ps. 107:40-42).

- Hiding, rest

God protects us as he hides us from the world. "'Because he loves me,' says the Lord, 'I will rescue him; I will protect him, for he acknowledges my name. He will call on me, and I will answer him; I will be with him in trouble, I will deliver him and honor him. With long life I will satisfy him and show him my salvation'"

(Ps. 91:14-16). During this season of rest, God comforts and guides. He shows us who he is and how much he loves us. When we seek him and repent of what we have been, God shows us his mercy and grace, and he lavishes his love upon us. When we are still in his presence, we know him better.

- Waiting

If we depend on God and wait on him during a season of waiting, he builds character in us. We come to know his sovereignty. With open and forgiving hearts by the power of the Holy Spirit, we grow up in our trust in him. "For in the day of trouble he will keep me safe in his dwelling; he will hide me in the shelter of his sacred tent and set me high upon a rock.... I remain confident of this: I will see the goodness of the Lord in the land of the living. Wait for the Lord; be strong and take heart and wait for the Lord" (Ps. 27:5, 13-14).

- Out on a mission

When we seek the Lord to be our lead and guide on the mission he has established, we become salt and light in the world. He gives us his Word and the words to convey his Word. He fills us with compassion for his people. "The Sovereign Lord has given me a well-instructed tongue, to know the word that sustains the weary. He wakens me morning by morning, wakens my ear to listen like one being instructed" (Isa. 50:4).

- Wanting more

God also gives us seasons of wanting more. If we seek him, he will fill us up and grow us up to be more mature in him in his time. He has promised us life to the full. He is our abundant life. In drawing closer, he gives us more of himself. "Better is one day in your courts than a thousand elsewhere; I would rather be a doorkeeper in the house of my God than dwell in the tents of the wicked. For the Lord God is a sun and shield; the Lord bestows favor and honor; no good thing does he withhold from those whose walk is blameless. Lord Almighty, blessed is the one who trusts in you" (Ps. 84:10-12).

"What is Your Offering, My Father, Creator, and Savior God?"

You invited me to your table, Lord, laden with
All your bounty to offer. What do you have
For me to partake from your heart
Full of kindness and lavish generosity

You pass to me your love, comfort, and joy
When I receive it, you sustain me today
In the night, you remind me you're beside me and ahead
To start a new day with more of you to offer

As you create a new me at your table
Empty of self, ready to partake, to be filled by you
My eyes open to your provision greater than I imagine
Heart hopes, waits eagerly, and becomes more truly yours

Receiving way, way down in the blackness of me
I behold his grandeur, his love, his holding onto me
Then I reach up and he grabs me
And seats me at his table in high places only he can take me

CHAPTER SIX

GOD CALLS US TO PRAISE

Praise the Lord, my soul; all my inmost being, praise his holy
name. Praise the Lord, my soul, and forget not all his benefits —
who forgives all your sins and heals all your diseases, who
redeems your life from the pit and crowns you with love and
compassion, who satisfies your desires with good things so that
your youth is renewed like the eagle's.
(Ps. 103:1-5)

Now when Jesus saw the crowds, he went up on a mountainside
and sat down. His disciples came to him,
and he began to teach them.
He said: "Blessed are the poor in spirit,
for theirs is the kingdom of heaven.
Blessed are those who mourn, for they will be comforted. Blessed
are the meek, for they will inherit the earth. Blessed are those who
hunger and thirst for righteousness, for they will be filled. Blessed
are the merciful, for they will be shown mercy.
Blessed are the pure in heart, for they will see God.
Blessed are the peacemakers,
for they will be called children of God. Blessed are those who are
persecuted because of righteousness, for theirs is the kingdom of
heaven. Blessed are you when people insult you, persecute you and
falsely say all kinds of evil against you because of me.
Rejoice and be glad, because great is your reward in heaven, for in
the same way they persecuted the prophets who were before you.
(Matt. 5:1-12)

Partaking with Him and Partaking of His Table

In order to partake of the life God offers us, we must respond to his invitation. Accompanied by the complete and finished work of Christ, God offers life and all of its benefits to those who believe. We must consider what that means. God pursues us out of great mercy and lavish love; we respond to that love in faith he initiates, and then we come to know him by faith when we experience his fullness through a personal relationship with him. In the very first step of faith, God covers our sin—past, present, and future. We have no shame in the Lord's eyes. As God's sons and daughters, we receive his faithful care: "Send me your light and your faithful care, let them lead me; let them bring me to your holy mountain, to the place where you dwell" (Ps. 43:3).

And there is so much more. We often stop at the first step; we know we believe, but we don't go the journey. The more is in the partaking, the sharing in the fellowship of our great God. God is the author and perfecter of our faith, but he is also the author of relationships. In his intentionality, God wired us with a need to know him and a need to be in a relationship with heaven's Creator. He also wired us to be in relationship with other people. When we come to the table and sit with our Father, Savior, and Lord, we partake in a relationship with the Author of the universe, the Sovereign Lord of all. Mind-blowing as it is to realize, we share in God's presence, in the knowledge of him, and we engage in the measure of the fullness of God through Jesus Christ.

Partaking with him and his table opens the mystery that was revealed in Christ Jesus and continues in his pursuing heart. For the joy set before him, the Creator and Savior of the world has mercy on us as sinners and offers us life more abundant. Our partaking of God's truth and grace is the wonder of all wonders. It cannot be fully described because it is immeasurably more than we can ask or imagine. God's truth and grace are powerful and abundant, and if we remain with him, his promises remain with us. He gave us eternal life when he did not even spare his own Son's life. At the table when we are with Christ, God shares himself with us as we partake of his life—life to the full.

In response, we worship with our hearts in spirit and in truth. We offer our praise to the One and Only.

The Perfecter of Our Faith

The writer of Hebrews talks about "fixing our eyes on Jesus, the pioneer and perfecter of faith. For the joy set before him he endured the cross, scorning its shame, and sat down at the right hand of the throne of God" (Heb. 12:2). What does it mean for Jesus to be the pioneer (or author) and perfecter of our faith? We know he is the author because he created us to be in relationship with him, and he draws us near by pursuing us and providing the means by which we come to know him. The "perfecter" of faith is an interesting concept. Jesus gives us "the way and the truth and the life" (John 14:6). He is the One God sent to rescue, serve, and save by the ultimate sacrifice. Before and during the Lord's time on earth in human form, he knew our weaknesses and temptations. While he is the Almighty, holy and just, who lived in bodily form, still he has great compassion on us. Jesus came to save us and to transform us into the persons the author and perfecter created us to be.

This again is the provision of the walk of faith. When walking by faith with Jesus, he reveals who he is and who we are. We come to know how much we have yet to learn and how much we need him on this journey of life. As we come to know Jesus and to see him in our daily walk, we know his greatness, kindness, and grace. We realize how we have fallen short and how much work he has to do in us. It is work that cannot be done by anyone except the Son himself. The only requirement for the work is that we come to the giver of mercy and the sovereign Father of all.

As we come, God begins the change in us. He tells us in his Word that "we know that when Christ appears, we shall be like him, for we shall see him as he is" (1 John 3:2). This is beyond comprehension, but the journey of faith requires we believe what Scripture says is true. And when we do, we believe God because he says it and we know him to be telling the truth. He cannot do anything else. He is the perfecter of our lives and of our faith journey with him. When we determine to walk by faith, God gives us the capacity to receive his invitation and the steadiness to remain with him. This does not happen all at once, but as we stay with him along the way.

It is the same with the perfection of our faith. God transforms us with the measure and in the increments he deems are appropriate for us to fall within his purpose and his plan. As the apostle Paul has said, "being confident of this, that he who began a good work in you will carry it on to completion until the day of Christ Jesus" (Phil. 1:6). We cannot speed up our growth, nor can we determine when and how it comes. Ours is to go with Christ where he leads. He does the rest. Just as he is the author of the walk, he is also the destination and the One for whom we make the journey. The steps of our walk lead us straight to him as he perfects them out of his great love for us. Not only did the Lord create the walk for us and provide for us along the way, but he also becomes the rear guard for the journey. Jesus is the perfecter of our faith:

> Therefore, since we are surrounded by such a great cloud of witnesses, let us throw off everything that hinders and the sin that so easily entangles. And let us run with perseverance the race marked out for us, fixing our eyes on Jesus, the pioneer and perfecter of faith. For the joy set before him he endured the cross, scorning its shame, and sat down at the right hand of the throne of God. Consider him who endured such opposition from sinners, so that you will not grow weary and lose heart (Heb. 12:1-3).

For the Display of His Splendor

The trees are brilliant with color in the fall sun. We welcome the glorious tones of red, orange, and gold, and store away their beauty in our mind's eye. The trees turn into their magnificent shades while standing in the sun and they remind us that unless the sun shines on creation, it does not reflect God's beauty. The beautiful fall leaves unveil his majesty and call forth in us awe and gratitude for who God is and what he has done.

In Isaiah 61:3 God's Word says Sovereign Lord provides for "those who grieve in Zion—to bestow on them a crown of beauty instead of ashes, the oil of joy instead of mourning, and a garment of praise instead of a spirit of despair. They will be called oaks of righteousness, a planting of the Lord for the display of his splendor." His people who remain in him will become oaks of righteousness—like trees well rooted with flourishing branches. They grow by his hand; he grows them up to be sturdy and strong, and to provide shade and beauty. The colorful fall foliage displays his splendor; may we be people of God for the display of his splendor as well.

What would God's splendor look like on us?

- Living life to the full
    - Honoring God who made us and becoming our authentic selves
    - Loving and offering the grace and truth of God to those around us
- Becoming
    - Allowing God to grow us up and to adhere to his discipline
    - Resting in heaven's promises, plan, and purpose
- Suffering, remaining, and trusting him in adversity
- Gratefulness—receiving and believing

The heart of one who displays God's splendor wears his honor and hope and reflects the brightness of a heart remaining in the presence of God and flourishing in his grace and truth. Our hearts must be tended, and God knows best how to tend them. After all, he made us, and he knows how to nourish and grow us and fill us with life—the life only he can give. The Sovereign Lord is the great mender and healer of broken hearts. This awareness of who God is comes by way of his pursuing us and then by our choosing to seek and follow him.

The Creator made us for his pleasure, and he wants us also to enjoy him forever. The display of his splendor could only be that which reflects God himself in a way that truly honors and depicts the One who loved us first. It is in this light that we must focus on the One who loves us. With him in view, we will become the splendor for which he has made us.

The Table Contents

God's faithfulness, presence, and complete joy make the table an amazing place to be. And in his presence, God covers us with his abounding love, compassion, boundless mercy, and truth. Yet, not all bounty is wonderful at first. At the table with God some deep and profound transformations can occur in our lives. During these times, God's mercy extends to us while our hearts rend. In the midst of our darkest hours, his never-failing love appears in the form of hidden treasure as he makes himself known to us: "I will give you hidden treasures, riches stored in secret places, so that you may know that I am the Lord, the God of Israel, who summons you by name" (Isa. 45:3).

When we come to the end of ourselves, God awakens in us our cry out to him. God wakes up within us a desire to be taught by him, and then he gives us new ears to hear and new hearts to know him. God allows us to stay where we are, but he also changes our perspective when we turn to him. He shows us his mercy and we want to be merciful. He gives us hearts to forgive. God receives us empty and in turn provides himself—to all the measure of fullness.

A Few of the Table Contents

Cover

Faithful care

From struggle and suffering to transformation, from tears to joy

Waiting—dependence on him

Moving the mountain

Empty to be filled

Weaknesses into strengths

Following Jesus—surrender

His mercy extended

Trust precedes strength

Power of the present in his presence

Power of being taught by him

Awakened listening

Using the gifts he gave us

Complete joy

Complete Joy

"We write this to make our joy complete" (1 John 1:4). The necessity to create originates with our Creator God who is the Word and who was the Word from the beginning. John says he writes because it completes his joy. Writing about the hope of our Lord Jesus Christ brings the joy full circle, for sharing the love and joy of Jesus Christ gives even more joy.

The full circle is the presence of God himself. Around the circle are the effects of his relationship; moving to the right, his Word and truth guide our days. He gives us purpose and significance because he is our Father God and we are his children. His light and life are reasons for being, and they bring hope and light to the world. Since he brought us to a spacious place of truth and freedom, we desire to share his light and life with others. We want to write and speak about God because he told us to do so, and also because the Spirit he placed within us compels us to tell of his great work in our lives. Sharing the stories of the Lord's faithfulness makes our joy complete. His story in our lives is full circle. The sharing of his hope for those who struggle in this life is for all of us.

Scriptures on Complete Joy

For seven days celebrate the festival to the Lord your God at the place the Lord will choose. For the Lord your God will bless you in all your harvest and in all the work of your hands, and your joy will be complete. (Deut. 16:15)

The bride belongs to the bridegroom. The friend who attends the bridegroom waits and listens for him, and is full of joy when he hears the bridegroom's voice. That joy is mine, and it is now complete. (John 3:29)

I have told you this so that my joy may be in you and that your joy may be complete. (John 15:11)

Until now you have not asked for anything in my name. Ask and you will receive, and your joy will be complete. (John 16:24)

Then make my joy complete by being like-minded, having the same love, being one in spirit and of one mind. (Phil. 2:2)

We write this to make our joy complete. (1 John 1:4)

I have much to write to you, but I do not want to use paper and ink. Instead, I hope to visit you and talk with you face to face, so that our joy may be complete. (2 John 1:12)

He is Our Cover

We are not wired to shield ourselves from our own sin, or to shelter ourselves from harm. As much as we might like to think we can cover ourselves by being good or doing good things, we cannot cover our own sin. God must do that for us, and indeed he has done this through his Son, Jesus. He takes himself and covers us with his life and death so we may not die but live with him eternally. This displays a love like no other. God shelters us from harm by keeping us safe from the ways of the world and from ourselves. Psalm 91:1 says "Whoever dwells in the shelter of the Most High will rest in the shadow of the Almighty." Believers in Christ the Messiah have shelter and rest in the shadow of the Almighty; the arms of Jesus save us and keep us safe while we live our lives in him.

The writer of Hebrews asks, "How much more, then, will the blood of Christ, who through the eternal Spirit offered himself unblemished to God, cleanse our consciences from acts that lead to death, so that we may serve the living God!" (9:14). With God as our cover, we cross over to live in praise and worship in the spacious place he provides.

He is Faithful

Because God is faithful to us, we cross over the threshold to the abundant life. He is faithful and trustworthy; he is who he says he is and he does what he says he will do. He is there with arms open wide, wooing us to himself and loving us into his grasp. He demonstrates his love as he has already done in Jesus Christ by his divine grace, desiring a relationship with us. Paul tells us of "this love that surpasses knowledge—that you may be filled to the measure of all the fullness of God" (Eph. 3:19). The abundant life is being filled with the fullness of God.

Out of the Father's faithfulness comes huge blessings to his children. We may enjoy the blessings of God's character and compassion. Isaiah 61:1-7 portrays the character of God in the life of Jesus as anticipated by the prophet Isaiah:

> The Spirit of the Sovereign Lord is on me, because the Lord has anointed me to proclaim good news to the poor. He has sent me to bind up the brokenhearted, to proclaim freedom from darkness for the prisoners, to proclaim the year of the Lord's favor and the day of vengeance of our God, to comfort all who mourn, and provide for those who grieve in Zion—to bestow on them a crown of beauty instead of ashes, the oil of joy instead of mourning, and a garment of praise instead of a spirit of despair. They will be called oaks of righteousness, a planting of the Lord for the display of his splendor. They will rebuild the ancient ruins and restore the places long devastated; they will renew the ruined cities that have been devastated for generations. Strangers will shepherd your flocks; foreigners will work your fields and vineyards. And you will be called priests of the Lord, you will be named ministers of our God.

You will feed on the wealth of nations, and in their riches you will boast. Instead of your shame you will receive a double portion, and instead of disgrace you will rejoice in your inheritance. And so you will inherit a double portion in your land, and everlasting joy will be yours.

When we are brokenhearted, he comes to bind us up. We may receive freedom through him when we have been enslaved or imprisoned by persons or things of this world—or by our own devices. If we are without sight, or in the dark, the Lord supplies what light is necessary to see. He regards our shame and disappointment with compassion, and he delights in giving us honor and hope—a double portion for that which was lost. God restores our lives and, in our despair, he brings a reason for praise. He makes us into crowns of splendor and oaks of righteousness for his name's sake.

Abundant Life is Both Joy and Pain

Abundance means plentiful and includes the "muchness" of life, including the hard stuff. When Jesus speaks of the abundant life, he is definitely referring to a life of abundant joy. But he also says we will have pain, too. How does one know the abundant life, with the fullness of joy, without having pain, loss, or struggle? We often pray for a life without pain. Yet if we were to have a life without pain, we might also have a life without joy. Life to the full is one including amazing joy and, often, much pain.

Jesus said, "The thief comes only to steal and kill and destroy; I have come that they may have life, and have it to the full" (John 10:10). The life Jesus speaks of is life to the full, or abundant life. It is a life full of good, not just of joy, but goodness, hope, truth, grace, mercy, and pain. This pain is in line with the sufferings of Jesus when he bore our pain and paid the price of our sin by his suffering on the cross. In a real sense we do not know Christ until we know suffering. The apostle Paul wrote, "I want to know Christ—yes, to know the power of his resurrection and participation in his sufferings, becoming like him in his death" (Phil. 3:10).

To that end, it is amazing grace knowing the One who died so we might have the abundant life. We are wired to be incomplete without Christ. It is treasure to have a personal relationship with our Father God, the Creator of the universe, through his Son, Jesus Christ. In him, with him, and for him, we have an abundance of Jesus through the indwelling of the Holy Spirit. He makes it possible for us to know him and to live in fullness, whether in pain or in joy, because we have the hope of Jesus within us.

Followers of Jesus Struggle, Too

Jesus said that we would have struggles. In fact, it is guaranteed. The apostle Paul was himself imprisoned, flogged, beaten, hungry, thirsty, naked, cold, shipwrecked, and concerned for Jesus' followers. But he knew it was a race worth running. When God called Paul to preach about the boundless riches of Christ, he received the call and obediently followed the Savior. We will also struggle, but "our struggle is not against flesh and blood, but against the rulers, against the authorities, against the powers of this dark world and against the spiritual forces of evil in the heavenly realms" (Eph. 6:12).

We sometimes wonder, when we suffer, if our choices led us to the wrong path. We are followers of Jesus, yet we can mistake our suffering for our own doing, or perhaps for something not in God's plan. This is a lie of the Evil One. What God teaches on this is that we are to submit to the mighty love and power of God if we want to change what he has allowed in our lives—whether hardship, loss, or betrayal. Furthermore, as his daughters, we are to be humble and strong, loving and persevering on our journeys. These are the traits of our Father God, who empowers us by his Holy Spirit to live in his likeness and go the distance.

The transformation God makes in us is slow and lasting, and his love is wide and deep. He reveals himself in his love and his mighty hand on our lives. To follow God means we accept he is in the lead and providing the capacity to follow him and the strength to go the entire way—but also molding our character to be more like Jesus as we go. Only a Father who is rich in mercy and bold in kindness would design a relationship like this one. He loves us immeasurably more than we can imagine.

What are We Doing With the Waiting?

We always seem to be waiting on something or other, whether it is in the grocery store checkout line, the traffic light, or on something much bigger in life, such as a health concern, or waiting for a relationship to heal, or waiting for a child to come home. The real question becomes, What are we doing with the waiting?

Does waiting set our minds on the eternal? God is the giver of time, and time includes waiting and eternal life. God desires that we wait on him and place all of our wants and desires in him. God has a plan and a purpose for us, and he is waiting for us to be ready for what he has in mind. His purposes will not be thwarted.

Father God,

Thank you for your waiting places. Help us to be still and to listen and expect you to show up as you always do.

Guide us into the purpose you have for this time and place.

Help us to follow and obey you.

Grow in us a desire to please you in all ways—to love and speak truth and to serve people you place around us.

Father, help us to praise you in the waiting.

Waiting on God Comes in Transitions

The gospel says to live on our own is death, but to live in God is life. In order truly to live, we must die to our old ways and to our old selves and follow Jesus.

How do we choose to live each day? God has given us good minds to choose. He has also given us a free will to determine which way we will go: to serve ourselves or to serve him? When we love and choose to follow God, we have purpose and meaning.

We are not taken in by whims or schemes of the world. We are his and he is our shepherd, coaxing us and giving us direction according to the plans he made before the beginning of the world.

God gives us the means by which to do whatever he has determined. He goes before us, with us, beside us, and behind us. He wants to reveal himself to us, to share a word with us, to confide in us. As we wait for sacred direction, we wait with anticipation, fervor, and with a longing for his face.

Waiting sometimes comes in transitions. We must rest in the Almighty's arms, but sometimes we get anxious about today and the future. Are we going to feel this present sadness this afternoon, or tomorrow, or for a long time? We know God has got this, and we are not the first to experience this transition. But not wanting to miss what God is doing, we strive and fret all over it. God does not want this kind of perspective in our relationship.

Are we waiting on God, or is he waiting on us? Whichever it is, waiting is a time for reflection and remembering what the Lord has done. It is also a time to seek Jesus and see him for who he is. He is in this spacious place for us at this time in our lives.

Father God, we seek you.

We want to know you better and to come and rest in your presence.

Draw us into your arms, and open our eyes and hearts to you.

We don't want to miss you.

Thank you for this time and place, a spacious one in you.

Our Empty for His Fullness

Even when we are overwrought and crying out to God, he asks us to come. The empty, broken, and hurt places are his specialty. We may not be able to utter a word, but God's Spirit can: "The Spirit helps us in our weakness. We do not know what we ought to pray for, but the Spirit himself intercedes for us through wordless groans" (Rom. 8:26). He shows us he is with us, by a word, a whisper, a prayer. He prays the words for us because he knows.

God knows how we feel. When we are sad, he is sad. He knows the shame and the pain. He utters his Word in ways we know. He understands our empty; he receives it as if it were praise and gratitude. His answer is always, "Never will I leave you; never will I forsake you" (Heb. 13:5). Whenever we turn to God on empty, he takes it and gives abundantly.

It is in the emptying that God shows up and pours out his abundance. According to the gospel of John, he came that we would live life to the full: "The thief comes only to steal and kill and destroy; I have come that they may have life, and have it to the full" (John 10:10) We have no capacity on our own to be full. But God does. What we lack is the spacious place for him. Often we try to fill the space or do something for the Lord. The more we realize we have nothing to give, the better we are able to see and receive him. We start by relinquishing what we think we have, because it is nothing compared to what God has. He wants to take our lack, our empty, and even what we think we have, and give us his bounty.

Through Jesus, therefore, let us continually offer God a sacrifice of praise—the fruit of lips that openly profess his name.

Weaknesses into Strengths

God tells us we can rest like weaned children: "My heart is not proud, Lord, my eyes are not haughty; I do not concern myself with great matters or things too wonderful for me. But I have calmed and quieted myself, I am like a weaned child with its mother; like a weaned child I am content" (Ps. 131:1-2). We tend to lay our issues at his feet and then pick them back up and carry them. But we are not able to carry burdens because he did not wire us to do so. God wants us to be children to his fathering. He teaches us how to be his children; our weakness becomes his strength.

God has already gotten things right for us for all time. Jesus came for just that purpose, to make things right between God and his family. As children of the Father, we have peace with God through Jesus. We must not try to get things right more than we place our hope in God. Jesus makes us right with God, and he has shown us that our need to set things in order turns into the very essence of our praise to God for already having done it. His rightness is our strength. It is a sweet revelation from God to know our weakness is his strength!

When we fix our eyes on the One who is sovereign and loves each of us unconditionally, we do not have to worry about whether or not someone is dissatisfied with us or something else in their lives. We are to trust the One and Only and choose to please him above all others. God will change our view and give us the capacity to focus on him and, in addition, he will increase our desire to please him above all others, including ourselves. Our weakness is his strength!

All we can be originated from our Creator God. He knows our every wrinkle and restless thought. We do not have to fret over anything. Instead, we have to take it to him. Our weaknesses can become our stumbling blocks to the relationship he has for us. But God uses our relationship with him to bring us closer and to make us stronger. What follows are some things that bother us. We should let them go and turn our focus back to our Father God, the Almighty.

Not Blocking God's Way

When we are utterly helpless to hand over a hard thing to God, we must cry out for help to give it up. The desire for God can only be met by God, and our need for a new self has to be less than our desire for God. God will make us new in our meeting with him.

God, who is so rich in mercy, continues to pursue us in new ways, some really beautiful ways and some really difficult ones. Sometimes I am the one who gets in the way of God's pursuit. God wants to give us more, but we have to give ourselves up in order to have him more. As he teaches, we have to lose our lives in order to have life.

When I get in the way of God's pursuit, I am blocking his flow. His blood runs in my veins, yet I have cut it off by fearing the unknown and being afraid of doing it all wrong. His pleasure in blessing us continues in spite of us, but our lives of fullness increase when we decrease our efforts to save ourselves.

In order not to block God, we must let go of what we ordinarily would do in trying to save ourselves. He has already saved us through our Savior, Jesus Christ. The One who saved us continues to live within us. We must allow God's extraordinary gift to flow by moving out of the way. Praise God from whom all blessings flow!

Surrender and the Holy Spirit

We have the gift and the capacity to know our Father God in an intimate and powerful way. He gives us love, truth, and power to believe and follow him. In our fleshly nature, we want to do it our way. However, if we lean on the Father and follow his lead, we will have the Holy Spirit's power flowing through us to be, do, and receive whatever he has for us. When we receive the flow of God's love and power in us by his Holy Spirit, we are receiving God himself coming down to us and enabling us to live in him and through him. Yet, as we have noted, we often create barriers to this flow.

God will not allow anything in our lives as his daughters to permanently harm us. He will never leave us to our own devices. He will love us, protect us, rescue us, and give us whatever we need in life's journey. But it is more than that. He is God. He is our Father. Thus, his flow within us is for his glory and our good— more than we imagine.

The flow of God within us as revealed in his Word says that the Holy Spirit will guide, teach, comfort, lead, and give us power and love to spread God's Word. By him and through him, we will be guided by his truth and enabled by his power to speak the truth and to love God and others. By the flow of the Holy Spirit within us, we may know him and follow him as he planned before the creation of the world.

Fearing more hurt and betrayal, we sometimes want more control of our lives. God will not disappoint us, but we still act out of unbelief in who he is. Whenever we do this, we stop the Holy Spirit's flow in our life. But if we yield to him and hold loosely the things we are guarding, he will allow his power to flow and to transform us into daughters who depend more on him. His flow shows us who he is and what he wants for his children. If we keep our eyes fixed on him and allow his flow in our lives, the barriers come down and the full force of God triumphs—whatever small fear or Great Mountain seemed impossible at the moment.

In order to have life, God has taught us we must offer up our own. Just like the flow of God's Spirit within us, we must allow it to flow within the areas where we have set up barriers—to good, to life, and to God. God allowed his blood to be spilled on the cross in his Son's life so we may have his life and his power flowing in us. Jesus' power is released in his blood—his very life given for us, to us, and through us with his Holy Spirit. Praise him!

The Fullness We Miss When We Try to Control

What do we miss when we try controlling our lives? Knowing our Father God? Growing our faith in him, increasing our knowledge of him, healing old wounds, restoring relationships?

If we rely on the Father, we are vessels for the Almighty. If we fear we are not equipped for his work, we hinder the very fullness he has given and we impede the flow of God's abundance in our lives. When we cry out to him, he pours out his love on us. He is always pursuing us with his mighty and merciful grace. We must awaken and receive what he has to offer. Let us have the faith to allow his flow of grace in our lives.

What are we afraid of that is more powerful than the relationship with our Father God? He moves mountains, and his creation displays his handiwork. He establishes kingdoms and rulers, and he appoints armies and angels. Our Father God knows us intimately and yet he continues to invite us into relationship with him. We can stop and start and run away and come back, and his grace remains.

What are we missing when we do not yield to our loving, compassionate, and holy God? We miss out on his goodness, mercy, joy, and peace. And these are not the only blessings we miss. Skipping over a blessing or two may seem like a small price to pay for controlling a situation we hold tightly. Who are we to think we understand what the God of the universe is doing as he works out his plan for the entire world? How do we know that it is just a small thing to miss out on a moment with our Father God? Our human tendency to make God small prevents us from knowing who he is in our lives.

Our Father God and Lord Jesus Christ come down to remain with us so we can remain with him in the Holy Spirit. We stay because he gives us the capacity to stay. We follow him because his Holy Spirit enables us to follow him. Without God's Spirit we cannot choose him. Why would we try impeding his flow within our lives when he *is* our lives? We can only believe him, follow him, and choose to do so with his power running through us. We want to go with the flow, the power of which is the same as the Holy Spirit exerted when he raised Jesus from the dead and seated him in the heavenly realms: It is "his incomparably great power for us who believe. That power is the same as the mighty strength he exerted when he raised Christ from the dead and seated him at his right hand in the heavenly realms" (Eph. 1:19-20). Going with the flow as vessels for God makes us ready for his grace and power flowing and our faith growing, as we receive his fullness of life.

His Mercy

God rewards us according to our righteousness, as the psalmist has written: "The Lord has rewarded me according to my righteousness, according to the cleanness of my hands in his sight" (Ps. 18:24). This sounds like a huge order, and it is. However, out of God's rich mercy that he showed us in his Son, he credits us with his righteousness when we come to faith. In addition, Scripture tells us that God deals with us according to the cleanness of our hands. Again, this sounds like a commandment we cannot attain. But God sees the cleanness in our hearts through his Son's blood. We are clean because of his wonderful gift of grace. Because God has chosen to give us a way to become righteous and clean before him, he then deals with us accordingly out of the richness of his grace and mercy.

All this is difficult to fathom. Our great God is not to be understood but trusted with all of our hearts, souls, minds, and strength. We must fully lean onto him, and he will provide the path, provision, and his presence along the way. When we have a difficult time receiving God's gift of grace, we must ask him to help us trust him and receive what he has mercifully and abundantly given. He answers out of his great love for us.

It is the love he has for us that propels us to step out in faith. It is not something we can do on our own. Faith, in the original decision and for the daily journey, becomes again the motivation to follow God in all we are and do. Our Father God showers us with gifts of salvation, righteousness, and cleanness. He makes us holy and blameless in his sight, and then he grows the faith within us to believe it and continue to make him our heart's desire.

The great gift of righteousness, which is being right with our perfect and infallible Father God, Creator of the universe and Lord and Savior, is the biggest gift we will ever receive. But God never stops giving himself to us. Through the Holy Spirit, he never leaves us or forsakes us. The Holy Spirit grows within us the desire to know the Father and to live as he would have us live—receiving and praising God for the full measure of himself within us.

In the Present and Not in Hindsight

We want to live "life to the full" instead of looking back at it in retrospect. If we surrender whatever is in the way of our stepping out in faith, we have him. To live as recipients of the divine gift of his Son through his life, death, and resurrection, we must choose moment by moment to live and receive the abundant life.

Often we go through hard times, but with 20/20 hindsight, we see God's hand and his fullness all the way through it. If we were to surrender our lens to God's, perhaps we would not have to look back but look upon him and his fullness right in front of us. A lack of faith, or unbelief, is what inhibits our sight and prevents us from seeing. We tend to believe something is going to be difficult, so it is. But we can ask God to give us fresh eyes, and new and softened hearts, to expect him to show up and be with us through whatever the struggle or new adventure.

God prepares us and goes before us in the unfamiliar. He sets things in place in order for us to walk through, and he guides us and protects us as we go. After we have passed this way, he brings things together. His yield from the journey is his work; ours is to walk through in trust and obedience while being conformed to his image along the way.

Living abundantly in Christ is a decision to trust him with all things. Along the way, we get the choice to live in his fullness. We can choose him and the abundant life in this moment, for the Great I AM is now.

Taking the Table with You (your prayer within us)

Dear Father,

Help me to take you with me today.
I want my heart to burst with your bounty,
ready to love and to serve the ones you place before me.

As I have received the dessert of your choosing, and my heart is
brimming over, I can say I have tasted and it is good.
Let my life be full of praise for you.

May I take the love and the abundant life out with me
and allow it to show as I live, walk, learn,
and grow through this journey of life.

I know that the table is set and ready as the Lord loves his people
and is waiting for them to come. May I bring someone the Lord has
chosen to come. Do I have the privilege of encouraging someone to
the table he has set for us?

Let us live in praise and gratitude
for the One whose table is ready.

"Teach Me"

This mind of mine seeks to know
You, Lord, instead of the places it roams
Teach me in the choices
Dark corners and walled off partitions

You in the light, you in the dark
Guide to heal and guard my heart
It is you I trust with the hard
Knotted and tangled, wounded and scarred

Take me, hand-held to where you lead
To know you, even if painful, indeed
Search me for I know I may not like what I see
But your grace—abundant, rich and free

When you stand me up again
To behold without disdain
Your clay, transformed by your hand
I see the Potter who loved me more than sand

I know I have seen him
His love changed me
Amazing Grace teaches and frees
It is for all the world, you see

The Power of God within Us

The power God gives us is real and to be used in our lives. "The Spirit God gave us does not make us timid, but gives us power, love and self-discipline," according to Second Timothy 1:7. As children of our risen Lord, our Creator and Savior God, we have been anointed with gifts and power, and with the Holy Spirit living in us.

God desires that we pursue the passions he has laid on our hearts. Only he can help us get rid of the ways we err. And only he can help us to pursue what is good. He wants to extinguish what is harmful within us and "to fan into flame the gift of God, which is in you through the laying on of my hands" (2 Tim. 1:6). We are to plant and watch how he brings in the harvest.

God gives us good gifts to use, and we want to use them for his purposes—starting today. When he displays his work in the world and within us, we must praise our Father God, the God of the harvest!

To Partake of God's Table

The definition of *partake* from the Merriam-Webster's Collegiate Dictionary is:

- to have a share or part of something along with others

- to join with others *in* doing something: to take part *in* something

- to have some of the qualities *of* something

In other words, when we partake of something, we experience the taking along with others; we share in the experience. We join with others to take something in. As we partake of God's Table, we join along with the fellowship of others who have also chosen to come and to partake of God's offering to us in Christ Jesus. It is offered to all, and we choose or choose not to receive the invitation or come to the table and take part with him. Christ is the head of the table and he offers us himself in abundance. We experience his love, truth, and grace in a relationship with God and with other believers at the table with us, all of whom he loves and created for his purposes. We grasp who he is, the love he has for us, and who we are in him when we come to his table to partake.

To partake also means to share in the journey of following Christ and receiving his bountiful blessings along the way. He has invited us to sojourn with him, to partake of the many seasons of life, including the pain and suffering required to know him and the fellowship of others in relationship with him.

The essence of the meaning of partake includes sharing with other people. It is in joint participation that we actively receive something in our relationship with Christ Jesus. When we know the Lord, we share a relationship with others. It is through these relationships that we know him better. Fellowship with others is essential, and the joining of all God's children together is the body of Christ, empowered by the Holy Spirit in each one of us.

God's passion for us is evident in his unfailing and never-ending love through Jesus Christ. His provision for our souls in eternity is far beyond the scope of our imagination, much less our asking and receiving. We can partake of God's mighty and merciful gifts of provision.

As God's children, our inheritance is assured. God works his purposes out according to the plan he constructed before the beginning of creation. We know God's passion for us through his plan, purpose, provision, and through the indescribable gift of his Son, through whom we may partake of God himself. We are privileged to share his bounty; in fact, who are we to reject his gifts? Who are we to not partake? As the children of the Father, his provision is not only for his glory, but for our good. He is God, and there is no other. Are we going to say Yes to his offer of provision?

When the Israelites were to enter the Promised Land, Moses turned the mantle over to Joshua as God commanded him. Joshua, directed and guided by God just as Moses was, knew that God had promised the land and would lead them into it, as he had sworn to their fathers. The Israelites had been on the move for years, and now they were going to be able to rest in the land the Father had given them. God told them he would guide them into the land and would fight for them. He offered them rest, his arm for the victory, and his continued guidance.

Ever since, we have been in search of rest from the world, a sure leader and victor in our battles, and guidance for our lives. Often, we stay on the move just as the Israelites did, some of them for their entire lives. When we focus on the moving or whatever is in focus at the time, we miss the guidance and the victory God has for us.

In our relationship with God, he provides the way for us to have peace with him through Jesus Christ, the Son of God. By heaven's grace we may come to God's table to receive his bounty, because of what Jesus did for us. And because we have chosen to receive Jesus into our lives, we inherit life to the full. God allows difficult things, and if we choose to partake in a relationship with him, he uses all of our experiences to transform us into the persons he designed us to be. Are there giants in our land that we can't conquer? Yes, but there is also God's bounty. Just as the Israelites grumbled and were afraid of entering the Promised Land, we grumble at our own circumstances. The Israelites found amazing goods of fruit and honey. As God's children, we are likewise highly favored. We are made in God's image, and we have a glorious inheritance as his children.

God is in the business of blessing us with his limitless bounty. The truth is that all of God's offspring have an unimaginable opportunity to partake of God's goodness. If indeed we know we are God's children, we must turn to him for our very lives. We must approach our journey as Joshua approached his by having strength and courage and acting like God is going to provide. And he will provide rest, his arm of victory for the battles, and his guidance. Perhaps we would see God better if we did not to focus on our difficult circumstance or ourselves. We would be able to hear his voice, know his Word, and follow his clear guidance. And then, best of all, we would have the rest he has already given. He provides, and we partake. Praise him for his bountiful gifts!

His Discipline

Scripture says "The lions may grow weak and hungry, but those who seek the Lord lack no good thing" (Ps. 34:10). Even so, we sometimes think our lives have nothing good in them. How could God allow the things that are happening? We are not God, and we do not have his knowledge and perspective. Indeed we have to trust him with our lives and everything in them.

When God corrects us or allows difficulties for our good, we may not necessarily feel that "those who seek the Lord lack no good thing." But our Father may be trusted. We know this because we have experienced his goodness, compassion, unfailing love, and faithful care through his Son, Jesus. God corrects or disciplines us in order to bring something better out of us. In other words, he prunes as necessary: "I am the true vine, and my Father is the gardener. He cuts off every branch in me that bears no fruit, while every branch that does bear fruit he prunes so that it will be even more fruitful" (John 15:1-2).

God faithfully cares for us and extends his hand to lead us, but he will not force himself on us. If we do not surrender to him, we will not have the good he is offering us. The question is not whether what God is offering is any good. Rather, it is whether we are going to receive it and humbly obey him. God is looking at our hearts and finding either a yielded heart that wants to know him better by obeying, or a heart still self-reliant and stubborn and not ready to receive the good he has for us.

The Gifts of Disappointment and Pain

What in one's life expands one's capacity and gives life? It could be leading a small group Bible study, or serving at a homeless shelter, or encouraging a new follower of Christ. By being the vessel to carry his message of love and truth, could God be showing his love and power through the spacious place he provides when we serve him?

God created us with a plan for each of our lives. He has given the Holy Spirit to equip us for living and giving in this large and needy world. What gives one energy and fills a desire to give back? If we have not found the spacious place God has for us, we can ask him to show us. God has prepared a place for all of us, and it will be apparent when the time is right. It could be we already know where this spacious place is but we feel inept to ask about it. Sometimes we have to jump in, even when we do not feel prepared, because God is using the very thing to increase our faith and our capacity to know him better. Other times, God has something in mind, and to find out about it we have to wait. He is getting us ready for his good work.

What is also amazing is that God does not waste anything in our lives, especially our hurts and disappointments. The very things God uses as he equips us and heals us are the places that have caused us pain. He makes them a great vehicle through which to show how much he loves us and allows hard things to display the richness and beauty of his love and power. Our disappointments and betrayals bring great pain, but through them, God shows his love in ways we could not have imagined. He has demonstrated his power to heal us and transform our lives beyond expectations

As followers of Jesus, we must lean upon him to know him. As we do, he will also show us how to know him better. God shows up as we live our lives in his very presence. He makes us into his vessels to display his goodness, righteousness, and truth. As he does so, we know him all the more. We are his children for the display of his glory. Praise God!

"The Goodness of our Great God"

I trust the goodness of our God
For life's journeys—mountains and valleys
Its joy, waiting, struggles, and pain
He has shown me his ways, who he is

His presence carries me through the disappointments
His lavish love pours forth comfort when I've gone too long
without hope
His harvest of joy coming up from the seeds of tears
Assures me again of his abounding grace

God taught me to be a mother when I was afraid
Compelling me to know him and his love
For the generations he loved me to love
Showing his compassion and healing beyond my dreams

God taught me to be his daughter when I was afraid
Out of order it seemed for a grown woman
What perfect order he brings for his children
His plan beyond our imagination—paradox, abundance,
fullness of joy

From little girl scared to dream to full-grown woman
complete with dreams
Borne of God's love and mercy, his choosing before creation
To allow our brokenness only to be made whole
By the only One who could, did, and continues to grow and fill us
with his fullness

How is it that I have come to see the goodness of our great God
By his mercy he has revealed himself to me
Oh that I remember his goodness to me and tell what he has done
Because he chooses to be merciful, compassionate,
and abounding in love

Crossing Over—the Abundant Life

Through the goodness of our Great God, he transforms us, his daughters. These are some of the life-affirming characteristics the Father gives through the Holy Spirit as we worship and praise the One and Only who bestows them upon us:

1. Believing receives

The Holy Spirit gives us the capacity to believe who God is and what he has promised.

2. Faith has momentum

As we take the step of faith in believing God, the Holy Spirit multiplies our steps of faith.

3. Hope expects

When we make the proclamation of faith, God not only gives us more faith, he also gives us more hope in who he is and what he has done.

4. Joy fills

As the Holy Spirit gives us the capacity to remain close to him, we have joy in his presence and more joy in our lives.

5. Love waits

God has shown us he is patient, kind, and compassionate. The heavenly Father pursues and waits upon us to come to him. With the Holy Spirit, we too have the ability to wait upon the Lord as he makes us into who he created us to be. When we wait, God is making us ready for what is to come. In the waiting, he reforms us to love him back and love others as he does.

6. Obedience frees

In his wisdom, God has given us a spacious place in which to live and abide in him. He has also given us his wisdom and knowledge of whom he has created, and the boundaries and conditions upon which he has made his promises. When we obey God, we live in complete freedom from our sin and whatever enslaves us.

7. Longsuffering transforms

God knows our very frame of which we are made. The perseverance we have in the power of the Holy Spirit becomes a crucial part of our character building for a life of abundance in Jesus Christ.

In Relationship

It is in relationship that we know one another. It is in relationship with our Father God that we come to know him. God wired us to be in person-to-person relationship, loving one another, making sacrifices for each other, and seeing the best in the other person. But do we live in relationships like this? While some would say that the highest of joys has been birthed in relationships, others would say their deepest hurts have come in relationships. Many of us lack the knowledge of how to live in relationship with one another.

All the things that happen and all that comes out of relationships either points to the goodness of God, or makes it necessary for us to cry out to him for help. The greatest joy comes from relationships, but the worst pain resides in them as well. God wants to use relationships for his glory and our greatest good—for this is how he works. He takes our struggles and, if we allow him, he uses them to heal us. Thus, God can make them into something bringing us great joy. Relationships may cause us to cry out to God; we cannot in and of ourselves make them work. Love is from God, and actually all goodness comes from him. If God is in the relationship, we have the capacity through him to make them work—to love, sacrifice, and see the best in another. But if God is not in the relationship, it will not live up to its potential. At its best and worst, it can be disastrous.

God uses the most difficult of things to bring us closer to him. Relationships have a way of drawing us to God. When a significant person in our life disappoints us, a friend betrays us, a relative no longer associates with us, a child rebels against us, or a spouse leaves us, we are broken until God heals us. Relationships become broken, too, and God heals them as he heals other difficult things.

God uses relationships to show us his goodness, love, presence, power, and grace. When we see one of these traits in another, we know it comes from God. God wants us to know him, and in drawing near, we come to know the great God of the universe, the One and Only Savior.

So it is with relationships. We know the abundance of God through our relationship with him, and we know it through relationships with one another, the people he has placed in our lives. He lives in us when we become followers of Christ, and he gives us the capacity to love and live in relationship. He also gives us the power to grasp his love for his people. Paul prays that we, "being rooted and established in love, may have power, together with all the Lord's holy people, to grasp how wide and long and high and deep is the love of Christ" (Eph. 3:18).

We cannot fathom the vastness of the love of God, nor are we able to comprehend the power he gives us to love and live as his holy people. The fullness of life God gives comes through relationship with him and with his people.

God's Hand in My Life

I was afraid to be a mother; perhaps I am afraid to be a daughter, too. My reader may ask, "Don't you have the order backwards? Doesn't being a daughter come first, then being a mother?" If you have read my story in *Real Struggles, Real Hope: A Journey to Truth, Trust, and Freedom*, you know that God drew me near as I traveled the journey of becoming a mother. He showed me that while my daughter did know I loved her, God loved her and he loved me, too. God took me on a pilgrimage beginning with seeing the divine hand in my life from very early on until adulthood. It was like a frame-by-frame view of the different people he placed in my childhood and then in my adult life who were his messengers of love and kindness to me. It was as if he said, "You do not need to have the perfect family in order to know my love. I will hold you in my arms and then hold your hand and guide your steps. You must follow my loving hand extended to give you hope in the midst of hurt and struggle."

After having made the pilgrimage of being a mother who has the glorious knowledge of God's love for me and my children, I have a new journey. God's new word for me is that I am his daughter, and so are my readers his sons and daughters. I am his daughter, and it is enough.

The pilgrimage begins as we learn to live in praise of him who teaches us to be his daughters of the King of kings, God himself.

CHAPTER SEVEN

GOD CALLS US TO PLEASE HIM

This day I call the heavens and the earth as witnesses against you
that I have set before you life and death, blessings and curses. Now
choose life, so that you and your children may live and that you
may love the Lord your God, listen to his voice, and hold fast to
him. For the Lord is your life, and he will give you many years in
the land he swore to give to your fathers,
Abraham, Isaac and Jacob.
(Deut. 30:19-20)

Therefore, since we are surrounded by such a great cloud of
witnesses, let us throw off everything that hinders and the sin that
so easily entangles. And let us run with perseverance the race
marked out for us, fixing our eyes on Jesus, the pioneer and
perfecter of faith. For the joy set before him he endured the cross,
scorning its shame, and sat down at the right hand of the throne of
God. Consider him who endured such opposition from sinners, so
that you will not grow weary and lose heart. (Heb. 12:1-3)

Loving Father, Thriving Daughter

Our plea from our vantage point on this earth, so full of God's goodness and love is, "Holy Father God, let your will be done on earth as it is in heaven." There are also on this earth fallen human beings and their puniness, apathy, and hate. But God wired us for something greater than ourselves. He made us into relational human beings, created by him to be in relationship with the Father and one another. God set up the world for us to be connected to each other—father, mother, husband, wife, daughter, son, sister, brother, friend, extended family members, and church and social and work relationships. We are to get along and honor one another in relationship.

Being a daughter is just one of the many relationships we have on this side of heaven. God made us women to be his daughters. He has also made us the daughter of others—indeed a father and a mother, or someone who filled those roles for us. They were human; some followed God, and some did not. Inevitably, these persons got some things right and some things wrong. God made us for relationship with him so we could know his perfect goodness and love, and to be able to live with his help in relationship with others. There are many aspects of a daughter-mother or daughter-father relationship. The daughter is to love, respect, and obey her parents, to receive their love and affection, and embrace what they have to offer. She is to remember them and honor them.

Yet, in our fallen world, sometimes parents fall short and are not responsible adults. Sometimes they come up short when caring for and providing for the needs of their children. Often they neglect their responsibilities for their children in order to maintain their own lifestyles. Or they demand too much or are too critical. They may not be disciplined themselves, and they may not discipline their children. Some may live through their children instead and demand too much from them. Their version of love does not value the child, nor does it encourage the child to grow to be who God created them to be. In the emptiness, God can come in to provide for the child and to love and honor the child. He also can teach the parent, mother or father, to provide for the child. There are also times when the daughter falls short in her relationship with the mother or father. God can also love, heal, and make the parent or child whole where his or her lack exists. It is in the brokenness that God comes and shows us how to receive his love and hope. I grew up in an environment where my mother was with me physically, yet her brokenness kept her from me. When God showed me who he was and revealed the truth in his Word, I came to know what real love is. I could trust him and his love for me and for my mother.

In the midst of human brokenness, God allows us to know him as the perfect parent. We are his daughters and sons, and his love is unfailing and unconditional. We cannot earn it, nor is it dependent on anything else. Furthermore, it never ends. He comes in and dwells within us so that wherever we are, he is. He pours his life into us, encourages and exhorts us, gives us purpose, and charges us to live a life worthy of God's call. He disciplines, teaches, and demonstrates his love through the undeserved gift of his Son, Jesus. We come to know that he is the giver of all good things and that we have a glorious inheritance in him. In addition, God teaches us how to love, honor, and obey by surrendering our lives to him as his daughters, to worship him in grace and truth, and to receive all he has to offer us. When we are lost, God reminds us that he has done great things for us, that he has changed us, and that we are his children. All things we need for life and godliness are on offer: "His divine power has given us everything we need for a godly life through our knowledge of him who called us by his own glory and goodness" (2 Pet. 1:3). We are indeed children of the praiseworthy King.

In the Community of Faith and In the World

It is sometimes difficult to know the difference between a daughter of God in the faith community, and a daughter of God in the world. There are so many hardships and fractures in the fabric of both our faith culture and the world that often we cannot distinguish the person of faith from any other person.

How is a daughter of the King set apart from a woman living in and of the world? What makes her thrive? God sets his children apart, but he does not intend for them to set themselves aside from serving others, both inside and outside the community of faith and in the world. In and through Christ, God enables his children to live and serve. Therefore, a daughter of the King is a servant— broken, yet being made whole through her relationship with him and with others. She is in relationship with our heavenly Father, and she is also in relationship with those around her, whether a spouse, child, parent, sibling, friend, coworker, authority, church leader, or any other person God has established in her range of experience.

Through relationships, some broken and some healed, I have learned that God created us to be in relationship with him and one another. As a daughter of the King, the Father of all relationships, the center of his plan for all humankind is to love and be loved, first by him, and then by others. The world is a broken affair, and so are all the people in it. This is the gospel message for all people God sent his Son to save. God uses relationships to reveal our sin, allowing our rough edges to be smoothed by one another in relationship. In the world and in our communities of faith, we are first and foremost broken people. God shows us that we need a Savior.

The broken relationships in my life with my family of origin have been most hurtful. I thought I could work hard enough to make them better. It was only when I relied upon God and not myself that my relationships were at a place where God could work in my life. He showed me how I needed to be in relationship with him and with others.

When God is the center of our lives and interests, he uses all things for his glory, especially in our relationships. This includes relationships with those we live with, work with, and associate with through the community, church, work, and school. In fact, relating to those around us is significant for maturing us through

God's transforming work of Jesus Christ. When we are yielded to Jesus and one another, our hearts are humble and repentant, and we have the courage to be who we were created to be. When I was young and hurt by family relationships, I did not know a huge part of myself. I was lonely and afraid, ashamed and withdrawn, and not repentant, or courageous. Yet, God placed many people along my path who demonstrated encouragement and love in their hearts. As I began understanding the truth in God's Word, I began believing fewer and fewer lies of the Devil. I was not as afraid to live.

God uses our brokenness, which is deep and buried in shame, to bring us home. He shows us who he is and what he has done for us, and then he shows us how to love others and ourselves. He shows us this particularly in the broken places being made whole in him who broke himself so we may live wholly and fully in relationship with him. No longer having to fix what is broken, we can allow Jesus into our broken places and heal our broken relationships. God reigns in righteousness in the broken; he does not despise a broken and contrite heart: "My sacrifice, O God, is a broken spirit; a broken and contrite heart you, God, will not despise" (Ps. 51:17); he comes with good news for the broken-hearted to bind them up: "The Spirit of the Sovereign Lord is on me, because the Lord has anointed me to proclaim good news to the poor. He has sent me to bind up the brokenhearted, to proclaim freedom for the captives and release from darkness for the prisoners" (Isa. 61:1).

It is not shameful to hurt. We can stand in God and give him the pain, and we can allow him into the broken places. He takes our shame and rolls it away, and in its place he gives us a double portion of blessings and honor: "Instead of your shame you will receive a double portion, and instead of disgrace you will rejoice in your inheritance. And so you will inherit a double portion in your land, and everlasting joy will be yours" (Isa. 61:7).

We need a Savior. He comes to bind us in him, cover our shame, make us right, replace the old with the new, and make us like him. God is the source of all that binds us, and especially what binds us to one another. He is the One and Only who indwells us and guides us in relationships. Just as he is the One who provides for us and is our rescue and strength on life journeys, through the power of the Holy Spirit, "Each one will be like a shelter from the wind and a refuge from the storm, like streams of water in the desert and the shadow of a great rock in a thirsty land" (Isa. 32:2).

Our great God determined our days on this earth and for eternity. His plan and purpose for each one of us is greater than we imagine. We are daughters of the King, the One and Only, who gave us breath for such a time as this. Our journey becomes one with those who also were given life on this earth for such a time as this!

People and the Life of Faith

Through our relationships and in our communities of faith, we experience the life of faith. Difficult people, loving people, and all the people in between come across our paths, and we are not equipped to relate to each one. But God is. We can fix our eyes on the problem person, or we can turn our focus to what God says counts. How am I to love this person? Why don't I want to interact with them? Will I please God in this situation? Do we need to be a doormat to every bully we encounter? Are we to be always available to a needy person who wants to monopolize our time? How are we to love them and honor them as God does with all his children?

Walking by faith requires that we take the next step while being solely dependent upon God. He guides us in each of these not-so-simple scenarios and relationships. Perhaps God wants us to deal with our own insecurities in wavering in the presence of a strong-headed and forceful person. Perhaps he wants us to be a friend to a needy person, but not necessarily a people pleaser, as opposed to being a God pleaser.

I have been a people pleaser most of my life. The bully demanded and won her way, and the needy person latched onto me. That happened because I did not want to make either unhappy with me. It was all self-focused, not necessarily other-focused. Yet God's perspective is that we are to love others because he loves us.

Perhaps God is trimming the rough edges off of us through our communities of faith and our relationships. A difficult family member can bring out the worst in us; God may allow this to help us remove planks out of our own eye: "You hypocrite, first take the plank out of your own eye, and then you will see clearly to remove the speck from your brother's eye" (Matt. 7:5). Or maybe God allows a selfish teammate at work who really gets under our skin to give us a glimpse of a similar trait in our own lives.

I spent many years focusing on behavior I did not want to do. This turned out to be terrible destruction. It was an unfruitful way to live. God wants to come into our lives so we can be the light and life for the world. With my sole focus on *not* being like this or that, I did not have my eyes on Jesus. He is the One who changes perspectives and the One and Only who can bring fruit from the transformation in my life. Until God turned my attention to the love and light of Jesus, I was fighting an old fight without the new life in my view. He is the One we seek, and through him we may have relationships honoring and reflecting our relationship with our great God.

God's Love Letter to Us

We are all the brokenhearted. We are all the captive. We are all the blind. Jesus has come for all of us in all our brokenness— not just broken hearts but in all the ways we are in bondage to sin.

When we do not have compassion for others, or when we do not want to serve the other person, we are blind to who we and they belong to. Either we are captive to our own sin of self-centeredness, and we do not know it, or our hearts are so broken we do not see the other person and we cannot empathize with their plight. Jesus came for each one of us and he is pursuing us with his wild and unfailing love. God's love letter to us is his inspired Word, the Bible. We learn of his journey with his people. We also learn how we are to know him and his plan for us—to give us a future and a hope with him: "For I know the plans I have for you," declares the Lord, "plans to prosper you and not to harm you, plans to give you hope and a future" (Jer. 29:11).

I have experienced some of the most wonderful moments in my walk of faith with those who have stood with me in the joy as well as the pain. Their faith, love, and support have been the words and arms of Jesus. God's presence became real in my midst through the very presence of these dear believers. My pain became their call to action through tears, warm embraces, and words of comfort. They came through their calls, their cards, and their being with me.

Recently I have walked through a most joyful time in my life. I have experienced the joy shared among friends who have been walking the walk of pain and struggle. They shared in my joy as if it were their own. There is nothing more profound or loving than knowing the pain one has and yet coming full on with their joy for you. Jesus comes through his people, and we know him through them.

We can never do this walk of faith alone, not without the Lord and not without others to shore one another up in the faith. People are an integral part of what God does with us in the walk of faith. He makes his presence known to us through others; he combines the voices and deeds of all of us to love and action for all the world to see. He not only makes us more dependent on him through our relationships with others, but he also uses our interdependence on one another in ways that are greater for the whole.

Glory and Arrows—Living in a Fallen World

What do we do about the arrows of rejection, fear, hatred, and other encounters with evil in our fallen world? God's Word says to stand, wear the full armor of God, and combat the arrows: "In addition to all this, take up the shield of faith, with which you can extinguish all the flaming arrows of the evil one" (Eph. 6:16).

God's glory is revealed in his creation and in us. He continues revealing his glory in order to make himself known to all people of the world. His revelation of Jesus, his Son and our Savior who was born over two thousand years ago, was prophesied and fulfilled through the covenant relationship God made. That covenant promised that the Messiah would come through the Hebrew people to save humankind.

Amidst God's glory are the attempts of the Evil One to hurt and maim us, and to foil God's plan. Yet Scripture assures us that none of God's purposes will be thwarted: "I know that you can do all things; no purpose of yours can be thwarted" (Job 42:2). As God's followers, we will be persecuted and suffer at the hands of the Enemy. God allows this for his glory; he has certain victory through his defeat of death.

How can God's glory be known through the arrows of rejection, fear, and hatred? This is the grand work of God. As his Word says in Paul's letter to the Romans, "We know that in all things God works for the good of those who love him, who have been called according to his purpose" (8:28). In Genesis 50:20, we find, "You intended to harm me, but God intended it for good to accomplish what is now being done, the saving of many lives." The arrows become the vehicle through which God reclaims and restores what was stolen from us and what was done to us.

We all suffer. We struggle through hard times and difficult circumstances. Sometimes we wonder what could be accomplished through a particular wound, betrayal, illness, failure, or loss. Only God knows. He does not inflict the wounds or cause the harm, but he uses them for his glory and our good. This means God's glory will be made known to another—in other words, someone will come to know him, and it could be that we come to know him or know him more. God does not waste anything.

How then should we live with the arrows? We must of course wear the armor of God:

> Finally, be strong in the Lord and in his mighty power. Put on the full armor of God, so that you can take your stand against the devil's schemes. For our struggle is not against flesh and blood, but against the rulers, against the authorities, against the powers of this dark world and against the spiritual forces of evil in the heavenly realms. Therefore put on the full armor of God, so that when the day of evil comes, you may be able to stand your ground, and after you have done everything, to stand. Stand firm then, with the belt of truth buckled around your waist, with the breastplate of

righteousness in place, and with your feet fitted with the readiness that comes from the gospel of peace. In addition to all this, take up the shield of faith, with which you can extinguish all the flaming arrows of the evil one. Take the helmet of salvation and the sword of the Spirit, which is the word of God (Eph. 6:10-17).

We live with the arrows by accepting God's truth and our right standing with him, our readiness to go forth in peace for all mankind, our faith in God as our shield, the salvation he has worked for us, and his mighty sword, the Word of God. However, after the arrow has penetrated and left its wound, and much later its scar, what must we do? We must allow God into our lives, especially in the places where we hurt. Sometimes we know an arrow is coming; other times, it happens out of the blue. God already knows. He is waiting on us to cry out for help. Our hurting places may become the means God uses to reveal himself to us in healing ways—ways far greater and better than we imagine. God has a plan for us at such a time as this. His ways are higher than our ways. The prophet Isaiah wrote, "As the heavens are higher than the earth, so are my ways higher than your ways and my thoughts than your thoughts" (55:9). As we trust God with the arrows and our broken places, including our own sin, the light of his truth and the love of his heart become the means by which we see him and his glory, made known in the flaming arrows of the Evil One.

God Meets Us in the Broken

Because God loves us and meets us in the broken, he pursues us, comes to us where we are, and meets with us. He created the earth and all that is in it, and when he breathed life into us, he made us in the image of himself. Yet, we wanted our own way, not God's way. Still, he loved us more. Jesus, the Father's only Son, born to us on earth, died a horrible death in our stead, and rose again, defeating death, so we can live with him eternally. As he leaves the earth, he sends the Holy Spirit to breathe new life into his children.

God heard his children cry and parted the Red Sea for them to walk across on dry land. Jesus walked on water to show the wonders of his great love for us. He heard the cries of the hearts of men. He loves us more.

Through the prophet Isaiah God told us he would send his Son to bind up the brokenhearted, to set the captives free, and to give sight to the blind. The proclamation is recorded in the gospel of Luke: "The Spirit of the Lord is on me, because he has anointed me to proclaim good news to the poor. He has sent me to proclaim freedom for the prisoners and recovery of sight for the blind, to set the oppressed free" (4:18). In the temple in Jerusalem, Jesus went to the front to speak and delivered these words from Isaiah. The promise is fulfilled in him. He loves us more.

In Jesus, God comes to us, saves us, breathes life into us, binds us up, and does whatever it takes for us to know him. He meets us in the broken because he loves us more!

GOD MEETS US IN THE BROKEN

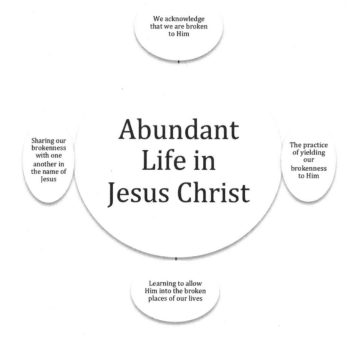

We acknowledge that we are broken to Him

Sharing our brokenness with one another in the name of Jesus

Abundant Life in Jesus Christ

The practice of yielding our brokenness to Him

Learning to allow Him into the broken places of our lives

Meeting and Collaborating with God Yields Transforming Work

When we allow God into our innermost being, where we are the most vulnerable, lost, despairing, and broken, he begins an amazing transformation in us. God works in our broken places. His strength is made perfect in weakness, according to the apostle Paul: "But he said to me, 'My grace is sufficient for you, for my power is made perfect in weakness.' Therefore I will boast all the more gladly about my weaknesses, so that Christ's power may rest on me" (2 Cor. 12:9). God's power resurrected Christ from the dead, and that same power is our strength. That is what Paul meant when he said God reveals his power in our weakness. Jesus allowed his own body to be crucified so we might live with him in eternity.

The Lord's work of displaying his divine love in our lives actually began while we were sinners. Jesus saw us in our brokenness as the joy set before him: "Therefore, since we are surrounded by such a great cloud of witnesses, let us throw off everything that hinders and the sin that so easily entangles. And let us run with perseverance the race marked out for us, fixing our eyes on Jesus, the pioneer and perfecter of faith. For the joy set before him he endured the cross, scorning its shame, and sat down at the right hand of the throne of God" (Heb. 12:1-2). We, the broken ones, are God's redeemed. He takes us as we are, and through our broken places shines his beautiful light.

As darkness is light in God, human brokenness yields life in Christ. His promises are true for all the broken. Jesus works in our brokenness to fulfill his promises, which will never fail, and to yield the harvest of hope and light through the life he gives in its stead. Our broken lives are exchanged for his holy and wholly abundant one.

- Our broken lives acknowledged to God by us and redeemed in Jesus Christ

- Our broken place offered to him becomes the place where we meet him

- Our broken lives yielded to him is a practice bringing health and healing

- Our broken lives shared with others become abundant lives

There is always brokenness in us, but through him and by him, hope and new life spring up from the very broken places where he meets us.

Broken Places—Where God Meets and Loves Us

God loves us despite and because of our brokenness, and he offers his grace. God's light shines through the broken places. The mystery of the gospel is that "God demonstrates his own love for us in this: While we were still sinners, Christ died for us" (Rom. 5:8). The Lord loved us enough to die for us. He offered brokenness in our place and poured himself out so we might live. An unfathomable and wonderful truth is that when we receive God's grace, his love and light live in us and pour out through us.

We are fully alive when receiving more of him in the broken places. He comes to fill where we cannot. And when he does, he then gives more and more. Therefore, it is through human brokenness that God gives abundant life to the full. It seems counterintuitive, yet in order to live the life God intended, we must acknowledge our brokenness and turn to him to save us from ourselves and our desire to fix ourselves. Christ's broken body resurrected from the dead becomes the life he wants for us, where our brokenness is resurrected through him living in us.

Not only does he make our brokenness our meeting place with him, but he also gives us himself in its stead. The steadfast and beautiful light of Jesus Christ lives within to remind us, teach us, and share with the world that in the broken, God creates transformation and wonder. The power through Jesus Christ increases through the steps of faith taken by his broken and faithful followers. The faith that has momentum is the faith of the ones walking by faith. Each step becomes a place where God meets and extends his arm to save, strengthen, love, and reveal his presence.

When acknowledged as something hindering one from God and acting upon by a step of faith in Jesus Christ, the broken place, the dark place, the place deep within finally gives over to Jesus. The mystery of the gospel is transformed into truth.

Jesus Christ broke himself for all so all could live life to the full. As we the community of faith share in each other's brokenness, we come together and are bound to one another by Jesus Christ in our broken-heartedness. He changes us through our suffering by drawing us to himself and creating a new place within that desires him more. The change in and through the broken places is new and alive, and it shines with the glory of Jesus Christ, the light of the world in and through us!

Broken—Being Right in Our Own Eyes

Being right in our own eyes is worse than being wrong in God's eyes. We have no rightness of our own; all sin is wrong to God. If we see ourselves as right on our own, we are prideful and not surrendered to God. He offers us his mercy, and when we receive the unwarranted gift of grace through Jesus Christ, he also divinely credits us with his own righteousness. It is only through this rightness of relationship with the Father through Jesus Christ that we have any rightness at all. On our own, we are surely capable only of self-righteousness. And yet another component of this gift of grace is that God himself, through his loving kindness, sees us only through the eyes of Jesus. That is to say he sees his own Son when he looks at us. God is holy and just and he cannot look upon sin; in his divine and merciful plan, he sees us as he sees Jesus. There is no rightness in our own eyes, only the rightness of Jesus. Through the Son's blood, we have a relationship with our Lord and Savior. The righteousness of Jesus becomes righteousness within us. He covers our sin and delivers us as right in God's eyes.

Being right in our own eyes is a form of brokenness, just the kind of brokenness from which Jesus came to rescue us. Though we present hard hearts, Jesus comes in love and truth to give us hope and life—hope in him for fullness and glory. This means we have a chasm in our souls that can only be filled with Jesus Christ. We yearn to be right with God, and we chase after all the things of this earth to be right but which will not fill us. He made us to need his fullness and glory, which he provides in Jesus Christ. We only have to give up our brokenness to gain his fullness. Let us go to him for our rightness and let him bind us up with his fullness and fill us up with himself—a gift beyond all others.

How God Answers Us—His Fullness for Our Brokenness

The life Jesus offers us is called the abundant life. He came to bind up our broken places and dwell within us to give us the completeness for which we yearn. He came to free us from our enslavement to the sin that keeps us from fellowship with him, to guide us when we cannot see, and to open our eyes when we live in darkness. "The Spirit of the Sovereign Lord is on me, because the Lord has anointed me to proclaim good news to the poor. He has sent me to bind up the brokenhearted, to proclaim freedom for the captives and release from darkness for the prisoners, to proclaim the year of the Lord's favor and the day of vengeance of our God, to comfort all who mourn" (Isa. 61:1-2).

How do we live the abundant life Jesus offers? We must acknowledge that Jesus is Lord and Savior and that we need him to direct our lives. We must change our direction, which is the meaning of repentance. We must change our attitudes and behavior regarding sin, and we must allow Christ in our hearts to love and guide us. And we must throw down whatever hinders us from the life God has given. The author of the book of Hebrews has written, "Since we are surrounded by such a great cloud of witnesses, let us throw off everything that hinders and the sin that so easily entangles. And let us run with perseverance the race marked out for us, fixing our eyes on Jesus, the pioneer and perfecter of faith. For the joy set before him he endured the cross, scorning its shame, and sat down at the right hand of the throne of God" (Heb. 12:1-2).

Why would Jesus offer us the abundant life? It is an unfathomable gift but, simply, he offered it to us because of his great love. His Word tells us he loves us unfailingly: "The Lord is compassionate and gracious, slow to anger, abounding in love" (Ps. 103:8).

We receive the abundant life when we come to faith in God. He gives us the fullness of himself in Jesus Christ. We experience his fullness as we depend on him and take one step of faith at a time. God rewards our steps of faith; the more we yield our broken places in the deep parts of us, the more we experience God. His fullness fills the cracks of our brokenness and emptiness. As we acknowledge our brokenness and allow him to work in our broken places, he meets us in the dark and carries us to the light in his presence. In time, we surrender our shattered pieces as we become more familiar with his Word, knowing his love and truth and replacing the lies we once believed. Because God offered his lovingkindness and faithfulness on dark days when we were right in our own eyes, we have received the gift of knowing him better and trusting him more—thus, the abundant life.

Tethered to Him by Choice

The deepness within us desires salvation. We only have to receive Jesus Christ, who knows our every whim and whimper, every tear, and each broken relationship in our lives. The deep brokenness within us shouts out to God for his remedy—Jesus. Only the Lord's love and truth bring healing and health to our lives.

God's children are tethered to him. We are not coerced, but we are pursued and held and carried by the Father as much as we choose to let him do so. "In all their distress he too was distressed, and the angel of his presence saved them. In his love and mercy he redeemed them; he lifted them up and carried them all the days of old" (Isa. 63:9). God fits us to him when we allow him into all of our nooks and crannies, into our deep and dark places, our barred-off places. He comes to dwell within, not forcing himself into any part of us we do not allow him in.

Not only does he hold us close, he also makes us his own for all the world to see. He makes us to stand out, to be noticeable, because he wants everyone to know him and his love. He clothes us with his gifts and robes us in salvation and righteousness, as the prophet Isaiah said: "I delight greatly in the Lord; my soul rejoices in my God. For he has clothed me with garments of salvation and arrayed me in a robe of his righteousness, as a bridegroom adorns his head like a priest, and as a bride adorns herself with her jewels" (Isa. 61:10). When we choose to wear the royal garments of the Almighty, we are the display of his splendor. He rewards us generously and repeatedly for being his children, a gift he has bestowed on us. He chooses to allow us this privilege because "in a desert land he found him, in a barren and howling waste. He shielded him and cared for him; he guarded him as the apple of his eye" (Deut. 32:10).

Receiving the Father's love and being held closely to him, we become new creatures covered in the newness of God inside and out. This covering becomes familiar as we wear it. As new creations, we are still vulnerable to the world's ways, so we must constantly shed whatever would take us away from God. The brokenness within us drives us to want to take over God's place in the heart. We just want it fixed our way right now. But that is not the way of God through Jesus Christ. Because we cannot save ourselves or fix ourselves, he has given us a new way.

In our brokenness, we are tethered to the Almighty. He takes us as we are. He loves us where we are. He comes close to hold and to carry us. He makes us into new people—even those of us bound and determined to fix things. His plan A is Jesus, and Jesus is for us. He comes to free us from ourselves and all that is broken within us, and to give us his new life and fullness only through him. His newness fits us. His love and truth fill us in the dark, broken, weary, and unsatisfied places.

Psalm 51:6—Truth in the Inmost Parts

"Yet you desired faithfulness even in the womb;

you taught me wisdom in that secret place."

The salve God has for us is sometimes painful, but it is always curing. It is the truth of his Word. It hits just the right spot and sears through wounds as it goes deep within, providing the healing effects that are necessary for health and recovery. God's Word touches the deepest parts of us when we least expect it. It is mystery and treasure, a mighty force of reckoning, and a healing salve to our brokenness.

Sometimes difficult and painful memories haunt us in the present because we have not dealt with them in the past. Hurtful words today also take us back to yesterday, when pain and despair were an everyday thing. When we present them to God, however, he deals with them one by one and applies his remedy. This is the way it goes with painful memories and words: We think of something hurtful and ruminate over it until we turn to God, who takes the thought and reminds us of who he is and what he has done. Eventually we hear God say we must turn this entirely over to him and, in doing so, we forgive the person in question, as well as ourselves. Many times we see ourselves as accountable for the hurtful event, and we often are. We could have done something to prevent the hurt. We should have seen it coming. While we are playing God in our lives, the real God reminds us we are his children and he is our Father. Our brokenhearted and empty places yearn for divine love, and yet we turn inward to fix them. When will we learn? But God, who is a gracious and compassionate God, one slow to anger and abounding in love, a God who relents from sending calamity (Jonah 4:2), comes again to our rescue with his truth and love.

In the fifty-first psalm, David turns to God and repents of his wrongdoing. After he committed adultery with Bathsheba, David writes, "Have mercy on me, O God ... Wash away all my iniquity and cleanse me from my sin. For I know my transgressions, and my sin is always before me." It is a beautiful song describing authentic pain and remorse for his actions against the Lord. He says a remarkable thing in verse six, which resonates over and over because it is the truth in God's Word for us: "Yet you desired faithfulness even in the womb; you taught me wisdom in that secret place." God desires that we have his truth in our inmost places. When we have God's Truth, we have his life and healing. The image that comes to me is the application of salve on a deep wound or cut. I even imagine dark crevices hidden to us, and places we do not allow ourselves or anyone else to know about or reckon with. God's salve is for every part of us, and when we allow him there, we experience his full and abiding love piercing us and making us fully alive.

There are things we drive way down in our secret places, such as hurtful memories tucked away so we do not think about them anymore, embarrassing moments that caused us pain when we were young, and times when we despaired because we had no dream or hope of one. God knows each painful memory and is waiting to turn the difficult times into wonderful ones. David wrote, "My heart is not proud, Lord, my eyes are not haughty; I do not concern myself with great matters or things too wonderful for me. But I have calmed and quieted myself, I am like a weaned child with its mother; like a weaned child I am content. Israel, put your hope in the Lord both now and forevermore" (Ps. 131). Putting our hope in the Lord is not a quick fix or magical thinking, but God will remedy the difficult and painful times by his power and love in all the broken places.

"Truth in the Inmost Parts (Psalm 51:6)—A Poem"

Truth to my broken
secret
dark
walls

Comfort to my sorrow
rejection
loneliness
grief

Courage to my new
beginning
ending
spacious place

Strength in my struggle
Calm in my anxious
Peace as no other gives

Allow my broken and empty, scared and weak
The place where you call my name (Isaiah 45:3)
Come Holy Spirit into every piece of me

The Way of Healing

God loves us and relentlessly pursues us through our work, family, friends, and church, and still we are holding back. Perhaps we are seeing for the first time. We hear him, know him, love him, and we want to know him better. Yet, we hurt, and we don't know why. Things that used to satisfy us no longer do; other things do not measure up.

We see hurt in the faces of our children, and we know this hurt. Mothers believe they should be able to keep their kids from hurting, or at least be able to comfort them. But we cannot. It seems that no matter what we try or how often we pray for God's intervention, things do not get better. The pain continues, and we are impotent in our child's life—and often in our own.

God is God of all the broken things in the world. He is the One who binds us up and holds us up, and he continues holding us tethered to him to guide, protect, comfort, heal, free, and love with an everlasting love. We are the broken, the imprisoned, the sightless, and we will continue living in darkness until we allow God into our lives. He knows us and will take all of our broken pieces and give us new lives set free to live in wholeness and abundance. But it all starts with the acknowledgement that we are broken.

We cannot know God until we recognize our own need. And we will not know him until we acknowledge we need him. In fact, he is all we need. He requires that we choose him, and then he comes into our lives. God's life breathed into his children is the transformation that attracts the broken to the maker of wholeness and healing.

This need for the healing we all require can only be met by God in Jesus Christ. In order to demonstrate the way of healing, we can consider our relationship with Jesus. If we have deep wounds and allow God into the dark crevices of our broken places, he does what only he can do. He applies the salve of love and truth while transforming our brokenness into a conduit through which to display the work of Jesus Christ in our lives. We are all connected to the One and Only through our brokenness. Only our Savior brings healing to the broken places. However, using our own brokenness as a way to point others to Christ, we may share connections with our community, family, and those we meet along the way of life.

The gospel points to our deep need for connectedness with our heavenly Father through Jesus Christ. We believe and grow in the knowledge of Jesus Christ and his love and truth. And in him we share our brokenness as the community of faith, and by his presence and work in our midst we rise up to live full and abundant lives.

What will Blame and Shame Gain?

There are things in life too complicated to understand. Another's struggles, particularly a family member's pain, are usually not problems we can fix. However, we can share in the pain of another. There are many things for which we share blame and for which we are to blame. Yet, we can come to know the One of whom we ask forgiveness for all the things for which we are to blame. As a result of God's grace, we can receive the rest from our shame. The Lord carries the blame and the shame for us, and he is the One who forgives us. He has taken our sin and cleansed us of it. We will be hurt, but we are not ashamed to hurt. We will be blamed, and we will be sorrowful, but in his grace we no longer carry shame.

Jesus stands in our place. He rescued us from shame and blame, including all that is unfair. He has won the victory over all of our sin, once and for all. Though perfect, Jesus died in shame from the blame heaped upon him. We lay claim to his gain for us. Our Savior has rescued us from the blame that is ours and from the shame for our sin for this day and forever. In Jesus' name, no more shame, but gain for all believers everywhere.

A Clear Purpose as We Walk by Faith

Our purpose becomes clear through the walk of faith. We come to know God's love personified in the person of Jesus Christ. As we follow him, he makes his dreams known. We receive the love he has and we share in the journey he planned long before the foundation of the world.

The individual relationship we have with our Creator is a mystery that was prophesied and fulfilled through the coming of the Father's only Son, our Savior and Lord. It is only through the Son that we have life and life everlasting. Life everlasting begins with our decision to believe in and follow Christ and to receive the grace and truth of our Creator. His purposes and plans never fail; his purpose for us is to receive what he has already given and to remain in relationship with him throughout our time on earth. Through this relationship, we know God in a personal way and we become more like him as we mature in faith. And as we mature in faith, he becomes the purpose of our very lives.

From this personal relationship with our Creator and Savior pours forth the benefits to others placed in our midst whom we serve. When we love and serve God, we become the servants he calls us to be, loving with all our hearts, souls, minds, and strength, and loving others as ourselves. Our purpose in life is to love God as he first loved us—and to keep on loving him. He uses us to love one another and to love and serve those around us, including our family, friends, peers, community, world, and even our enemies. When we love them, we want to introduce them to the One in whom we find life. Our Savior's plan is for all to know and love him and to spend eternity with him. He gives us the privilege of loving and serving his people so they, too, may know and love him—and spend eternity with him.

What is our purpose for such a time as this? Just as God pursues us and loves us, we are to seek him with our whole heart. He will show us the purpose for which he created us. The very life for which we are searching is within our grasp and in his arms.

God's heart—His Private Transformation in Us to our Public Proclamation of Him

"God's heart"

For us
Goes before, with, behind
In us
To teach, comfort, and guide

Loves us
Rescues, restores, rebuilds
Pursues us
To save, hold, and keep forever

Treasures us
Gives us his Son, One and Only, perfect, fully God and fully man
Shows us
The wonder of his great love

Merciful to us
Reaches down from heaven to rescue us
Provides us
With grace, the way to live with him forever

Compassionate with us, kind, and
Abounding in love for us
His heart for us
Makes us the apple of his eye

Erases our sin and shame
When he gives us Jesus
Believe and receive him
God's heart becomes ours

No more threat of shame, dishonor
Disappointment or despair
What a sight to see
God's heart in me

From Private Release from Shame to Public Praise of the Author

"Starts with a Hurt Word"

Starts with a hurt word
Turned inward at first
Covered by shame
Twisted becomes pain

It's not the hurt anymore
Shame hidden at core
Blame heaped upon pain
Until one knows not the source

The accuser attempts again
With slurs, jabs, and disdain
In my defense I argue
Only to go under farther

No more I say to the liar
I have an advocate, my Father
Not only is He the holy and just
Victory is his; Satan, you're but dust

From blame to shame
Accuser is his name
No more shame from hurt and pain
In my Savior I have double the gain

Double portion Isaiah quotes
In him we have the most
Instead of shame we have double
The gain as he rescues us from trouble

He covers our sin and shame
Hidden in him our gain
Double the portion we sing his name
For he is mine and I am his forever

"Double Portion (Isaiah 61)"

In private, he removes my shame!
In public, he allows me this privilege of sharing his name.

He is my portion
Abundance from above
Christ Jesus, it is he
Life to the full for me

Heart bound by his own
Freeing my eyes to see
Not only my pain gone
Jesus' face of love alone

He came to earth to die
Rose on the third to life
Shedding my shame
Life of freedom gained

Jesus comes to save
And to earth he gives heaven
Double apportioned
To the ashamed, despairing

Double portion it is
Life in his without shame
Life lived through him
Singing his praise

His Great Love

To be able to share in the wonders of God's great love is to know personally our heavenly Father and Savior. He takes our broken hearts and pours out his love to us. In the broken places, God mends and restores, rescues and rebuilds, and takes away the destructive ways and replaces them with his brand new life-affirming ways.

Knowing him is being vulnerable to his heart and allowing him into the broken places, even those places we haven't allowed ourselves. We cannot know him and be hardened to his ways. He wants us to expect him to show us the wonders of his great love, because it is indeed what he has done for us. Through his Son, he has done the wonderful—once and for all time.

Our guarded natures have no place with our Creator, Savior, and Lord. Yet, we hide in our shame and respond in our disappointment. We try going back to our old ways of closing ourselves off, controlling our lives (so we think), and living independently from him. We find it does not work out well. We need a Savior. We need our relationship with him as he designed it.

In order to know the wonders of his great love, we must know him on an individual level. He is the wonder. His heart of unfailing love pursues us. He comes to us when we seek him with all of our hearts. When we allow him in and choose to trust him, he gives us his saving grace, the gift of righteousness. In the place of our hurt, shame, sin, unforgiveness, and depravity, he gives us honor. Our hearts become like new, because a righteous, just, and holy God has claimed them. Only he can give a gift like this one.

He is the One and Only, and he gives the main thing we desire—the rightness of a relationship with him. God's great love for us is the most magnificent gift and the greatest wonder of all.

All Good Gifts

All good gifts come from our heavenly Father: "Every good and perfect gift is from above, coming down from the Father of the heavenly lights, who does not change like shifting shadows"

(James 1:17). In Christ he comes, saves, and graces us with unfathomable power and love. A relationship with the Father of heavenly lights is what our hearts desire, and yet we tend to go elsewhere to fill the void. God in his infinite wisdom, love, and mercy gives us a void only he can fill. All good gifts come from him in his Son, Jesus. All honoring relationships are good gifts from God—consider David's relationship with Jonathan, Mary's relationship with Elizabeth, Paul's relationship with Timothy, and many others.

God covers, gifts, guides, teaches, and encourages us through many different people. From our family of origin to this day, God has provided persons to influence our lives for the good. There are those who will guide, protect, love, and encourage us as we serve God in the world. There is no mistaking his intentionality in this as we have all received huge blessings through God-ordained relationships in our lives. God brought many faithful Christian women through my own growing up years so I would see what he wanted me to become as a woman and as his daughter. These women were my mentors and friends who knew about the encumbrances of my earlier years and who acted as my encouragers and confidantes through difficult as well as joyful times. They stood in the gap for me to grow and mature into the woman God planned for me to become. He bestowed on me good gifts that I in turn offer to others on their journey to help and sustain them along the way. When we bless others with the good gifts God has given us, we in turn know the Blessed One more intentionally and more abundantly.

Canopies

Tall trees with their branches and leaves in the air stretch across our view and form a canopy, a protection of sorts, for shade and for beauty. It makes us think of other canopies. Do we as the body of Christ form a canopy over one another, shielding each other from going it alone or providing for ourselves what we could not provide without the community of faith? Perhaps during the hard times we are the protective covering needed for our brothers and sisters of the faith as they walk through dark times, seasons of pain and suffering, and also circumstances too difficult to bear on one's own without the help of another.

Trees stand tall. Their branches receive from the tree trunk what they need to grow and produce leaves and fruit. If we stand firm in the One and Only and receive from him what we need to grow, we can also produce a canopy with others for the covering, shade, and protection of one another in Christ. He is the source, and we may become the vehicle by which he delivers love and kindness, protection and refuge, and truth and strength to stand in joy through tough times.

We yearn to grow in God, to stand tall and firm in him, and to live in love and truth with one another. We receive from him and pour out through him what the world needs. Our heavenly Father in Christ Jesus gives us himself so we can know him and live out his love and truth for the sake of the world. This is his purpose and ours.

Each one will be like a shelter from the wind and a refuge from the storm, like streams of water in the desert and the shadow of a great rock in a thirsty land. (Isa. 32:2)

The Rewards of Faith

The reward for a life of walking by faith is real and abundant. It is life to the full. In a life of faith, God gives us the wherewithal to keep on keeping on when times get hard. The writer of the New Testament book of Hebrews tells us, "Do not throw away your confidence; it will be richly rewarded" (10:35). As we hold onto our confidence in the faith, and as we believe in the promises of God and their fulfillment in our lives, we become the Christ-followers he created us to be. "Blessed is she who has believed that the Lord would fulfill his promises to her!" intoned Elizabeth (Luke 1:45).

God is faithful in all he does. He fulfills his promises and never forsakes us. Furthermore, he gives momentum to our steps of dependence on him. He grows our faith as we take small steps. Not only that, he increases the impact of our small steps for the Kingdom. As we trust in God's faithfulness, he takes our tiny offerings and uses them for heaven's glory. The gospel message is that because Jesus died and lives again, we may serve with clean consciences, pure hearts, and with the truth and love within us that only Christ can impart. As vessels of his making and empowering, we offer back the treasure he bestows.

At times the true believer is hard pressed to stand and deliver the good news message. But God creates new expectations and rescues his children who are persecuted and strained when they continue calling on and pressing forward with him. Through these experiences of walking by faith, God enables us to stand and depend on him. We know God better, take hold of the promises he has made, and remember who God is and what he has done. The rewards of growing the tiny mustard seed of faith and knowing God better are just the beginning. In his faithfulness, God continues the rewards to his faithful children in ways we cannot imagine.

God bestows more of himself as we entrust more of ourselves to him. His more is infinite, and he enjoys supplying it.

"God is Faithful"

God is faithful
He never leaves
Nor forsakes us
He is our reward

He gives us faith
Increases our steps
In hard times and pain
He comes to our rescue

His children take his hand
They let him lead them
To the infinite supply
He has in store

Keep on keeping on
With hearts fixed upon him
His reward is waiting   ·
And abundantly more

"The Momentum of Faith"

He is the power in my steps
He is the love in my choices
He is the truth in my words
He is the action in my deeds

He is the hearing in my listening
He is the sight in my seeing
He is the heart of our hearts
Wonder of wonders—collaboration with God.

Come as you are, broken and empty
A vessel waiting for purpose
Carrying you, no help he needs
From you. He has given all for you.

Wake up, arise, shake off the dust
Clothe in the new for he lives
In you and you are alive
With purpose, his. Come.

Power in my steps, love in my choices
Truth in my words, action in my deeds
Hearing in my ears, sight for my eyes
Heart of my heart, wonderful Jesus.

Come as you are
Broken and empty
He is waiting
To give you his all

The momentum of faith is the extension of God's arm. In our brokenness, we allow him to carry us and be his vessels, frail as we are, for his purpose and plan for all the world to see. As we allow God's steps in us, our vessels are strong because he lives in us, for all the world to see.

"Call from Above"

Call from above
Turn my ear; lift my soul
To receive from you
Word of heart impart

Give yes to me
Answer you with all
Inside transform
To pour love out

Broken places
New you impart
Piece by piece
You remold my heart

Share my shattered
Dreams and inside
The vessel treasure
For him it mattered

Tiny steps, forward momentum
Walking by faith
Collaborate with God
God moves mountains

"Oh, that I Would Hear Your Voice"

Oh, that I would hear your voice
Revive a fire within
Satisfy a longing
Give me a word

Show me how to pray
To ask, seek, find
With you at the helm
And I at your feet

If I speak of you, Lord
Allow me to love first
Shine forth you in me
Only you and you alone

I ask for your favor
The energy rekindled for you
Satisfying my soul
Heart full in response

Father, friend, and faithful Lord
Allow my steps to be bold
With eyes focused on you
My heart transformed by your love

More than Enough—His Portion for Us

God promises to give us a "double portion" as foretold by the prophet, Isaiah, in 61:7: "Instead of your shame you will receive a double portion, and instead of disgrace you will rejoice in your inheritance. And so you will inherit a double portion in your land, and everlasting joy will be yours." Instead of our shame, we will have double the gain. Jesus came to fulfill this prophecy. What does it mean? God's promises are true, and he never fails to give us what he said he would. It is certain that Jesus is much more and gave us much more than we can comprehend. Yet, what does "Instead of your shame you will receive a double portion" really mean? Jesus came so that we would not be shamed any longer, so we would not be enslaved to sin. He came so we could live freely and become what God intended us to be. What is the Lord's intention in his double portion for us?

Instead of our shame, God came in the flesh for us to know the power and grace of the Lord Jesus Christ—and not have to live up to the law, which of course we cannot do. Why? Because no one can live up to the law. Shame follows when we attempt to follow the law; we can only be enslaved by it. God intends for us to follow him, to know him, and to know how much he wants to give us.

In the times of the prophet Isaiah (8th century BC), the double portion inheritance was the portion given to the eldest son. God promises his children an inheritance double to that of their shame. While the shame of our old lives as sinners before our lives in Christ is large, God promised an inheritance twice the size of our shame. As we come to know the Father and the Son better, we receive the power and grace only the Holy Spirit can bestow. In doing so, we know the great God of the universe who is unfathomably gracious and giving. His generosity cannot be matched, and he wants us to experience what knowing, loving, and serving him is all about. The relationship the God of Israel wants with all of his children is demonstrated in Jabez crying out, "Oh, that you would bless me and enlarge my territory! Let your hand be with me, and keep me from harm so that I will be free from pain" (1 Chron. 4:10). This is a cry to know God, to believe him, and to receive the bounty he has stored up for those who follow him. The aim of our heavenly Father is that we personally know the giver of life and blessings, and to be part of his intention for the world.

"Awake, Put on Your Garments of Splendor, and Be Free"

Awake, awake, Zion,
clothe yourself with strength!
Put on your garments of splendor,
Jerusalem, the holy city.
The uncircumcised and defiled
will not enter you again.
Shake off your dust;
rise up, sit enthroned, Jerusalem.
Free yourself from the chains on your neck,
Daughter Zion, now a captive (Isa. 52:1-2)

The Word of God is true. Jesus died in order for us to live fully alive and awake in him, to be clothed with strength in him, and to be free in him. We have removed the chains from around our necks. God's promises are true, and they will always be true.

He is God, and there is no other. We can believe in him, and we can believe him, because God does not lie or change his mind.

We are wholly known and loved in Christ, and we are ready to rise up in faith. He clothes us in the new and frees us to live as he intended, before the creation of the world. It is an act of faith to live fully in Christ, to be wholly known and loved, and to walk with him in faith. It is also an act of faith to wear the new garments and to display his love and splendor as we live out the love he has poured upon us. We are to arise, dress in the splendor he has provided, put on the new, and know we are free to be the people he has created us to be.

Garments of the Lord for Us to Wear for His Renown

"I delight greatly in the Lord; my soul rejoices in my God. For he has clothed me with garments of salvation and arrayed me in a robe of his righteousness, as a bridegroom adorns his head like a priest, and as a bride adorns herself with her jewels" (Isa. 61:10). God gives us his garments, including the robe of righteousness. He gives this out of mercy for us. We must wear it, for with it, he enables us to receive. He equips us to believe; he helps us trust him. Without God's mercy and power, we could not receive, believe, or trust. We would not become righteous, nor could we wear the robe of righteousness.

Because God gives us his garments, we can become our truest selves by wearing them and walking by faith in them.

Walking by Faith, We WEAR what He Gives Us

W Wired to know God, we become our truest selves by wearing what he gives us

Wide open to being clothed in the new

E Enter into God's presence for peace, joy, and victory

Expecting God

A Abide, remain, choose to be with him

Allowing him in to lead and love

R Rightly related to the Father by Christ

Running to him with all

By his mercy, we are his! Because we are his, we wear the mystery of God. He wires us with a deep need, which he satisfies and fills. He does this through our personal relationship with him. We have a deep need to be with him and to know him, the One who knows us.

From No More Shame to Proclaiming His Name

The prophet Isaiah tells us that the Spirit of the Sovereign Lord anoints us "to comfort all who mourn, and provide for those who grieve in Zion—to bestow on them a crown of beauty instead of ashes, the oil of joy instead of mourning, and a garment of praise instead of a spirit of despair." Isaiah continues, "I delight greatly in the Lord; my soul rejoices in my God. For he has clothed me with garments of salvation and arrayed me in a robe of his righteousness, as a bridegroom adorns his head like a priest, and as a bride adorns herself with her jewels" (Isa. 61:2-3; 10).

We are clothed in the Lord with these things as "a planting of the Lord for the display of his splendor."

- Crown of beauty
- Garment of praise
- Garment of salvation
- Robe of righteousness

As daughters of our most high God, we step out:

- By his grace
- In faith
- By his righteousness
- For his glory

- Enabled by the Holy Spirit

We step out to the acknowledgement of who he is and whose we are, so the world may know the Sovereign Lord.

Becoming Who We Already Are

Deep inside, an inner voice tells us we can be more. We are more. Sometimes we stop listening to the inner voice only to give in to whatever is comfortable and familiar. We resist change. The inner voice becomes noise in the background. Yet as God's children, we know we are guarded as "the apple of his eye" (Deut. 32:10) and kept as "the apple of your eye," hidden in the shadow of his wings (Ps. 17:8). Not only does the Lord favor us, but his love endures forever and he does not abandon the work of his hands (Ps. 138:8). And the New Testament also says, "He who began a good work in you will carry it on to completion until the day of Christ Jesus" (Phil. 1:6).

As children of God, we walk with Him not to continue to pursue our own paths, but to follow his. As we do, God's heart, which is rich in mercy, beckons our hearts to yield to him. We know his great love and we want to be in his presence. He changes our hearts to be like his while we stay close. He made us and knows our very frame. He also knows our every step in and out of faith. As our sovereign and faithful Father God, he develops us into who he created us to be.

It is his voice we hear when we know we are more. He made us to be more than we see, and more than we know. Being a daughter of our loving Father God is a privilege beyond measure. God has so much he wants to share with us. All we have to do is approach God and follow him. If, however, we do not first decide that he is Lord, his bounty is beyond our reach. But with the decision to accept him, he blesses his daughters and sons with himself and all his abundance.

With him, we are not left to our own notions of who we are and what life has to offer. Instead, our Savior and Creator is the Lord of our lives who guides, teaches, transforms, and leads us on his path and plan for our lives. And all the while, we experience his riches and bounty during the journey. He develops us into those he knew before creation.

God's clear design and intention is for us to become who we already are. As we come to know him and his voice, we become the creations we already are for his glory.

The Depths of God

"Oh, the depth of the riches of the wisdom and knowledge of God! How unsearchable his judgments, and his paths beyond tracing out! "Who has known the mind of the Lord? Or who has been his counselor?" "Who has ever given to God, that God should repay them?" For from him and through him and for him are all things. To him be the glory forever! Amen" (Rom. 11:33-36).

We could not fully understand our Father God even if we tried. This is not to say he does not reveal hidden things to us, especially in his written revelation. Indeed, the great mystery of God in Christ was that over two thousand years ago he stepped from behind the veil and became incarnate as a baby in a manger in Bethlehem. God is the author of creation and time, even though he works outside the parameters of time. When the time is right according to our sovereign God, he shows us himself and brings to light the things he planned before the foundation of the world.

"As the heavens are higher than the earth, so are my ways higher than your ways and my thoughts than your thoughts," we are told in Isaiah 55:9. And yet, through the Son God allows us to know who he is and what he says he will do. The apostle Paul reveals in his letter to the Ephesians (3:1-13) God's plan for humankind through his Son, Jesus.

> For this reason I, Paul, the prisoner of Christ Jesus for the sake of you Gentiles—Surely you have heard about the administration of God's grace that was given to me for you, that is, the mystery made known to me by revelation, as I have already written briefly. In reading this, then, you will be able to understand my insight into the mystery of Christ, which was not made known to people in other

generations as it has now been revealed by the Spirit to God's holy apostles and prophets. This mystery is that through the gospel the Gentiles are heirs together with Israel, members together of one body, and sharers together in the promise in Christ Jesus. I became a servant of this gospel by the gift of God's grace given me through the working of his power. Although I am less than the least of all the Lord's people, this grace was given me: to preach to the Gentiles the boundless riches of Christ, and to make plain to everyone the administration of this mystery, which for ages past was kept hidden in God, who created all things. His intent was that now, through the church, the manifold wisdom of God should be made known to the rulers and authorities in the heavenly realms, according to his eternal purpose that he accomplished in Christ Jesus our Lord. In him and through faith in him we may approach God with freedom and confidence. I ask you, therefore, not to be discouraged because of my sufferings for you, which are your glory.

Do we apply the wisdom of these verses to our lives? Or, when we do not understand God's path or his judgments, do we sometimes cry out, "Why?" or "What are you doing?" To question God's motives or actions does not help us trust Him. He desires that we come to him with all of our emotions—from nagging questions to all-out despair. What is helpful is to seek him out, know him better, and allow his heart to join with ours by remaining close to him.

We will not understand God's motives all of the time, but if our hearts are in order we are able to trust the God of the Bible. He shares with us who he is and what he says he will do, which is to love us and never leave us. And when we trust the God of the Bible, remarkable things happen not only within us but also in our surroundings. Perhaps they are remarkable because our view has changed. Either way, God shows us that he is God, that he is good, and that he is enough. God shows us by way of contrast that we are not enough. How much greater it is that he has wired us to know him, the One and Only, and to have access to all of the Father through Jesus Christ the Son.

So it is as he has said. He is God, and there is no other. He is to be praised even when we do not understand, or when we think we do, or when we still have questions. When we do agree, he takes our very tiny steps and shows us his glory, to which there is no end.

God is Greater than Our Hearts

"If our hearts condemn us, we know that God is greater than our hearts, and he knows everything" (1 John 3:20). Sometimes, when we have confessed a sin and turned away from it, it keeps making us feel askew and abnormal inside. But God knows our hearts well, and when his Holy Spirit resides in us, there is no condemnation.

"God is greater than our hearts" is true, and it makes sense. God is greater than anything about us. But when it comes to our hearts, we hold them tighter. We think that if there is condemnation in our hearts, God must still hold the sin against us. Yet this is not the truth. "If our hearts condemn us, we know that God is greater than our hearts, and he knows everything." Also, the apostle Paul testifies in Romans 8:1, "Therefore, there is now no condemnation for those who are in Christ Jesus."

If we continue thinking we are all bad or not doing enough to remove our sin, we are not trusting God with who he says he is and what he says he does. God has forgiven us of all our past, present, and future sins. There is nothing we can do to persuade him to erase our sin, because he has already erased our sin when we chose to follow him. In fact, we will never deserve God's free gift of grace. He gives it, and at the same time he invites us to trust him.

"If our hearts condemn us, we know that God is greater than our hearts, and he knows everything" (1 John 3:20). This Scripture gives us a heads up that God already knows the condition of our hearts, and we cannot make them right on our own. Nor are we to judge them. Our sins do not go away in trying to make them go away. Rather, they go away when we trust our Father God in Jesus Christ to do the transformation in us. In other words, we must let go of our hearts and let God make them into the kind of hearts he designed—hearts that are new, that love him, and that trust him wholeheartedly. The heart that Jesus transforms is one that has courage, and one that lets him break it in order to make it whole. God cautions us before giving us new hearts in Christ Jesus. We no longer as his daughters and sons hold onto our divided or deceitful hearts. He has given us new hearts, and we now have the capacity to be loving, whole, courageous, and fully surrendered.

If we hold onto Christ, he will give us the rest and peace we long for when our hearts are restless, broken, wrenched, and torn apart. God takes all things and makes them new—that is, if we let him. The new may not be as we anticipated. He is greater than our imaginations can conjure. His ways are not our own. When we cannot love as we hoped we could, he changes us. He arrives as we cry out in anguish over a hurtful past. He gives us more than we think we can handle, but he is with us and will not let us go. His timing is always right and our hearts can always rest in his. God is greater than our hearts, and he knows everything.

God's Gift of Righteousness

"Righteousness goes before him and prepares the way for his steps" (Ps. 85:13). God rewards us with His righteousness when we follow Jesus as our Lord and Savior. We cannot come to rightness with God without the gift of God's grace through His Son, Jesus Christ. It is only by this gift, undeserved and free, that we may have peace with our God, who is holy yet accessible through the sacrificial lamb of his only Son, Jesus. God credits us, his children, with a right relationship with him when we choose to accept his Son, his gift of grace, his unmerited favor toward us.

This is God's way in our lives. We cannot earn or achieve peace and a right relationship. We must surrender and follow. He is our lead. He was first our Creator, then our Savior and Redeemer, and now he is our Lord. In order to be in right relationship with him, and for him to see us as holy and blameless (that is the only way we can be in relationship with him), we must surrender our lives.

We are not able to surrender our lives without the Lord's help, however. He gives us the capacity through the divine call on our lives and his indwelling of the Holy Spirit in us. God gives his children a way to call him Father, and then he gives us the capacity to trust and obey his call and commands.

As God's offspring and children of the promise, we are called to be "right" with our Creator. Then God calls us to a journey where he has ordered the steps and goes before us. He goes with us in the journey and behind us after it. We have to walk in his steps and keep on keeping on. Rightness with God gives us the way, and walking in his steps gives us the life. It is a life prepared, known, and planned by our loving Father just for his beloved.

The Blessing of Our Loving Father God

"The Lord bless you and keep you; the Lord make his face shine on you and be gracious to you; the Lord turn his face toward you and give you peace" (Num. 6:24-26). Our loving God always makes himself available to us. And when we allow him to teach us who he is and how he loves us, he continues rewarding us with kindness. We continue growing in God's love as we continue receiving it.

The Lord's blessing is so important to our lives. As his offspring, we live in his blessing. We may not know or receive it, however, as he would like us to receive it. He wants us to look toward him as a flower looks toward the sun—not only receiving the nourishment it needs for daily existence and growth, but also for the warmth and presence of God that makes life itself possible.

God's face, grace, and blessing are tantamount to a life in Christ Jesus. We would not be able to turn our hearts to the Lord without his turning his face to us. This is as true today just as it was when the Father sent the Son to be born on earth, to die for the sins of the world, and to return to heaven to be at the Father's right hand. As we go to Christ for life to the full, we cannot go without his favor and blessing. He makes it possible to come in confidence that he is waiting to shine on us and to give us the grace and faith we need to turn our faces toward him. We trust him to be able to do it time and time again.

Thank you, Jesus

for shining your face upon us to enable us to come.

We praise you that you have given us the great blessing of your presence in our lives. For without you, we could not and would not turn toward you. Please help us to keep looking to you and for your face, grace, blessing, and peace.

Amen.

God's Healing

As children of the King, do we have broken places, or are we held captive to things from our past? Do we feel there are dark crevices in the soul screaming for hope? In order to thrive as daughters, we must receive the Good News. According to the prophet Isaiah, the Servant of the Lord came "to open eyes that are blind, to free captives from prison and to release from the dungeon those who sit in darkness" (Isa. 42:7). He is with us and he will never leave us. As believers, we must allow him access to the places where we are broken, imprisoned, or living in darkness.

THE YEAR OF THE LORD'S FAVOR

"The Spirit of the Sovereign Lord is on me, because the Lord has anointed me to proclaim good news to the poor. He has sent me to bind up the brokenhearted, to proclaim freedom for the captives and release from darkness for the prisoners, to proclaim the year of the Lord's favor and the day of vengeance of our God, to comfort all who mourn, and provide for those who grieve in Zion—to bestow on them a crown of beauty instead of ashes, the oil of joy instead of mourning, and a garment of praise instead of a spirit of despair. They will be called oaks of righteousness, a planting of the Lord for the display of his splendor.

"They will rebuild the ancient ruins and restore the places long devastated; they will renew the ruined cities that have been devastated for generations. Strangers will shepherd your flocks; foreigners will work your fields and vineyards. And you will be called priests of the Lord, you will be named ministers of our God. You will feed on the wealth of nations, and in their riches you will boast.

"Instead of your shame you will receive a double portion, and instead of disgrace you will rejoice in your inheritance. And so you will inherit a double portion in your land, and everlasting joy will be yours.

"For I, the Lord, love justice; I hate robbery and wrongdoing. In my faithfulness I will reward my people and make an everlasting covenant with them.

"Their descendants will be known among the nations and their offspring among the peoples. All who see them will acknowledge that they are a people the Lord has blessed."

"I delight greatly in the Lord; my soul rejoices in my God. For he has clothed me with garments of salvation and arrayed me in a robe of his righteousness, as a bridegroom adorns his head like a priest, and as a bride adorns herself with her jewels. For as the soil makes the sprout come up and a garden causes seeds to grow, so the Sovereign Lord will make righteousness and praise spring up before all nations" (Isa. 61:1-11).

In the sixty-first chapter of Isaiah, the prophet speaks of the year of the Lord's favor where he adorns his head like a priest, and as a bride adorns herself with her jewels. For as the soil makes the sprout come up and a garden causes seeds to grow, so the Sovereign Lord will favor. He was sent "to proclaim the year of the Lord's favor and the day of vengeance of our God, to comfort all who mourn, and provide for those who grieve in Zion." As God's children, we are living in the year of his favor. He brings us good news in Christ. Jesus came to bind us up where we are broken, including especially our hearts. God sent Jesus into our lives for eternity. He is here to heal us, give us freedom, and reveal himself to us. The Father also sent the Son to give us hearts and eyes to know him.

Isaiah 61 are the beautiful words of Scripture Jesus read from the scroll in the temple (see Luke 4:16-21). Through him we may now know the good news of God's redemption. We may be healed, set free, and have sight where before we lived in darkness. In addition, Isaiah 61 tells us that in God's view—and ultimately in humanity's view also—we wear a crown of beauty, the oil of joy, and a garment of praise. We also wear the garment of salvation and a robe of righteousness, because we have been made right with God through Jesus. In the future, as God through Jesus transforms us, we become his oaks of righteousness for the display of his splendor. He works in us and grows us up to be grand old oaks from the tiny seeds he planted in us. And the best news is that he does it for the display of his splendor so the entire world can know him.

But that is not all God does through his Son. He takes all of our sin and brokenness and develops us into the children we were designed to be. As thriving daughters of God, God uses our broken places, our imprisonment, and even our blindness for his purposes in our lives and the lives of the generations. He rebuilds, restores, and renews the damaged places in our hearts and lives. For our decision to follow Jesus, he gives us himself. He takes our shame and gives us a double portion, just as he did in the Old Testament as the inheritance of the firstborn. He gives us the inheritance of all, the double portion, instead of the shame we have known. In shame's stead, God gives his all in order for us to be able to live freely and share what he has done for us. This is the way of our loving and gracious Father who gives life abundantly.

God's Grace

God mercifully offers to exchange our shame for his grace. In a profound mystery, he pours deep and rich mercy where shame and pain used to reside. The exchange is beyond compare: Jesus' death and resurrection in place of our sin and unrighteousness. Who would do such a thing? Only a great God who loves his children and wants to live in relationship with them. Only a wonderful Creator who is holy and righteous and wants the same for his children. We do not deserve it, nor will we ever earn it, yet he gives it.

All of this means we are now rightly related to a perfect, just, and holy God, our Creator and Savior. We may come to him with freedom and confidence in our worship, praise, confession, thanksgiving, and intercession. He receives us fully and gives richly of himself. He sees us as perfect because he could not look at us in any other way. And if that were not enough, he will not stop loving us, nor will he ever leave us.

The exchange of our shame for his grace is the holiest, most beautiful, most unfathomable, and most magnificent in the universe. When received, it becomes the transformation of one life into another, molded by our Creator for reflecting on who he is to us. God comes to dwell in our lives to love us and mold us into the ones he planned before creation and formed inside our mother's wombs. His plan includes the exchange, the swap.

If we do not turn our lives, plans, and innermost parts over to God, we will remain fixed upon things that will never satisfy. God himself is the only one who can fill the vacuum inside of us. The exchange of our shame for his grace makes it possible. We turn ourselves over to the One who created us and knows us better than we know ourselves. He loves us perfectly and wants us to be like him. When God fills the vacuum inside, we are new and whole—not shamed and broken. He takes our broken lives and reshapes them into what he had in mind from the beginning. His mercy for our sin; his grace for our lives; his wholeness for our brokenness; his life poured into us when we say *yes* to him. His answer is always *yes*.

God's New is Always Springing Up

Growing up in God, maturing in him, and knowing him at a deeper level is a powerful and worthy-like-no-other pursuit, one of his making. God is in charge of how quickly and how deeply we grow up in him. If we put in the time seeking and obeying him, he does the rest. In fact, without the help of the Holy Spirit's indwelling, we would not be able to seek and obey him. God, the author of our relationship with him, is also the grower and harvester of the seeds he plants within us that lead to our maturing and knowing the Master.

It is choice-by-choice, step-by-step that we grow in our relationship with our Father. He alone knows what it takes for us to grow spiritually, to walk with him consistently, to be tethered to him constantly, and to be transformed into children of God.

God's mercy falls down on us, making it possible for each step of faith to spring up to salvation. He pours out his mercy in quantities greater than we know, and yet he continues making the small seed of faith grow to fruition in salvation and in other works: "For we are God's handiwork, created in Christ Jesus to do good works, which God prepared in advance for us to do" (Eph. 2:10).

God's unfailing love continues without our doing anything. He does not require a sacrifice; what he requires is a devotion to him, a step-by-step faith walk, and a heart yielded to the One who created all and conforms all to his purposes. In Jesus righteousness rains down and God's new is always springing up. Will we receive what he has to offer? While God's mercy is extravagant, we will not be made right without Jesus. When we take the small step of faith—small like a mustard seed—God creates in us and springs up in us a heart like his, a righteous one, one made right with God. No hope is larger than this. Let us spring up and perceive the new mercies he has given, and let us receive the new life in our Lord Christ Jesus. Let us live life as he planned—to the full as growing and maturing followers of the One and Only.

Yearnings Met by God

A daughter longs for many things, all of which are met by God, because a loving Father God fulfills the yearnings of his children. In order to thrive, daughters must turn to God to meet her longings. After all, God has wired us to long for him, and he is all we need for a full life. There are several categories of longings, including the longing to dwell in safety, the longing for the assurance of goodness in the future, the longing for health and well-being, a longing for love and courage, and, last but not least, a longing for purpose or calling.

Let us call these five categories home, hope, healing, heart, and harvest.

Home —to dwell with God (I have a dwelling place with God).

Hope—assurance of good things in future (I have assurance of goodness).

Healing—health and well-being (I will be better).

Heart—love, courage (I am loved; I can be strong).

Harvest—accomplishment of purpose and plan (I have calling and purpose).

Home

Through Jesus, God the Son, the way for us to be right and at rest in the Father is provided. Jesus is our home. He is our safety net, our refuge, and our place to call our dwelling. We all need a place to call "home." Whether we go out from and return to an actual physical place, or just know in our heart of hearts there is a place within us giving us peace and security, we long for it. When we are restless or weary, we want to be home. As God's children, we long for him, and he is the only place actually bringing rest and restoration—God's arms through Jesus Christ.

In the Old Testament, the tabernacle, and ultimately the temple of the Lord, was where God dwelled. He rested amidst his people wherever they were. In their times of wandering, they set up a tent for God's dwelling place. The psalmist writes often of being near God and wanting to live with him. For example, in Psalm 27:4 we read, "One thing I ask from the Lord, this only do I seek: that I may dwell in the house of the Lord all the days of my life, to gaze on the beauty of the Lord and to seek him in his temple."

Today, God still dwells among his children. We have him with us through the indwelling of the Holy Spirit in our hearts. When we choose to follow him, trust him, lean into his ways, and follow his heart, we know we are at home with him. He says, "Here I am! I stand at the door and knock. If anyone hears my voice and opens the door, I will come in and eat with that person, and they with me" (Rev. 3:20). He stands at the door and knocks, and we must answer the door and let him in. When he comes in, we are in his presence, where our longings are fulfilled for home in the presence of Almighty God.

There are days when my personal mantra is, "I want to go home." God is present whether I acknowledge him or not, and yet I feel unsettled or anxious to be somewhere other than where I am. I believe God may be pursuing us to come sit with him. He wants to show us where our real home is—with him wherever we are. He is all we need. He is more than we imagine.

Hope

We yearn for the assurance of good things in the future. God has called his children to "hope." In the New Testament Paul writes, "I pray that the eyes of your heart may be enlightened in order that you may know the hope to which he has called you, the riches of his glorious inheritance in his holy people" (Eph. 1:18). God has given us a longing for good. In order to live a full life, we must have hope. The hope we yearn for is God himself.

When God sent Jesus to live and die for us and then rise again, he gave us hope for today and for eternity. In addition, he sealed our hope with the promised Holy Spirit to live with us and give us the capacity to hope and have faith—the "confidence in what we hope for and assurance about what we do not see" (Heb. 11:1).

God comes to show us hope. When we do not have hope, we become heartsick, as the book of Proverbs opines: "Hope deferred makes the heart sick, but a longing fulfilled is a tree of life" (13:12).

Healing

As children of God, we long for good health and well being. God, the great physician and healer, knows our very frame. He allows hard struggle, pain, and illnesses to bring us back to him so we can know his great love for us.

God's healing is for the body and the soul. He allows our hearts to be broken in order to make them whole again. It is only through a relationship with Him that we will be made whole. The prophet Isaiah wrote, "Then your light will break forth like the dawn, and your healing will quickly appear; then your righteousness will go before you, and the glory of the Lord will be your rear guard. Then you will call, and the Lord will answer; you will cry for help, and he will say: Here am I (58:8-9).

Heart

Deuteronomy 33:12 says, "Let the beloved of the Lord rest secure in him, for he shields him all day long, and the one the Lord loves rests between his shoulders." God's children long for his heart. We are his beloved. He loves us, shields us, and if we go to him with our problems and worries, we will rest between his shoulders.

This Scripture is such a lovely image of a child at rest with her Father. The love of the Father comes alive with the picture of a child atop his shoulders. The child not only has a better view of the world, but she is also in a place secure from harm. She can be a child while the Father protects and loves her with all of himself. This is what God does for his children.

God's heart is greater than we imagine. Not only did he send his Son to die for our sins, he did this when we rejected him, ran from him, and denied he was God's Son. The gospel of John records that "For God so loved the world that he gave his one and only Son, that whoever believes in him shall not perish but have eternal life" (3:16). The Father loves us with an everlasting love. God's heart is good, and we long for a good heart that loves us unconditionally. We yearn for God's heart, which is faithful, abounding in love, compassionate, and slow to anger.

God promises to love us and not to leave us. He tells us to be strong and courageous: "Have I not commanded you? Be strong and courageous. Do not be afraid; do not be discouraged, for the Lord your God will be with you wherever you go" (Josh. 1:9). We long for God's good heart and unconditional love.

Harvest

Perhaps most of us yearn to have a life's purpose and to be used for something greater than ourselves. God made us for his glory, so we are wired for heaven's plans and purposes. The Lord declared to us, "I know the plans I have for you ... plans to prosper you and not to harm you, plans to give you hope and a future" (Jer. 29:11).

We have a great need to contribute to good works. Paul says that "we are God's handiwork, created in Christ Jesus to do good works, which God prepared in advance for us to do" (Eph. 2:10). God's children long to do good. In Christ, we have the capacity for good works to contribute to God's harvest. Our longings are met in Christ Jesus, including the yearning to contribute, to have purpose, and to have a calling outside of ourselves.

Crossing Over the Threshold to Rest and Joy

Jesus offers his life so we may cross over the threshold to attain rest and joy. Through him we can know God's great love for us. The invitation to rest and joy is addressed to all. Are we going to stand at the threshold and not cross over to the abundant life that only Christ offers? Just as bridegrooms carry their brides over the threshold into their new home, Jesus carries us over. May we not merely stand at the threshold to what he offers, but let us cross over the threshold to a new and abundant life in him.

While Jesus does indeed offer rest for our souls, he also offers rest for our minds and hearts in the Holy Spirit dwelling in us. He comes to help us with our striving or worrying—rest for our minds. And he shows us we are to trust him with our most valuable relationships and our deepest concerns and sorrows—rest for our hearts. Most of all, Jesus comes to offer Himself with his presence and love.

Out of his great love for us, God was merciful and he made us alive in Christ Jesus—even when we were dead in our transgressions. The apostle Paul put it this way: "For we are God's handiwork, created in Christ Jesus to do good works, which God prepared in advance for us to do" (Eph. 2:10). God covers our sins, he forgives our transgressions, and he puts us into a right relationship with him through Jesus Christ. By his grace we are saved.

God made it possible through knowing his heart for us to find rest. God's love is unfailing and endures forever. Because his Holy Spirit lives in us, we may grasp how wide and long and high and deep his love is for us, and how it can fill us up with all the fullness of God. Paul said exactly that: "I pray that you, being rooted and established in love, may have power, together with all the Lord's holy people, to grasp how wide and long and high and deep is the love of Christ, and to know this love that surpasses knowledge—that you may be filled to the measure of all the fullness of God" (Eph. 3:18-19). All Christians can cross over to this kind of love, and it is a step we must take for the life he promises.

We know God loves us, but do we really understand how much? Even though we may not comprehend the extent and quality of God's love, we do want to know him and his heart for us. When we cross over into his loving arms, he shows us with each step the full life he provides. God never takes his eye off us, and if we listen, he not only counsels and guides but he teaches us how to know him and his love. As the psalmist wrote, "I will instruct you and teach you in the way you should go; I will counsel you with my loving eye on you" (Ps. 32:8).

God is our refuge and protection, and if we are in a low place, he is our deliverer. God reminds us about what he has done for us in the past, and who he is to us in the present and the future. In God's compassion, he forgives us, as Psalm 32:1-2 assures: "Blessed is the one whose transgressions are forgiven, whose sins are covered. Blessed is the one whose sin the Lord does not count against them and in whose spirit is no deceit." We are blessed because we are in a right relationship with God, who has forgiven us, covered our sins, and does not count our sin against us.

Isaiah 30:18 says, "Yet the Lord longs to be gracious to you; therefore he will rise up to show you compassion. For the Lord is a

God of justice. Blessed are all who wait for him!" God longs to be gracious and offers us compassion. Out of his great love for us, out of his riches in mercy, he gave us the gift of grace, his Son Jesus. According to First John 1:9, "If we confess our sins, he is faithful and just and will forgive us our sins and purify us from all unrighteousness" (1 John 1:9) God loved us all so much he gave his only Son so we would not perish but have life eternal. The famous verse in John 3:16 is very clear: "For God so loved the world that he gave his one and only Son, that whoever believes in him shall not perish but have eternal life."

God does not overlook our sins; he deals with them in a firm and enduring way by giving us his only Son, who died on the cross to pay the penalty in our stead for our sin. The Father's love is unwavering. Not only does he forgive us, but he also covers us. The covering is the blood of Jesus by which we are redeemed. First Peter 1:18-19 says, "For you know that it was not with perishable things such as silver or gold that you were redeemed from the empty way of life handed down to you from your ancestors, but with the precious blood of Christ, a lamb without blemish or defect." Jesus' blood paid the penalty for our sin, just as if we had never sinned, and it made it possible for us not to endure the wrath of God that we deserve. As Paul wrote in his letter to the Romans, "Since we have now been justified by his blood, how much more shall we be saved from God's wrath through him!" (Rom. 5:9). By Jesus' blood, therefore, we who were far away have been brought near to God, as the Bible says: "But now in Christ Jesus you who once were far away have been brought near by the blood of Christ" (Eph. 2:13). God made peace with us by reconciling us to himself through his Son, Jesus. Colossians 1:19-20 defines what making peace is: "For God was pleased to have all his fullness dwell in him, and through him to reconcile to himself all things, whether things on earth or things in heaven, by making peace through his blood, shed on the cross."

Under God's compassion and cover, we are credited with righteousness through our faith in Jesus Christ. Our faith puts us in right standing with the Father. With a step of faith, we become his righteousness. We have done nothing to deserve this; quite the opposite, but that is the way of God's great love for us. His mercy is unequalled; his love unparalleled. He makes a way for us to be in relationship with him, and the way is through the sacrifice of the perfect One—God's Son. Second Corinthians 5:21 says, "God made him who had no sin to be sin for us, so that in him we might become the righteousness of God." God sees us as he sees Jesus, in right standing—his righteousness.

Out of his great love for us, shown in his great mercy, God has given us new life. We are forgiven, covered, and righteous—and offered a new and abundant life in Jesus Christ. Scripture says, "Therefore, if anyone is in Christ, the new creation has come: The old has gone, the new is here!" (2 Cor. 5:17).

The new life is here. We can cross over the threshold to rest and joy and experience God's great love!

> Therefore, brothers and sisters, since we have confidence to enter the Most Holy Place by the blood of Jesus, by a new and living way opened for us through the curtain, that is, his body, and since we have a great priest over the house of God, let us draw near to God with a sincere heart and with the full assurance that faith brings, having our hearts sprinkled to cleanse us from a guilty conscience and having our bodies washed with pure water. Let us hold unswervingly to the hope we profess, for he who promised is faithful (Heb. 10:19-23).

Jesus Lived the Abundant Life

Receiving the relationship with our Father God through his Son, Jesus Christ, is the first step to the abundant life. The abundant life is all about Jesus. After all, God loved us first. His commands are that we love him with all of our hearts, souls, minds, and strength, and that with each step we take in following him we are to choose life, not death. When we surrender our lives in childlike trust, Jesus gives us the means to choose him by increasing our faith each step of the way. It is in the emptying of ourselves daily as an offering to him that he fills us with himself.

Dying to ourselves allows more of him and less of us. As we overflow with the Spirit of Jesus in us, we may be able to pour ourselves out for another. God commands that we love others as we love ourselves; when we love and serve others, he says we are in fact serving him.

God's Son died a horrific death on the cross for us, and in doing so he suffered the scorn of his own people. Because of his pain and suffering, Jesus knows our own pain and suffering. In it, we come to know him better and receive more of him.

God offers us himself in the midst of our pain in order that we know what joy is. When we share in the pain and know God is there with us, we experience the joy of God himself. He delights in being in relationship with us, and we come to know that same delight. Intimacy with the God of the universe brings unexpected joy, even in the midst of our sorrow. When we are in our deepest anguish, and we feel that everyone has turned against us, God comes and fellowships with us. We know him and his presence; there is no other like it.

Jesus shows us how to live life to the full. He had an intimate relationship with God, the Father. He did what the Father sent him to do. He regularly went off and prayed in solitude to determine the Father's will. His closest relationships were mentoring ones with his disciples or with friends who were like family—Lazarus, Mary, and Martha. He sought the Father in every aspect of his work. He did not try to please others. He knew his mission ultimately was to bring glory to the Father in heaven through his message of the good news of the Kingdom.

Most people misunderstood Jesus while he lived on earth, but to those who were ready, he revealed himself on the personal level. In sharing stories of God's Truth, Jesus loved and showed mercy to many. He sought after people who would also share the gospel, whether in suffering or not. Jesus taught love, grace, truth, peace, and joy, and he exemplified them in his life, death, and resurrection.

Position, Power, and Privilege, the Three P's of the Abundant Life

POSITION

If we are at peace with God through Jesus Christ, we are rightly related. We are children of the Father, adopted as sons and daughters through Jesus, which is a glorious inheritance. We are seated with Jesus at the right hand of God in the heavenly realms. Paul assures us that "he chose us in him before the creation of the world to be holy and blameless in his sight" (Eph. 1:4). We are rightly related to God because our sins have been forgiven by God and covered by Jesus' blood. We have nothing to fear because God loves us and will never leave us. He is the Great I AM, and there is no other.

POWER

The power we have as children of God is greater within us than he who is in the world: "You, dear children, are from God and have overcome them, because the one who is in you is greater than the one who is in the world" (1 John 4:4). The Holy Spirit indwells each child of God when he or she believes in Jesus as his or her Savior and Lord. The power of the Holy Spirit is the same power God exerted in raising Jesus from the dead and seating him at his right hand in the heavenly realms. "I pray that the eyes of your heart may be enlightened in order that you may know the hope to which he has called you, the riches of his glorious inheritance in his holy people, and his incomparably great power for us who believe. That power is the same as the mighty strength he exerted when he raised Christ from the dead and seated him at his right hand in the heavenly realms" (Eph. 1:18-20). The Holy Spirit teaches, guides, and comforts. He gives us the power to love, obey God's Word, forgive, and be transformed by his Spirit within us.

PRIVILEGE

Each Christian believer has spiritual gifts to serve God and his church in this world. Through the power of the Holy Spirit, who makes us all one, we have the capacity to share the good news of the gospel and serve God's people. With the Holy Spirit within us, we are transformed into the image of Jesus. In him and through him we become his vessels to share the divine light and love in this world. We have the privilege to approach him and rest from the burdens of the world, and we go out with his leading and equipping to share and to serve. We also have the privilege of sharing in Christ's suffering as we live and serve his kingdom.

Questions Embracing the Position, the Power, and the Privilege

Who are we in Christ Jesus?

What have we received?

Are we exercising what he has given us?

How has God wired me and how am I fulfilling his purpose in my life?

Have I stepped out to share and to serve?

Am I living out my full potential in Christ Jesus for his kingdom?

The Position, Power, and Privilege—How then do we Pray?

As his children at his feet, privileged and honored to be called his own

As rightly related to God, covered, and forgiven daughters and sons

As children led, taught, comforted, and guided by God

As children with a delightful inheritance

As his people with power to serve (and a willingness to suffer in Jesus' name)

As sons and daughters seated with Jesus in the heavenly realms

As sons and daughters in love and willing obedience to our Father God

As children in awe of our great God who will always love us and never leave us

The Riches in Christ Jesus

God shows us himself through the riches he has given us. He loved us so much he gave his only Son to die for us so we can live with him forever. He demonstrated the love he has for us through his Son's self-sacrificing life, brutal death, and resurrection. God continues displaying his love and power through the indwelling Holy Spirit in those of us who believe. Through the power of the Holy Spirit, we can know him, his Word, his love, and his power.

God has given us riches in Christ Jesus. Because he is our Father, God is teaching us to sit in his presence and to know his promises. We must learn to trust him and receive what he has given—his righteousness and rest. We must rely on him and go out with confidence that he is changing us from the inside and growing us up to know him better and to follow him wherever he leads. We are his daughters and sons, and he is our Father, the Giver of all good things and the One who makes things new.

Without the Father, we do not have the forgiveness of sin and life everlasting he promised. Without him, we cannot be "new." We must recognize that God has given us the best when he came down to us in Jesus to offer salvation. In doing so, he brought us out of our bondage into a spacious place. He never leaves us to go it alone, nor does he forsake us on the journey. Whatever he commands us to do, he goes with us. We are his dearly loved children. With this divine rescue, God gives us the opportunity to know him and his Son better, and to live a new life of freedom.

When we choose to follow Christ, he allows us to know him in ways we never dreamed. God confides in his children and helps us know what he has promised. The psalmist says, "The Lord confides in those who fear him; he makes his covenant known to them" (Ps. 25:14). The Holy Spirit poured down from on high makes us grow and change in ways that otherwise would be impossible. Our bodies become vessels that house God's Holy Spirit—treasure in jars of clay. "We have this treasure in jars of clay to show that this all-surpassing power is from God and not from us" (2 Cor. 4:7). Only by his power can we grow through hardship or difficult journeys to become "oaks of righteousness, a planting of the Lord for the display of his splendor" (Isa. 61:3) The Father uses all things for his purposes that the world may know him, his love, and his power. His children have been transformed and made new so the world may see and know him.

Professing Our Acknowledgement of Who He Is and Whose We Are

Part of knowing God is acknowledging who he is and what he has done for us as his children.

I am okay

- o   not because of me

- o   not because of my hard work

- o   not because of my achievement

- o   not because of my relationships

- o   not because of past, present, or future

- o   not because of my family of origin

- o   not because of my husband (or wife) and children

- o   not because of my church, friends, or the place I live or work

I am okay because I am God's daughter or son by his grace, goodness, gift, and greatness. I look to him to be okay just as I am in my brokenness. I have a place in God's kingdom because of the Son's work and victory.

God's power

- o   provides

- o protects
- o rescues, delivers
- o gives us gifts and passion for our lives
- o enables to go on a pilgrimage to his table

I find truth in him on this pilgrimage, and he reveals hidden things to me to allow me to know him: "I keep asking that the God of our Lord Jesus Christ, the glorious Father, may give you the Spirit of wisdom and revelation, so that you may know him better" (Eph. 1:17).

As God's thriving daughter, I realize that

- o I am forgiven (Ps. 32)
- o I am living in God's presence (Ps. 84)
- o I am dependent upon God (Ps. 46)
- o I can place my hope in him (Ps. 62, 23)
- o I am thankful and I praise him (Ps. 92, 98, 100, 103)
- o I remember because he reminds me (Ps. 106, 107)
- o I desire my relationship with him above all (Ps. 139, 51, 16)
- o I pray, trust, and wait upon him (Ps. 143, 25, 40)

A thriving daughter must

- o Surrender and hold onto oneself loosely and grasp God's hand tightly
- o Allow God's power to flow from him to her, not barricading off parts of oneself
- o Realize that not surrendering is a barrier to God and stifles his power
- o Allow God's release of faith in her, which is the power to be loved and to love, to receive and extend grace, to do good work, to receive and extend peace

A beloved daughter knows no shame and "instead of your shame you will receive a double portion, and instead of disgrace you will rejoice in your inheritance. And so you will inherit a double portion in your land, and everlasting joy will be yours. (Isa. 61:7). She wears the gifts of newness and rightness with humility. She relies on the Lord and enjoys pleasing him. She receives rescue, healing, redemption, joy, and peace, and she enjoys the bounty of the relationship with God our Father and the Lord Jesus Christ. He defends her, trains her, grows her up, and matures her in a spacious place. She receives the love of a parent and allows God's help in the battles she wages and in the hard things in life. She has the boundless riches of Christ Jesus dwelling within her. It is life to the full!

"Listen, Oh Daughter"
(inspired by Psalm 45:10-11)

Daughter of Zion
Child of the One true God
He favors you, above all
And gives you his bounty and rest

Loving-kindness awaits you
Child of God, daughter of the King
Come and see, rest your head
Know his heart, enthralled he is by you

Why listen to man
Blind and confused
Scornful and deluded
His contempt is not a match for God's favor

Rise up, Oh Daughter, listen to his call
Great things he has done, abundant for all
Emboldened by him you behold
Proclaim his kindness as he foretold

Love birthed, kindness shared
Go the road he has prepared
No longer ashamed but blessed instead
To be the daughter, Oh God, just as you have said

"God's Children Blessed by His Faithful Care"
(inspired by Deuteronomy 33)

Fight the fight already won
Safe, secure in his arms
Favored among children all
Given refuge, protected from harm

Blessed on the heights and lowlands too
Man and God look to you
With fondness and gladness
God's light shines from within

Inheritance full from above
The best gifts earth and heaven come
Treasure from him, hidden riches pour forth
For his children, his beloved, all the more

He watches your going out, coming in
God goes before, with, and after you
Not asleep, he is the night watchman and day too
Only to keep his own in his faithful care

Let him fight your battles
Carry you through the night
Guard your steps and give you rest
He enjoys giving his all to you

What Does Your Heart Wear?

God looks at our hearts, not our appearance. What is your heart wearing? When God calls his children, he gives us new hearts. Is your heart new?

When God's children get rejected by the world and worn down by the oppressor, unbelief may set in—but it need not. He has made our hearts new, rescued, and redeemed. But sometimes, we wear our old clothing of sackcloth and ashes. This changes when we lean into God and trust him. That is when we wear his heart and his clothing.

What is the red dress symbolism mentioned earlier? The red dress my mother wore became her ultimate rejection of me on the day of my wedding. Yet, God in his pursuing and unfailing love used that situation to free me from rejection to receiving his truth and his love. Sometimes, we become confused by what the world gives us. We believe its lies. I believed the lie that no one could love me or think I was lovely, even on my wedding day. The truth becomes hidden from us. But God continues to pursue his children, to rescue, redeem, heal, and use them for his glory, a glory that cannot be hidden. In his glory, his children shine. He clothes them in his finest, his fullest.

And oftentimes we want ourselves to shine. We want the glory ourselves, but we cannot steal God's glory. He knows our hearts and loves us still. And we know deep within that our hearts are broken. We want to be loved, significant, and known. He is the only way for this need to be met—his love, his significance, his knowing, and his glory.

When we have him, we shine for his glory. He wants to make himself known through us. He knows us, and in relationship with him, we are loved, significant, and known. His glory shines in us, through us, and transforms us into being more like him—a significance that is unimaginable.

When we are in step with the Lord, his heart appears within us and loves others through us. We wear his heart for his people and his purposes and plans for such a time as this. God uses our broken places for the world to know him. When we are forsaken or rejected, we can cry out to our Maker and Savior God. He binds us up, releases us from the darkness, and frees us from our own imprisonment. He becomes the red dress of healing, freedom, and sight. He will use our enslavement as the means to free us. He did it for me.

The Practice of Faith: Our Hearts Clothed in Christ

The practice of faith is a daily discipline that keeps our eyes fixed on Jesus. Our focus is not on the temporal, but the eternal. And this does not mean only that we are waiting for heaven.

Practicing faith requires our focus to be Christ in our hearts, minds, and deeds on earth while knowing we are heaven bound. When Jesus Christ is first in our lives, our internal compass and our external behavior will exhibit his grace and truth. His love guides our relationships and fellowship with others and also extends itself outward into the world.

When we have the Lord, our hearts are full of hope. Trusting him provides a deep center, and when we fix our eyes on him, our hearts reflect what our eyes see. This hope comes from our knowing the One and Only. As we stay in his Word, we know him exponentially more. Our hearts clothed in Christ become our daily wear; we have him, and he is all we need, long for, and hope.

"Putting on Faith: Clothed in Christ"

Heart wears
What eyes see
Glory—Jesus in our midst
And yet, sin exists

God's heart within
New, hope, him, the view
But, brother betrays
Practice wearing heart still new

Feelings, not truth, unsettle us
Hearts in disarray slink back
Put faith on to move forward
Armor in place, God's heart the enemy wrestles

Holy Spirit, divine dresser
Shield my heart with your truth
Grow faith where my feelings test me
Shine your love through my heart's view of you

God's Favor

The miracle of God's mercy and favor overshadows and defeats our scorn and contempt, and replaces it with God's kindness toward his own children.

When we feel the contempt of another, we may experience pain, doubt, and shame. But this is not what God has in mind for us. We have his favor, and there is nothing whatever, no contempt of any kind, that can undo God's love for and acceptance of us.

Do we want approval or honor from another? Are we seeking a person's love over God's? God's favor is a huge thing. He is our Father God, Creator God, Savior God, and Holy God of the universe who is sovereign over all. When we call upon him, he answers us in love and never abandons us. God himself in Jesus Christ lived through horrific shame and scorn on the cross; his own people treated him with contempt. When we live to honor him, those who do not accept him as Lord will view us with the same contempt.

When we are scorned or shown contempt, we must take it to the One who knows better than anyone how to deal with disdain. Jesus received the worst treatment and yet won the victory over death and shame once and for all. If we take it to him and lean on him to help us, we receive God's vindication, favor, and rest, as only he can give.

Why take on the contempt of another when we can have the favor of the One and Only? We can rest knowing he knows above all what it feels like. He faced the cross of crucifixion without shame and with joy because he wanted us to know his favor where we once knew scorn and shame—"fixing our eyes on Jesus, the pioneer and perfecter of faith. For the joy set before him he endured the cross, scorning its shame, and sat down at the right hand of the throne of God" (Heb. 12:2). He endured all sin for all time and gave up everything to be Lord of the universe. And he showed us what his favor really means.

God's Tears and Ours

"His anger lasts only a moment, but his favor lasts a lifetime; weeping may stay for the night, but rejoicing comes in the morning," writes the psalmist (Ps. 30:5). The morning light is only a night away, and after that, there is joy in the morning. God allows our lives to have sad times, endings to things, death, leavings, and change. We mourn and he comforts us, and after a time, joy returns. Many times joy comes in to replace the deep sadness we feel. God is the author of joy for he brings joy to us by being with us. He heals us, and restores us to more joyful times. He makes good things out of difficult things, and he creates joy from sadness.

In the midst of sadness, we must remember that joy is coming. Psalm 126 is a reminder that God returns joy to his children: "Those who sow with tears will reap with songs of joy" (126:5). The psalmist assures us that God restores our fortunes like streams in the Negev. Of course, we all want to live in joy and not to have to endure pain or sadness. But life has cycles, and our seasons of joy must have them, too. The Holy Spirit enables us to have joy even during our seasons of sadness. We are not able in and of ourselves to make ourselves joyful, but God can. We have joy because of Jesus, who died for our sins and lives in us eternally. A child of God has joy because of the fruit of the Holy Spirit dwelling within. "The fruit of the Spirit is love, joy, peace, forbearance, kindness, goodness, faithfulness, gentleness and self-control. Against such things there is no law." (Gal. 5:22-23).

What if we do not feel joyful? The truth is that we may not feel joy at all times. Nevertheless, we may know joy through the power of the Holy Spirit within us. We have joy even if we do not feel it. In addition, we always have a reason to celebrate because we are God's children: "Now if we are children, then we are heirs—heirs of God and co-heirs with Christ, if indeed we share in his sufferings in order that we may also share in his glory" (Rom. 8:17). And, "If you belong to Christ, then you are Abraham's seed, and heirs according to the promise" (Gal. 3:29).

Jesus faced the shame of a horrific death, but he ran his race with perseverance because he was joyful over who he was doing it for—his children. "Endure hardship as discipline; God is treating you as his children. For what children are not disciplined by their father? If you are not disciplined—and everyone undergoes discipline—then you are not legitimate, not true sons and daughters at all" (Heb. 12:7-8). Instead of our having to conjure up joy, the Father has given us his Spirit to make joy possible, even in the midst of discipline. We have joy in his presence, knowing he is with us and will never leave us. God wants to comfort us and dry our tears, for the day of overwhelming joy is coming.

God Sustains

God says he has delivered us, and therefore he can certainly sustain us. "I am the Lord your God, who brought you up out of Egypt. Open wide your mouth and I will fill it" (Ps. 81:10). The Lord reminds us of his constant and faithful care, and if we remain with him, he will cause us to remember what he has done for us. In addition he will sustain us in the moment. Not only has God given us what we need for the present, he will provide for us in the future, too. God is faithful; he is gracious and abounding in love for his children. It is in sustaining us that God does his transforming work. We obey, trust, walk in faith, and wait. We can only do these things with the help and guidance of the Holy Spirit, so in a real sense it is God who gives us the power to choose to allow him to sustain us. And of course it is God who does the sustaining.

If we question whether we are on the right track, we have not heard God saying he will continue hearing and answering our cries. Sometimes we fail to know he has heard us because we have not gotten the answer we want. God wants us to trust him, and not to lean on our own understanding, for in the trusting, we know him better and we know that trusting him is the answer we are looking and waiting for. The Lord's nature is love and truth, and that will never change. Whatever our question, he loves us, sustains us, and does not forsake us.

When we are feeling lost and alone and without answers, we have to trust our sovereign God. Trusting can be done in a number of ways. We give all things up to God in prayer, and then we rest that he has it. While doing so, we seek him in his Word and trust Scripture promises and the character of the Almighty. We remember what he has already done for us, both in his work on the cross and also in the ways he shows us his rescue in our lives. When we think we have failed to hear him correctly, we ask him to guide us and change our course. Because he wants us close to him, our responsibility as Christians is to look to him for the way, the wait, the walk, and the wandering. And there will be wandering: We are human, and we will not get it right all of the time. But God in his rich mercy takes even those wanderings and weaves them into his handiwork and his beautiful plan for his glory and our best. As the apostle Paul wrote, "We know that in all things God works for the good of those who love him, who have been called according to his purpose" (Rom. 8:28).

Staying close to God is a choice we have to make with immediacy, at least hourly and daily. He will honor our choice whatever it is, but God will richly bless the hearts of his children who choose to allow his ways to sustain them and his heart to be their faithful care. In Psalm 81:10, God says to "Open wide your mouth and I will fill it." What we can take from this is to expect God, to allow the great and holy One and Only to sustain us with his unfailing love and truth.

God's Mercy and Resting in Him

The mercy of God is not what we deserve, but it is what we have been offered. God is compassionate, gracious, slow to anger, abounding in love, and faithful (Exod. 34:6). Out of his bountiful kindness, he desires to show us mercy and gives us mercy even when we are going the wrong way and following our own desires. Even after we have chosen to leave our old ways and follow God, we cannot come to him on our own. He has to soften our hearts to want to know him and his mercy. When we respond to his pursuing love and mercy, he gives us the courage and the faith to make the first step—and the ensuing ones as well.

This bounty of God to undeserving people who want what they want without regard to him is also a way God shows humankind that he is indeed God and that there is no other. He is always more than any of us can fathom; his ways are higher, and no one can compare with his deeds. He is just, compassionate, and loving. He is our holy, sovereign, almighty, and gracious Father who sent his only Son to die for our sins so we can live with him in heaven forever.

The potter knows us inside and out because he created us. He knows what we need and what we desire, and he loves us more than we can imagine. Who can question the One and Only? But we do. We want answers to the "whys" of life, all those lingering questions we have been unable to answer, like why there is evil and other terrible things in our world. God, who is almighty, sovereign, and gracious, does not change, even when we cannot understand why he allows such things.

Isaiah 65:24 says, "Before they call I will answer; while they are still speaking I will hear." It is comforting knowing that when we call on God, he already knows our cry and will answer us. It may not be the answer we want or think we need, but he answers. Sometimes the answer is to wait. Other times, he says no. And then oftentimes, he gives us the affirmative when he knows that this response is in our best interests according to his plan for us and all humankind.

In the Word, we are not told to understand God but to trust him: "Trust in the Lord with all your heart and lean not on your own understanding; in all your ways submit to him, and he will make your paths straight" (Prov. 3:5-6). God also gives us the means to trust him if we let him. He takes our tiny steps of trust and multiplies them until we are leaning into our Father God as a child who needs and wants to rest in his lap. In the long run, we will learn to lean into him and leave the "whys" resting upon his shoulders. After all, it is what he desires us to do and what will make us stronger in his love and more receptive to the grace he shows to his children. As we trust God and love him back, he gives us more of himself and his bounty of grace.

Trusting Him

We want to get at the why's of life not only to understand but also to clear our consciences. If we are God's children, followers of Christ, we stand clear before him. He has already done the work of atonement for us through his Son, Jesus Christ, but sometimes we still feel guilty. We cannot earn grace or forgiveness or clean consciences. Asking why so we can work our way in the clear is not a path to the answer.

God loves us and will never leave us. Trying to understand why we are in a painful circumstance will not help us put an end to the struggle. God's answer will always be to trust him. He is sovereign; he loves us and is with us through whatever happens in our lives. We may not understand why certain things are the way they are, but we can know him and rest in him during the process. The only way to avoid hard times or pain or struggle is not to be born on this earth. In the midst of our pain we may no longer ask *why* but *who*. *Yes* becomes our choice to lean into him, yes to the only One who understands, loves, and keeps us.

God Transforms Our Focus

When we are young in our faith, sometimes the lens through which we see God in our lives is blurry, or skewed by circumstances. The paradigm through which we experience life is not so well formed as when we are more mature in the faith. As we mature, our steps are surer and our hearts and minds know truths about God because of the journeys we have walked with him. We know he is a faithful God. We have experienced his slowness to anger, his grace, and his abounding love. To Moses the Lord proclaimed, "The Lord, the Lord, the compassionate and gracious God, slow to anger, abounding in love and faithfulness" (Exod. 34:6).

We not only know the Lord, but we believe him and the promises in his Word. When we step out in faith, as Abraham did, "By faith Abraham, when called to go to a place he would later receive as his inheritance, obeyed and went, even though he did

306

not know where he was going" (Heb. 11:8). God recognizes us as his children. Though we are already in God's family, not everything comes naturally or easy. Trusting God with each moment and every detail of our lives is still a daily decision and a choice. And with each step of faith to trust, we are building a life with our Father God and Savior, a foundation upon which all else depends.

We all experience the kindness of God in creation, in the love of another, or in his pursuit of us. And when he does pursue us, we must turn to him in humility and gratitude. We must "seek the Lord while he may be found, [and] call on him while he is near" (Isa. 55:6). Our perceptions of our lives, our journeys, even our daily moments hinge on this central relationship. His truths become more real to us when we spend time with him, when we experience his goodness, and when we turn toward him in gratitude. When we remember his hand in our lives, we know him better.

We are naturally independent and self-focused. Even so, God wired us for a relationship with him, and we are our best selves when we fix our eyes upon and worship him, the Almighty Father and Savior. Through the new lens of faith, we experience the kindness and favor of the Master, Jesus Christ. God gives us a heart to want to know him and the faith to follow him. He keeps on pursuing us through a personal relationship with Jesus Christ: As he pursues us and we come to him, he gives us the heart, eyes, and ears to know, see, and hear him through the indwelling of the Holy Spirit in our lives. He changes us as we live in relationship with him, and he transforms the lens through which we view life. He helps us want to know him more and guides us into all truth. He shows us how to love and forgive and live expectantly in the hope of his goodness; we cannot do these things on our own, but only through the power of the Holy Spirit living within us.

As we allow God into more of our lives, he gives us more of himself. We realize the unending supply of his goodness to us. He promised us that "the thief comes only to steal and kill and destroy; I have come that they may have life, and have it to the full" (John

10:10). As we live with him, we know the fullness of him who promised a full life to us. He is the portion we have waited for, the filter by which we know life. And because Jesus is our life, we do not have to be concerned about our circumstances. We know him. He is so much more than we have ever dreamed and way more than we imagine. He is "able to do immeasurably more than all we ask or imagine, according to his power that is at work within us" (Eph. 3:20).

The Loving Father Answers

The sun on the path today was bright for one minute, and then behind the clouds for another. It reminded me that our days with God are like that. We feel his strong and sure presence, and then we waver in our recognition of him. It is as if God is behind the clouds, rather than being present for the journey. But God is always present with us, whether we recognize his presence or not. Why is this so difficult to believe? We want faith to be sight right now. And he says in Scripture that "faith is confidence in what we hope for and assurance about what we do not see" (Heb. 11:1).

Some days, I hear the Lord through his Word when my heart knows the Scripture is just for me. Being in the presence of God and knowing he has spoken to me brings a sense of awe and expectation—a small glimpse of heaven. I want more, more of him. But I know it is not like that all the time. Sometimes, it seems as if he is far off.

God assures us that through the indwelling of the Holy Spirit, he is near to us. He lives within us by virtue of our faith in the Lord Jesus Christ. It does not get closer than that. Tethered to the Father, we go on the path of this life's journey. If we properly understand this connection, we will know the riches he has for us—and this includes moments with the bright shining sun and moments when the clouds are hiding it. God is with us, and he is never going to leave or forsake us.

Psalm 139 says "You have searched me, Lord, and you know me. You know when I sit and when I rise; you perceive my thoughts from afar. You discern my going out and my lying down; you are familiar with all my ways" (139:1-3). God knows wherever we go. He goes before us, with us, and behind us. Perhaps he is carrying us and we cannot see him because we are in his arms. Maybe we are waiting because God is preparing the road ahead. What if God is picking up the pieces on the road that was so difficult we could not see anything around us, in front or behind? Our Father God is "compassionate and gracious ... slow to anger, abounding in love and faithfulness" to his children (Ps. 86:15). He does not leave us on the journey, no matter if the path is sunny, dark, or unfamiliar. He is God, and he walks it with us every day.

At Home with God

We all yearn for home. We all need a place to rest, or to feel accepted and loved, where we are known and where we can be who we are without judgment, rejection, shame, or disappointment. The only place that fits this description is heaven. God has wired us all to yearn for heaven, a place that perfectly fits us, where we are the people he has created us to be.

God has chosen to live among us and to dwell within us. It is in this dwelling of God within by the Holy Spirit that we may know God and his love and acceptance for us. He gives us rest, not only in a physical and emotional sense, but also in a place to be who we are without being judged, rejected, shamed, or disappointed. He knows us and still loves us and accepts us just as we are. He resides in us and gives us a small glimpse of what living eternally with him will be like.

In the Old Testament, it was very important to the Hebrew people to find a resting place for God. God called his chosen children by his name and offered them his dwelling place. The Ark of the Covenant went with the Israelites wherever they traveled. God told them he would show them a place where he would dwell—ultimately that became the temple in Jerusalem, where they placed the Ark of the Covenant.

God in his abounding mercy, and according to his plan before he created the world, became our dwelling. When we come to him, we may rest in his presence, the most amazing dwelling in the entire universe, and including eternity. He not only chooses a place for his dwelling, but he also chooses one for us as well. In God's presence, we are at home.

Are we at home with God? Do we yearn for a true dwelling place? The Father says to call on him and he will answer with unfailing love by providing his presence and an eternal home.

Our Shame for His Grace

Shame says we are wrong or we have done something wrong. And it is true, but only in part. God gives us a new slate when we trust the Master as our God and Savior. We can say that things have not gone well, or that we have not realized our dreams yet. But shame and disappointment come from relying on another source to make things right. We cannot in and of ourselves make things right with God. As God's children, we need him, the perfect Father. He acknowledges our need; he lavishes us with good things. There is no shame or disappointment in him.

God knows every nook and cranny of our being. There is nothing we can hide from him. We may be hiding from others or even ourselves, but we cannot live in secret from God. He knows about any shame, sin, or disappointment we have, and he still holds our honor. When we admit our need and follow him, he takes away all that keeps us from him and bestows on us the highest honor of all, the privilege of being a member of the family of God. God makes us right with him through his Son, Jesus. No longer ashamed of who we are or what we have done, we can freely live in relationship with God and know rest, peace, and joy for our souls.

Why then do we hold onto our shame? What makes us carry it with us and try to hide it? Do we not want to be known? Perhaps we do not want to be known because we fear that no one would love us if they knew who we were or what we were capable of. But God knows, and he loves us. We were not wired to carry shame around on our backs. We are not in a position to be able to make things right with God, but he has already done so. He has carried our shame to the cross. What if we allowed ourselves to remember our sin, to talk to God about it, and then leave it with him? He would take it and give us grace in return. What if we were to carry his grace around in the place of shame—our shame for his grace?

We stand in his grace. "Since we have been justified through faith, we have peace with God through our Lord Jesus Christ, through whom we have gained access by faith into this grace in which we now stand" (Rom. 5:1-2). No longer are we guilty, but instead we are close to God, even called his own children. With this grace, God grows our hope, and our shame and disappointment diminish. God is greater than our shame and disappointment, and where we have not discovered it yet, he will lead us to it. He will show us that his plan for us is full of grace.

His Love Overpowers our Shame

Shame keeps us from coming to our Father God, but it is the very reason we need to come. Whether we have done something wrong, or something wrong has been done to us, we all have shame at some point in our lives. That is a natural part of being human. In its stead, most of us try to rationalize or cover up our shame; it is just too difficult to recall and discuss. It may seem trivial to another, but God knows our shame. We need to talk to him about it. In fact, it is the only way we will be made right. "Hope does not put us to shame, because God's love has been poured out into our hearts through the Holy Spirit, who has been given to us" (Rom. 5:5).

When we are ashamed, we feel the need to protect ourselves or to keep our real selves from being known. We may build barriers to keep secrets. We rationalize our behavior, and the shame grows. Later, we cry out to our Creator, Savior, and Father God, who takes us in his arms as his children and soothes us with his unfailing love, compassion, and desire to make us whole. This is as he intended when he made us. He covers us with his mighty hand and keeps us by his side to show us who he is and whose we are.

God has given love in shame's place over and over. He teaches us his truth and grace so we know when a lie is about to take over in our head and eventually in our heart so we can "take up the shield of faith, with which you can extinguish all the flaming arrows of the evil one" (Eph. 6:16). After all, it is the Evil One who uses our shame to keep us from our One and Only Savior and Father God.

As children of God, we have the amazing love of our Creator who knows our every need before we do. He has wired us to be connected to him in order to be who he made us to be. This relationship brings a right relationship with the God of the universe, who wants us to be whole, without shame, and with his honor and his name as his sons and daughters. He waits for us to give him our shame so he can lavish his love on us in its very place.

To Whom We Belong as His Daughters

As I was growing up, I loved for people to ask who I was and to whom I belonged. It was the way of the small town where I grew up. Everyone in my community belonged to a family, and that family was known by all in the community. It was a comfort to be known in that way in those days.

When a person in my community would ask who my father was, I would proudly proclaim my father's name. If that person were part of a group standing around talking, they would look at one another and say, "Yes, I know him, fine man. You know him, too, don't you? Yes, I can see that you are his daughter." If they had known him for most of their lives, they would share a story or two, either a funny one or a nostalgic or honoring one. As a daughter of his, I would walk away feeling good about belonging to his family, our family. After all, he was a loving, generous, kind, and honorable man of faith, and one who put others before himself. He was revered by his family and community. It was a privilege and an honor to be called one of my father's children.

However, when my family of origin took a turn for the worse after my father died, it no longer felt the same. We were broken, not only by his death, but also by the many things that continued happening in the years right after he died. Damaged relationships and difficult diagnoses do not make a family want to be together, much less get together and show love, empathy, and compassion. The more we tried, the harder it became.

It was during these years that not only was my family of origin stripped from me, my mother, sisters, and brother, but the honor of my family was stolen, too. It has only been recently that I have come to know it was bound to happen. The honor and privilege of family is created on the foundation God has given to us. It is by his design that we are part of families. It is also by his design that we are wired to need him above all. I had relied upon the family system and found it lacking through the years, but the fact that I was known and belonged gave me something I knew I needed in my heart of hearts. I yearned for the love shown in the community, the name recognition in the town so I could feel significant. My father's name provided it for me.

God in his wisdom and love for us has given us his name. We belong to him; he is our Father. And all that is his he has given to us. We are known by him, and we are known to the world by his name. When my family of origin needed rescue and could not be what I wanted it to be, I was devastated. Yet through God's pursuit of me in the struggle and pain of these broken relationships, I experienced his love in new and profound ways, as well as the real significance that comes from belonging to him. I have found that it is in the broken places that God shows up to reveal his love. Fractured relationships have given me the gift of dependence upon the Father. In the struggle and the pain, I have been forced to trust him. More importantly, he calls us into a right relationship with him. I must to leave the rest up to God.

As a daughter of the highest God, our Creator and Savior, the Lord Jesus Christ, I am loved, honored, and cherished. I belong to him, and in him I am known. To the world, I am known by him. God created our family of origin to be one in which we belong together and were known to each other. I treasure that he made us his family through which we could know him—the honor, privilege, and significance worth cherishing.

Our Inheritance

As small children, we hear things like, "you inherited your father's hazel eyes," or "your inheritance will include the acreage your grandmother's house is built upon." We know that something has been given or passed along or will be ours one day. I knew as a little girl that I inherited my father's hazel eyes, my mother's black hair, and that one day, the land where our ancestors settled would belong to my siblings and me.

The term *inheritance* is very personal. Perhaps it is a regional thing, or maybe it is something our family discussed more than other things. It seems God has strong intentions where inheritance is concerned. He spells it out many times in Scripture. His promise is that as his children we have a wonderful inheritance. It is something we can count on. As God's sons and daughters, we not only become like him in Jesus Christ, we also inherit the Kingdom on earth and in heaven. He says it is our inheritance because we are God's children.

The definition of *inheritance* in the Merriam-Webster's Collegiate Dictionary is "the acquisition of a possession, condition, or trait from past generations." God tells us in Scripture that we will acquire a glorious inheritance from him: "I pray that the eyes of your heart may be enlightened in order that you may know the hope to which he has called you, the riches of his glorious inheritance in his holy people" (Eph. 1:8). By his very nature God keeps his promises; our inheritance from him will not be taken away. On the other hand, an inheritance given by a person to another may be revoked, changed, or stolen.

My father always said to my siblings and me that we were to keep our land. He worked the land as a farm when he was a boy, just as his father, grandfather, and great-grandfather had. It was their family's land, and it was to belong to his children when he was no longer alive and living on it himself. My brother, sisters, and I loved the stories of our father's youth and how they worked hard and enjoyed one another when times were difficult and material possessions were not plentiful. He would say, "But we had the land!"

My inheritance, which in my mind was part of my family culture, which included family, faith, land, and community, grew over the years in significance to me. It became a huge part of my identity. I was not only a daughter to my father and mother, but I was a part of something bigger, which had been around for many generations. I believe my siblings felt similarly. When our father died, the inheritance he left with us became even more significant. My identity was in my family name and traditions; it had a way of defining me—in good and not so good ways.

I have come to understand that some of our ways need to be torn down in order to be fully restored and healed by our loving, Almighty Creator and Savior. Family traditions and culture in and of themselves are not bad at all; we all have a need to belong, to be known, and to live in community with others. When the family or culture of the family become stronger than or mean more than God and his desires for us, problems occur.

In my case, I placed significance on my inheritance not because of its inherent value, but because it was a treasure to me in its family significance—that of identity in the world and in belonging to it. I revered our family's position over God's place in my life. He was up there, but he was not top center.

I have watched my family of origin go through many hard years of brokenness. In many respects, I see that my own need for identity and belonging distorted my view of many things, including family and inheritance. God replaced the many lies in my life with his truth, and thus, his inheritance. Whatever inheritance we lost in my father's death was not the main thing. It was my need to feel a part of a bigger unit, my need to have an identity, and my desire to be significant. If we draw near, God never leaves us alone in our brokenness. He pursues us with power and healing, and he gives us freedom only he can give.

As I walk through the halls of the retirement community where my mother lives, I notice the history of it in pictures displayed for its twenty-five-year anniversary. My grandmother was one of its original members. It gave my father, her son, great joy to know before he died that she would have a place in it. My mother has lived there for more than fifteen years and is amazingly happy. Why do I share this part of my story on inheritance? My mother now belongs to this community with its traditions and family culture—things she really never fully embraced when I was growing up or when my father was alive. For her, too, our broken family of origin has been rebuilt to replace the old. She lives in a new one made up of persons from the community she has known most of her life, with her cousins and distant relatives, and with new ones—a community in which she has her identity and to which she belongs. It is her own.

God's inheritance is the one that truly matters. He promises it and he delivers. And with it comes healing and wholeness of the pieces that needed breaking and rebuilding. We will know God when we see him because we will indeed look like him. Eternity with God is the truly glorious inheritance worth living for.

Inheritance, a History Lesson

In the Old Testament, an inheritance meant the acquisition of land as God provided. Sometimes the Israelites fought for it and then settled on it, and sometimes they were told to go to a place they did not know, as in Abraham's case. He went when he did not know where he was going, but God told him to do it, and Abraham obeyed. Thus, God gave him an "inheritance." The inheritance was not only symbolic of God's provision, but it was also literally provision of a home for the present and for the future. The Jews knew their God through his provision, and the world knew their God through his provision. The Israelites were set apart in this way through the covenant the Lord made with Abraham. The promises of God reminded them of who God is and what he does, and that God remains the same. He also gave them a way to link their present with the past of their ancestors and the covenant he made with them. "Inheritance" was a promise of God to his children.

The promises of God are always kept. He still gives his children an inheritance, even though it may seem different to us as children of the new covenant in Christ Jesus. Through Christ we have a new way, not the way of the law, but the way of grace. With this gift, God fulfills the promise of eternal life in Jesus Christ to all who choose to follow him. We belong to the family of God, just as the Israelites did. We are connected to him through the gift of his Son, and we have all the rights and privileges of a son or daughter, including our inheritance of eternal life. Not only do we have this provision now and in the future, but we also have a history with God. The Father gives us his Son and he calls us his children. This relationship establishes us and roots us in his love, grace, and power with the indwelling Holy Spirit. This reminds us that we have this inheritance—belonging, promise, union, identity, expectation, hope, and fulfillment of his Word and calling on our lives.

Our History and God's Plan of Inheritance

The land of my inheritance is not gone. As a daughter of the most high God, my Savior and Redeemer, I have a new inheritance in Jesus! I am his treasured possession, highly favored and cherished. I cannot take the land of my inheritance with me, but I am going where he is—to a land known only by him and the ones who have gone before me. According to the prophet Isaiah, "Instead of your shame you will receive a double portion, and instead of disgrace you will rejoice in your inheritance. And so you will inherit a double portion in your land, and everlasting joy will be yours" (Isa. 61:7). I agree with the psalmist that "I remain confident of this: I will see the goodness of the Lord in the land of the living" (Ps. 27:13). Even though I do not know exactly what these verses mean in my life, I know that in God there is hope for this life and the next. His Word comforts me in ways I cannot fully explain. But it is of God, and it is God working in my life. To heaven's plan of inheritance I say hallelujah!

A child of the King of kings knows her inheritance. She knows it is safe in the Lord. She does not have to fret over things like this. God supplies her need even before she cries out to him, because he knows her cry before she calls, and he knows her needs before she does herself. Our great Father is sovereign and is working his purposes out for all generations from creation until eternity. As Job replied to the Lord, "I know that you can do all things; no purpose of yours can be thwarted" (Job 42:2). If the land of my earthly father is lost to me, then my Father God in heaven has something greater in store for me—and all his children.

I have chosen to let go of the circumstances that led to the affliction and anxiety that have caused me great pain. For the grudges I have held and any dishonor I have caused, God out of his kindness has given me great mercy and grace. Our heavenly Father bestows honor on all of his children. He regards us with the eyes of his heart, the heart that gave his only Son for saving our souls. The spacious place of my youth in the land my earthly father left us remains in the hands of another earthly owner. Yet God is the rightful owner of it all. And he has fitted us for another place—in the arms of Jesus, our truly spacious place.

Forgiveness

We are not made to carry burdens, particularly the load of unforgiveness. Jesus tells us, "My yoke is easy and my burden is light" (Matt. 11:30). But do we see it that way? We ask why we have to do this, or why we have to accomplish that? We feel more and more pressured to carry more stuff, including feelings and the loads of worry and anxiety. When our minds and hearts are loaded with things we cannot sort out, untangle, or put in proper perspective, we find ourselves troubled and weary. It is too much for us. The Lord's yoke does not seem so easy! But God did not design us to carry that much. We think we can carry a huge load, but the consequences are costly.

Jesus says we are to forgive others their wrongdoing. "For if you forgive other people when they sin against you, your heavenly Father will also forgive you. But if you do not forgive others their sins, your Father will not forgive your sin" (Matt. 6:14-15). The heavenly Father is the only judge. We fear that someone else's wrong will be expunged, or that the person will not get what they deserve for having wronged us. We may still try understanding why they would do such a thing to harm us, but whatever the thought process, it takes way too much away from our lives. The best thing we can do is forgive. Jesus has to do the rest in any event. We cannot in and of ourselves do the forgiving without the capacity of the Holy Spirit who helps us in the act of forgiveness.

If we do not forgive another, we are carrying that which we were not designed to carry. It takes us our minds, our hearts, and our focus, and it is the burden Jesus knew it would be to us. He came to lighten our loads, to carry the heavy stuff, and to rescue us from the sin that plagues us: "Therefore, since we are surrounded by such a great cloud of witnesses, let us throw off everything that hinders and the sin that so easily entangles. And let us run with perseverance the race marked out for us" (Heb. 12:1).

"Fixing our eyes on Jesus, the pioneer and perfecter of faith. For the joy set before him he endured the cross, scorning its shame, and sat down at the right hand of the throne of God" (Heb. 12:2). Let us turn our focus to the One who "for the joy set before him he endured the cross." Then let us run with all of our minds, hearts, souls, and strength toward him in the race set out before us. Forgiveness is a truly important aspect of the Christian life. Christ lived and modeled a life on earth for us, and he certainly knew the pain and death associated with forgiveness. Why would we think we could carry on without following the Lord's exemplary life? We find true life in his light load.

God will Help us Handle our Work and His Word

Second Timothy 2:15 reads, "Do your best to present yourself to God as one approved, a worker who does not need to be ashamed and who correctly handles the word of truth." God gives us the capacity to know him and his Word. His Word "is a lamp for my feet, a light on my path" (Ps. 119:105). We can correctly handle Scripture with the help of the Holy Spirit. His work in our lives is to know God personally, and he equips us with his guidance to know him more and more through the places he takes us, the relationships he gives us, and the struggles he allows. His Word with us is Jesus residing in and written on our hearts.

As he ministers to his own people who have suffered under false teachers who mishandled God's Word, Paul gives Timothy a charge to stand boldly "as one approved, a worker who does not need to be ashamed and who correctly handles the word of truth." It is a huge responsibility to teach and minister, but God has given us himself and the power within to know him, his presence, and his Word.

God's children go out into the world as messengers of truth and grace. In gratitude to the Savior, we surrender ourselves for the blessing and favor of having this privilege.

God is our Rear Guard

God is our rear guard: "But you will not leave in haste or go in flight; for the Lord will go before you, the God of Israel will be your rear guard" (Isa. 52:12). The Lord accomplishes his purposes in our lives as he continues working and weaving all things together for our good and his glory. His plans are not thwarted by our wrong actions; we have no power over the God of Israel. But God uses our mistakes and failures to bring together his plan for good.

As our rear guard, God takes all the things that have gone before and finishes the work. He protects what is his and guards it until he completes it. And that is what God does with us; he protects his own. He guards our lives and completes what he has started within us. He plans the harvest before even the tiny seed gets planted. In our lives, he takes our tiny seed of trust and grows it to fruition into a life of faith. He knows the harvest beforehand. We can take the step in front of us knowing God has the next step in his plan. He protects each step and the harvest.

Life is full of steps with twists and turns that we do not expect. But God knows what to expect because he has already been on the journey. He went before us just as he is doing now. His presence guides, guards, and protects his own. We are not responsible for the purpose, the plan, or the harvest and we certainly are not wired to be the rear guard. We may act like we are when we do not trust God with the outcomes. But God is working on our behalf with his purposes and his plans, and they are much greater than we know. If we look to him as our outcome, we do not have to be concerned about any other outcome or harvest.

God's harvest will come. His work will be accomplished. And indeed, he will be the rear guard. As God's children, his beloved, we know the One who goes before us, within us, and behind us—truly our rear guard.

Following our Loving Father God

"When I called, you answered me; you greatly emboldened me" (Ps. 138:3). Going forth on the path he has chosen for me, I follow. He leads and carries me from time to time. Even when traveling along valleys and up mountains, I am always on his firm foundation if I stay with him.

When I cannot go anymore, when I cannot stop blaming myself for my poor performance, or when I cannot get my heart set right, he hears my cry out to him. He hears my cry when I cannot trust him enough, or when I cannot be bold, or when I cannot even stand. The Lord makes me bold, carries me, helps me trust him and know his hand. He emboldens me to leave my burdens and my shame at his feet, and he shows me how to sing his praises.

Atop the mountain I go to shout the wonders he has done. He sets me high above to see what he wants me to see, to know, and to experience. All of a sudden it is not about me anymore. I see him.

Looking to God, I am beyond the shame and the disappointment. He is beyond all of my hopes and dreams. When I look inside myself, I find too much to be concerned about, but my Father God does not leave me to my own devices. He knows and cares for me even so. Not only is he infinite and available, he is everlasting and so is his love.

As God's children, we are not wired to be filled any other way than by divine grace, truth, and love. Nor are we to live by any other means. We are wired to look up, not in, to be made right by him, not ourselves, and to be connected to him, to draw life from him, and to live with him. When we know our own depravity and our need to be made whole, we see our smallness. And when we cry out as children to the One and Only, he fills us to see him and to be made right and whole.

Atop the mountain we go for the very life he gives for his children.

AFTERWORD

THRIVING DAUGHTERS FOLLOW OUR LOVING FATHER

The Journey of the Girl atop the Mountain

With her arms raised in adoration and praise of her Father God, he led her, carried her along unfamiliar paths, painful places, and hard circumstances. He not only led her, but also in joy pursued her to draw close to him on the journey. He wants to remind her on the journey that he is with her and will never leave her, and that he wants to give her the daily opportunity to come with him and choose to believe who he is and who she is to him. He wants her to see his hand to cover her, to hide her, to lead her, to protect her, to provide for her, to fill her up, and most of all to embrace her in love, truth, and grace. In addition, the Father is her shield from all that could harm her. He will teach her how to let him father her and how to be his child.

As the Father God shows her the way, she begins seeing all the choices in front of her to come and sit with him, to follow as they start out, and to believe him as they travel. She feels loved and known. There is purpose in the journey. It is the high adventure for which she was made, because she is thrilled with the new and the unknown. She feels a part of something bigger than herself. And at the same time, she yearns for rest and home, which he gives her as they talk and share. In the Father's arms are joy and peace like she has never known. The truest glimpses in her mind's eye of their journey together are her riding and resting on God's shoulders as they pursue his path.

The journey is more than she has imagined and greater than her dreams. "Why has it taken so long for me to go with you?" she asks. God says back to her, "You were not ready, and I do not force it. But when you are ready, I will take you on the sweetest and best of all journeys. I love you and want to be with you. Are you ready for what's next?"

"Loving Father, Thriving Daughter"

You remind me who you are, Father God
And where you have placed me
In awe and wonder I see
Your kindness bestowed going before, with, and behind me

God causes me to look up
His face abounding in love
Holy, yet approachable, God Almighty
In Jesus, he bids us come

Without his mercy we are lost
Within his grace we are found
Our positions secure, sons and daughters
Children of the King, Jesus

God is exalted
In Jesus he looks kindly on the lowly
We are blameless, favored, and cherished
By our Creator, Savior, Father God

He does not leave us
Or abandon the work he has begun
In us for he has a plan
You see—sons and daughters of the King

Thriving Daughters Follow our Loving Father God

Whether I am standing on the shoulders of our great God after he has picked me up, or atop a mountaintop, I am here because he brought me to this place. He wants me to take in the perspective and enjoy the view. It has been a long journey, but one he planned before I was born. Life is not all mountaintops; it has its valleys, too. In each case though, God is with us, and where he is there is joy and peace. Parts of God's path are long and low, some are steep and high, and some are just slow. It seems being a daughter has been a slow path for me. But being his daughter, really living as his daughter, has been a change of perspective for me in my life. It is also the reason I know I am riding on his shoulders and seeing the world as a father allows his child to see.

God creates majestic landscapes over the course of many years, so why wouldn't he take his time with each of his children? I am not the potter, nor am I the parent. He is our Father and our Creator. Who better than he to plan the course of our lives? And who better than he to love us, to give us perspective, teach us, and show us how to be followers of the Son?

It is on this mountaintop I stand upon God's shoulders and declare his love for all humanity. He brought me here to show me his view and to give me an image of heaven's bounty made for us. The little girl in the closet is no longer bound by space or by lies. The Lord has taken her to his truth and shown her who he is and how great is his love for her and all God's children. She is free to live as his daughter because God's children have access to the Father himself, who is the author of abundance.

Does life seem long and low, steep and high, or just slow? Are you ready for a new view? Will you allow God to show you his way, and go with him to know his love and bounty?

It is in the going that we know God and who he says he is. We have to learn to lean into him and the path he has set before us. It is no longer my journey, but our journey, God's and mine, and it is right. I am surer of the steps with the Father because I am following in his steps. There is purpose in it; I am not fretting over the difficulty, or the distance, or who is in charge, because the Author of eternity is. When we know him, we want to know him more. It is in the more of our loving Father God and the Lord Jesus Christ that we know the peak, and it is so worth the trek.

A STUDY GUIDE

FOR

GOD CALLS US:
DAUGHTERS EXTRAVAGANTLY LOVED

The purpose of this guide is to give readers or facilitators of a small group a few questions to ponder and pray on the journey of being a daughter (or a son) of our King of kings, our Father God, and the Lord Jesus Christ. These questions can be used for individual or group purposes. Some of them may help one come up with questions of one's own. In God's Word, and in his Word-made-flesh in Jesus, the Father shows just how much he loves us and wants a relationship with us. For group study, the lists of questions may be a way to discuss our own journeys and help us in deepening our walk with him as his daughters.

God Calls Us to More

In our walk with our Lord Jesus Christ, we cross over to a life engaged in a relationship promising to be one of sharing, serving, and growing. He tells us he has the abundant life for us. John tells us that "The thief comes only to steal and kill and destroy; I have come that they may have life, and have it to the full" (John 10:10). As daughters of our Father God, we want to live in this fullness. God calls us to more.

Study Questions:

1. Have you had a moment or period of time where you were awakened or called to a desire for more of God—for a fuller life? If so, what precipitated it?

2. Were you drawn more to Scripture, or to serve in a special way? Was this calling out of your comfort zone?

3. If you have been in a lull, would you know what to do to acknowledge your lack of desire for more of God?

4. Have you ever questioned your status quo? Do you want a deeper look at how God wants to use you for his kingdom?

God Calls Us to Remember

One of the greatest things about relationships is that in relationships we have a history and we remember our times together. The same is true of our relationship with God, except he is the Author of relationships. He made us to be in relationship with him and with one another. We have a history with God, and we remember what he has done for us, how he has rescued us, protected us, and given us many blessings. When we step out in faith and become daughters of our Savior, he gives us the Holy Spirit to dwell within, to be able to walk with him, learn from him, and follow him. He also gives us the capacity to remember the things God has shown us and how he has loved us from the beginning. We are truly daughters extravagantly loved. One of the best reminders that we are his daughters is to remember whose we are, who made us and who saved us.

Study Questions:

1. Name something God has done in your life and tell why it is significant.

2. Describe a good thing happening in the present.

3. Remember a hard thing from your past. What made it difficult?

4. Is there someone in your life now who needs kindness and attention?

5. What moment in your past is surfacing as a reminder that God was there in the kindness or attention shown to you?

6. How might you show up today as Jesus' hands and feet?

7. Prayer: *Father God, give me eyes to see, ears to hear, and a heart to know your heart for me. Give me a new heart to see others as you see them and to want to share with them what you have done in my life.*

God Calls Us to Listen

As we remember what God has done, and as we walk with him on the journey, we want to know what to do next. Sometimes it is clear, and sometimes it is not. Most of all, God wants us to know him. He wants us to come to him. Jesus tells us that our work on this earth is to believe in the One our loving Father has sent.

In Isaiah 55, God's Word tells all who are thirsty to "Come, all you who are thirsty, come to the waters" (55:1). He says to listen to him: "Give ear and come to me; listen, that you may live" (55:3). He gives what no other can; he gives what will satisfy. In Matthew 11:28-30, Jesus says "Come to me, all you who are weary and burdened, and I will give you rest. Take my yoke upon you and learn from me, for I am gentle and humble in heart, and you will find rest for your souls. For my yoke is easy and my burden is light."

Study Questions:

1. What does God call us to do on our faith walk? Have you made it more than that recently?

2. What reminders bring you to the Lord today? Do you remember to go to Jesus for rest, and to remember what he has sacrificed?

3. Do you lay down your burdens at his feet? Do you cling tightly and hold all else loosely, especially the burdens?

4. What is your thirst? Do you yearn for more from God? Have you told him about it?

5. Are you listening to God? What are you expecting from him?

6. Now, go. The Lord is holding you. He has already given you what you need for the journey, for he has given himself. If you are yearning, ask. If you are waiting, seek. Let go of what hinders you from receiving rest for your soul.

God Calls Us to Trust

God wants us to be his daughters. He has planted the seed in us to know him as our Father—our protector, guide, provider, comforter, teacher, and the one who encourages, inspires, and fills us with himself in unfathomable ways. Being God's daughters results in the journey of walking with him and listening to him as daughters who need to know him in order to live as he planned. Are we in need of knowing our Father in heaven in this way? Yes, *if* we are to hear our Father and know his love and plan for us to have life to the full.

Study Questions:

1. Are there glimpses in your life today that remind you when you grew in your knowledge of God?

2. Has your faith changed in recent months? How?

3. How do you handle doubt and anxiety? Does knowing who God is and what he promises help?

4. What does knowing God mean to you?

5. How does believing God change your perspective for this day?

6. The apostle Paul wrote, "I want to know Christ—yes, to know the power of his resurrection and participation in his sufferings, becoming like him in his death" (Phil. 3:10). Is this true, or has this been true, in your own life?

7. Do you believe suffering brings us closer to God? Have you experienced this personally?

8. What assurance do you have that you are God's child? If you are not sure, would you pray to him now to know you are his? *Dear Lord Jesus, I know I am a sinner, and I ask for your forgiveness. I believe you died for my sins and rose from the dead to sit at God's right hand to intercede for us with God the Father? I trust and follow you as my Lord and Savior. Guide me and help me to do your will. In your name, Amen.*

9. How can God intercede for you today?

10. Knowing Jesus as your Lord and Savior means living as his child. How does trusting him with your life change the way you live?

11. Have you experienced the Lord's healing in a transforming way?

God Calls Us to Remain

Jesus has come so we may experience his compassion and abounding love. When we live close and follow, we know him better with each step we take. Every moment that we trust Jesus more than we lean on our own understanding, we experience more of him. Each time we ask the Lord for guidance instead of relying on ourselves means we experience more of him.

Study Questions:

1. Are you in touch with God's heart and Word for you? Are you drawing near to him?

2. God hears you and knows your cry before you come, listen, and delight in him. His Word reveals his heart and desire for you. If you feel God is silent, cry out to him.

3. Are you running elsewhere to be nourished at this time? Where are you going for comfort, joy, relationship, and satisfaction? Draw near to God and come to his table.

4. Is your life full, or are you empty of dreams?

5. What are the good things bringing you nourishment at this time? Are they God's best?

God Calls Us to Praise Him

In order to partake of the life God offers, we must respond to his invitation. Accompanied by the complete and finished work of Christ, God offers life and all of its benefits to those who believe. We must consider what that means. God pursues us out of great mercy and lavish love; we respond to that love in faith he initiates, and then we come to know him by faith when we experience his fullness through a personal relationship with him. In the very first step of faith, God covers our sin—past, present, and future. We have no shame in the Lord's eyes. As God's sons and daughters, we receive his faithful care: "Send me your light and your faithful care, let them lead me; let them bring me to your holy mountain, to the place where you dwell" (Ps. 43:3).

And there is so much more. The more is in the partaking, the sharing in the fellowship of our great God. God is the author and perfecter of our faith, but he is also the author of relationships. In his intentionality, God wired us with a need to know him and a need to be in a relationship with heaven's Creator.

Study Questions:

1. Are you in God's presence and living fully? What does he have in mind for your relationship with him? Have you asked him about it?

2. Converse with the Lord about the hard things. Allow him into the difficult and painful places in your life. Know and experience God's love for you in quiet fellowship in his Word.

3. Worship and praise God for who he is. Thank him for what he has done in your life. Ask him to show you *more*.

4. In the Word, we experience God. He shows us himself, and Scripture transforms us to see him. Have you been reading the Bible? How has it changed you recently?

5. Do you expect God? He tells us to expect him. If we come to him, we can know he is there. Allow him in the inmost places. Even in the darkest, most painful places, God can heal and reveal treasure in ways we never imagine or expect.

6. Allow God's greatness in your life. To partake of his bounty, we must take what he has to offer—not just the good, but his good for us and for his glory for the entire world to see and know him.

7. Jesus is our perfect model for receiving what God offers. Even he asked not to have to take the cup of responsibility for the world's sins. But he gave his life for all of us as his suffering was the perfect sacrifice, once and for all, to give us the relationship with God we could not have without him. In order to relate to us, Jesus who knew no sin became the way for us to overcome sin and live with God. He took the cup he was offered. Come and experience what God offers for his glory and our good.

God Calls Us to Please Him

Being a daughter is just one of the many relationships we have on this side of heaven. God made women to be his daughters. He has also made us the daughters of others—indeed a father and a mother, or someone who filled those roles for us. They were human; some followed God, and some did not. Inevitably, these persons got some things right and some things wrong. God made us for relationship with him so we could know his perfect goodness and love, and to be able to live with his help in relationship with others. There are many aspects of a daughter-mother or daughter-father relationship. The daughter is to love, respect, and obey her parents, to receive their love and affection, and embrace what they have to offer. She is to remember them and honor them.

Study Questions:

1. In what ways do you know God loves you?

2. Are there ways you still doubt God's love?

3. Are there times when as a child of God you know you are thriving? How would you describe them? Where or when are you not thriving?

4. When you feel you are just treading water in your relationship with God, what is happening in your life? Have you discussed this with him?

5. What is God's requirement for a personal relationship with him?

6. If our work on this earth is to know God, how are you doing?

7. Could it be that God has the gift of thriving and abundance waiting for you? Receive what he has to offer. He says to come.